DATE DUE

DEC 0 9 1996		
JAN 3 1 1999		

HIGHSMITH   #45102

Yes, You Can, Heather!

Yes, You Can, Heather!

THE STORY OF
HEATHER WHITESTONE, *MISS AMERICA 1995*

by her mother,
Daphne Gray
with Gregg Lewis

10683

ZondervanPublishingHouse
Grand Rapids, Michigan

A Division of HarperCollinsPublishers

Yes, You Can, Heather!
Copyright © 1995 by Daphne Gray

Requests for information should be addressed to:

 ZondervanPublishingHouse
Grand Rapids, Michigan 49530

ISBN 0-310-20373-2

This edition printed on acid-free paper and meets the American National Standards Institute Z39.48 standard.

Edited by Sandra L. Vander Zicht and Lori J. Walburg
Interior design by Susan Vandenberg-Koppenol

Printed in the United States of America

95 96 97 98 99 00 01 02 /❖ DH/ 10 9 8 7 6 5 4 3 2 1

*To my family for a lifetime of love,
devotion, and strength—
and to my daughters and grandchildren,
who have brought me joy*

Contents

Acknowledgments

When such a momentous task as writing a book is undertaken, there are so many people who make it all possible. To all those who believed in my dream, please accept my gratitude and heartfelt thanks.

I have heard it said that a man can count himself rich if he has the priceless experience of one or two true friends in his lifetime. If this is true, then the Lord has blessed me with his richest gifts.

Judy Harper, Diane Steensland—thank you for giving Heather her voice and for being my mentors. To Patti Richards, Barbara Barker, and Monica Smith, thank you for giving wings to Heather's talent.

To Martha Marsh, Tricia Fergerson, Lesa Johnson, and Anita Tillman, you are always there for me through thick and thin. I couldn't have made it this past year without your help and support. Beverly Still and Joann and Cleveland Bryant, your strength and wisdom guided me through one of the roughest times of my life—and true you still remain. Jim and Vicky Davis and Wayne Smith, your unique friendship enriches my life always in so many ways and brings me joy and laughter.

To Julius Burnett and Larry Futrell, thank you for the good beginning with this project.

To my friends at Zondervan, especially my editor, Sandy Vander Zicht, whose creative approach and persistence paid off. Your commitment to this vision and unwavering support have been invaluable to me. And to Scott Bolinder, my publisher, for his encouragement and sagacious advice.

Thank you, Gregg Lewis, for your words have captured my thoughts and feelings in such a realistic manner that they made my story come alive. You are a master artist.

Mamá and Papá—to you I owe all, but I especially thank you for such a strong moral legacy. What a wonderful gift to give one's child. Now I pass it on to my children. You made my roots strong, and you gave me wings to fly—but you were always there with loving hearts and open arms.

To my brother Mike Gray and his wife, Lois, your help with the STARS booklet was greatly appreciated. To my sister Deborah Congdon and her family, and to my brother Jim Gray and his family, thanks for all the continuing love and support through all the years.

To Trey Ward, thank you for sharing your mom with Heather and me. You're the greatest!

And Stephanie Ward, my sister, your gift of love and support is never ending. You enabled both Heather and me to reach for our stars.

I want to thank my daughter Stacey Vera, her husband, Tom, my daughter Melissa Gomillion, her husband, Tony, and my daughter Heather for their encouragement and help.

And to my grandchildren, Shane and Tessa Vera and Sara Gomillion, for their indirect contribution of love. When their "marmalade" got really stressed, their sweet voices and very existence brought me such peace and joy. To them, I say our aspirations and dreams are our possibilities!

Foreword

The first time I stood on the stage in Atlantic City and looked out over the empty convention center, I was amazed not at its size, but at the fact that I was there. The journey to the Miss America Scholarship Pageant in Atlantic City did not begin four years ago when I first competed in a local pageant. It began when I was eighteen months old. Even then, God knew his plan for me and how to make that plan happen. He used my parents to mold me, for I was too young to understand his dream for me.

This book is written from my mom's perspective on how she reared me and her feelings about the choices she had to make. In many ways, our family was the typical American family. We were not fabulously wealthy, nor did we have a prestigious name. We lived in a nice ranch house in a middle-class neighborhood. On weekends my father would often take us sailing. My sisters and I attended public schools, rode a yellow school bus, and had afternoon chores like most of the friends we knew. We had two working parents, family financial problems, and sibling squabbles. Despite my deafness, it was an extremely "normal" life.

I gave my mother my Miss Alabama crown soon after I became the 75th Anniversary Miss America because she spent hours lovingly and patiently teaching me to speak and to listen with the help of my hearing aid. I believe she is a role model to other parents across the country. On my national speaking tour as Miss America, I have met many parents who have deaf children. Many of them tell me how my mother gives them hope.

I often thank God for the blessings he has bestowed on me. The greatest of these is the strength he provided me to carry on when I wanted to quit, and the dream he put in my soul when hope seemed lost.

What may come as a surprise to you is that you and I have much in common. If you can dream a dream, you too can accomplish it according to his will. God promises that "he who began a good work in you will carry it on to completion until the day of Christ Jesus" (Philippians 1:6). I pray that you will recognize the need for his help and believe in miracles from him. Hold fast to God's words and his strength through Jesus, and watch your dreams come true.

In Christ's love,

Heather Whitestone
Miss America 1995
John 3:16

$\mathscr{P}$reface

September 19, 1994

Dear Heather,

It's been only two short days since the Miss America Pageant in Atlantic City, and I'm on a plane headed back home. As I gaze out over the clouds, the hum of the plane's engine brings me a sense of the peace that had eluded me for so long. I'm surprised in the midst of the normal confusion of a typical Monday flight, packed with businesspeople and commuters, that this tranquil and nostalgic mood fills me. I can't help smiling at the thought that travel will become your lifestyle for the next year.

For the first time in eight days, I have had a chance to reflect on all that has transpired. Wow! Miss America 1995! Heather, I am so proud of you, but then I always believed in you and knew if you were ever given the chance, you would show the world what we, your family, had always known. I've always believed God saved you from death because he had another purpose for your life. God used your deafness to draw you closer to him, to strengthen you, and to prepare you for his master plan. You have become a tool, a vessel, through which his message of love and hope can be exemplified.

It is ironic in one respect and extraordinary in another, that twenty years ago, almost to the exact day, you lay in a hospital bed near death. The parallelism of these two major events in your life—your deafness and being crowned Miss America—happening within twenty years plus days of each other is eerie and uncanny. Our prayers were much different in 1974. Unlike the praise and exaltations uttered on the night of your crowning, those prayers were desperate pleas for life.

Unbeknownst to us, and all alone, sometime between September 14 and 21, 1974, you slipped into a world of silence. Yet, on September 17, 1994, you showed the world a different way to hear. I am astounded when I recall that on September 14, 1974, you were in a comalike state, unable to walk or stand. Yet, miraculously, twenty years later, you danced your way into the hearts of millions. The old adage that "God moves in mysterious ways" is more meaningful to me than ever.

Every mom wants success and happiness for her children, and I am certainly no exception. You, Stacey, and Melissa have given me more than my fair share of proud moments. Though each of you has chosen different ways to showcase your talents, you are each confident, honest, determined, and motivated young women. I realize I was firm with you girls. That probably was the teacher in me. On a deeper level was the mother's love and desire for you to be happy.

Each of you has expressed at times you felt I pushed too hard. Guilty as charged! My expectations were high for all of you because I knew your potential. For this, you can thank Grandmother and Granddaddy Gray. They instilled in all their children the belief that "a job worth doing is worth doing well" and "it takes no more time to do it right than it does to do it wrong." You girls had no means of escaping the passage of these moral teachings that bind a family together. "Train a child in the way he should go, and when he is old he will not turn from it" (Proverbs 22:6). That was the underlying motive for my convictions. I have heard all my life a parent has two main responsibilities—to provide each child with roots and a pair of wings to fly. So I make no apologies for the manner in which I raised you. I can truthfully say that I take pride in all you girls.

Many people have asked me if it is hard to let you go, Heather. I've always felt you were more vulnerable than the others, and it's only natural that I was protective. Have you not noticed that you invoke the same protective instinct in other people? I have always been honest and forthright with you, but I did screen as many of the negative aspects of life's lessons as I could. Moms tend to do this anyway, and your deafness made that even easier for me. But more importantly, I always encouraged you to try anything and to strive for excellence. I was there to support you, help you, guide you, and wipe away the tears when you were hurting. So what if you didn't hear all the gossip—you were better off without it. At times I envied you for this gift. It allowed you to not have preconceived ideas or negative opinions or fears of others. You give everyone a chance to be themselves and then form your opinion.

I've always told you to face your obstacles. For a profoundly deaf person, communication skills will always be your biggest challenge. When we correct your speech or make suggestions as to how to convey a thought, feeling, or concept, it isn't because we doubt your abilities. We only want to be a part of your support team and help you in your struggle. These actions were often questioned by you and others. Everyone needs to understand, this is a necessary part of the teaching method we have used for twenty-one years. Think about it. You are now Miss America. Obviously, the method works!

However, any anxieties I had were quickly dispelled in your first press conference. You handled the press like a pro. You were yourself and remained true to your beliefs. Instead of antagonizing them, you captivated them.

Can I let you go? Heather, you were never mine to keep! A parent's covenant with God is to raise, nurture, and release when the time comes. Sure it's lonely at times, and I do miss you. But I know in my heart it is time to let you go. It is part of God's plan for the roles of parents and children to change as time passes. I'm looking forward to the new and exciting relationship that we'll experience as adults. Once family, always family, and memories are the fibers that bind us together.

As I watched you those first few days in the various press conferences, I was overwhelmed at the interest and curiosity people had regarding your early years and deaf training. I became painfully aware of how little you remembered. You had lived a lot of those years in a cocoon of silence because of your deafness. Once language was established, I concentrated so intently on assisting you with your academics and therapy that there never seemed to be time to reminisce about our early lives. How we got you to speak didn't seem as important as maintaining your speech and progressing with the communication skills. You are even asking questions as to why your deafness is such a focal issue. To understand how miraculous your life seems to others, you need these early memories, and that is a gift I can afford to give you now.

How fortunate we are that so many of our family and friends are able to give you an account of those years and help fill in the missing pieces. I look forward to reliving those memories! Heather, this way you will have a unique opportunity to see yourself, not only through my eyes, but through the eyes of others. So it is with much love that I take pen in hand to write for you this account of your life.

Fly high, Heather, and set your sights on the heavens, for there are no limits. Reach for the stars, and help others begin their "star" journeys, as well. Let your "light" shine!

Love always,
Mom

CHAPTER 1

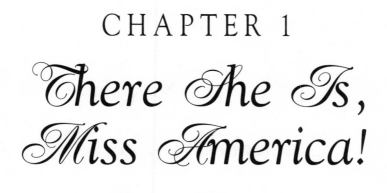

There She Is, Miss America!

September 17, 1994.

My lack of nervousness had begun to make me nervous. The relaxed sense of peace I felt seemed such a contrast to the tension and excitement I'd experienced during all the other pageants in which Heather had competed. Yet this was Atlantic City—and the final night of Miss America. Tonight would bring either the remarkable culmination, or the sudden and disappointing end, of my daughter's incredible dream. And the most pervasive sensation I'd had all evening was this disconcerting, yet clearly God-given, feeling of inner calm.

Even when Miss America's television hosts, Regis Philbin and Kathy Lee Gifford, announced the five finalists, I didn't worry. But then, since the second name called was "Heather Whitestone, Miss Alabama," I didn't have time to feel much tension. It was only when the five finalists moved toward the row of stools lined up at center stage, during what seemed like an eternal commercial break before the interview portion of the competition, that my maternal anxiety began to build.

What seat will she get? It's in your hands, Lord. Please let her be seated close to Regis and not at the far end, so she'll be able to understand his questions. . . . Oh good! She's in the second spot. That's perfect!

All five contestants looked stunning perched on those stools. As a burst of orchestra music signaled the end of the commercial break, a hush of anticipation settled across that vast convention hall. I wondered if the people in the balcony could hear the sudden pounding of my heart.

My nightlong calm evaporated as the last notes of music faded away. I hadn't worried at all about the evening gown competition; Heather had been elegant. She'd looked and walked great during the swimsuit segment as well. Then she'd justified my lack of jitters during the talent portion of the competition by captivating the entire audience with her electrifying performance—a classic ballet interpretation of the Crucifixion danced to Sandi Patty's inspirational number "Via Dolorosa."

But the interview was the contestants' last chance to impress the judges. Each finalist would be judged on her impromptu response to Regis Philbin's questions. For Heather, these next few minutes were to be perhaps the most difficult, most crucial, and most unpredictable aspect of the whole pageant. Heather's performance here would make or break her dream.

The group of thirty family members and close friends surrounding me felt the same tension that gripped my heart. I know my father did, because I was transferring much of my tension to him by clamping a desperate death grip on his left arm. My mother had him by the right arm. Because we'd been through this together at the Miss Alabama Pageant, I knew my sister Stephanie was fervently beseeching the Lord. And I silently echoed her prayer: *Oh, Lord, please let her hear and understand the question. Give Heather the words to say and help her pronounce them clearly.*

Up on the stage Regis was saying, "All right, we're coming down to the wire now. I'm here with our five finalists. I'm going to ask them each a question about their platform—the social issue that concerns them the most. This is where anything can happen because the answers the finalists give are worth up to ten points. Those points are added to their previous scores for a grand total, giving our judges a final decision. But, ladies, before we get to your platforms and the judging, I'd like to chat with you briefly and ask you some random questions to get to know you a little bit better."

First, he asked Andrea Krahn, Miss Georgia, how she'd felt about the Pageant's decision to conduct this year's swimsuit competition in bare feet. Andrea responded that it hadn't bothered her because she'd had three pedicures. When the laughter died down, Regis turned his attention to Heather and said to the audience, "You know, Heather Whitestone, our Miss Alabama, you may have read, is hearing impaired. No hearing in one ear, five percent hearing in the other. So I must ask you—you dance so beautifully—do you hear the music?"

Heather nodded and smiled. "I can hear some sound with my hearing aid. But what I do is feel the music and listen to the music . . . for a couple times. Then I count the number with the music and memorize it in my heart. And that's how I do it!"

As the crowd's approving applause sounded through the hall, I began to breathe again. Heather had understood the first question and responded confidently and clearly. *So far, so good.*

That initial round of icebreaker questions quickly ended, and Regis began again by asking Miss Georgia a couple of questions about her platform of "Parenting Skills: Solutions for Child Abuse."

Then it was Heather's turn, and Regis was saying, "All right, Heather, your platform [youth motivation] is entitled 'Anything Is Possible!' How can we remove the barriers that limit us from realizing our full and unique potential, as you did?"

Heather got a quizzical look on her face and said, "How do we remove the barriers . . . is that what you're asking?"

My first response was, *Uh-oh, she didn't understand.* But then we'd always taught her to repeat questions to make sure she'd understood. *So maybe it's all right.*

Regis was already rewording his question. "How do you let people know that anything is possible?"

At that point Heather launched right into her answer. "My good attitude helps me get through hard times. And believing in myself helps me to overcome the obstacles. I have found there are five steps that can help them become successful. That's why I created my STARS program."

Regis then asked, "You created a five-star point program?"

Heather quickly responded to clarify. "Stars have five points. So I thought that would help people remember these five important steps."

"You think if it worked for you, it should work for them?"

Heather nodded. "Oh, it worked for me! See, I experience this every day. And it really did help!"

As the enthusiastic applause again died down, a huge wave of relief washed through me. Heather had cleared her biggest hurdle. All those years of tedious daily speech therapy had paid off by giving her a chance at her dream. Now, as the remaining contestants answered their interview questions and the television took its final, and seemingly longest, commercial break of the night, there was nothing left to do but wait. And pray. And wait.

And remember.

So many things flashed through my consciousness. Twenty years ago this night, eighteen-month-old Heather had lain critically ill in the pediatric ward of a hospital in Dothan, Alabama, while her doctors tried to decide what was wrong and how to treat her. Since that terrible time, I had had to answer an endless list of questions about Heather:

Was it Heather's original illness or the drugs used to treat her that caused her deafness? *Even the doctors' opinions differed on that question.* What should parents do for a profoundly deaf child? *I'd certainly gotten plenty of conflicting opinions on that issue.* Were the experts right when they told us not to expect her to attain more than a third-grade education? *That had been perhaps the most devastating assessment of all.* Why even bother enrolling a deaf child in dance? *Most people considered only the limitations; fortunately a few saw the potential.* Could Heather ever hope to make it in the mainstream and ultimately find success and happiness in the hearing world? *Sometimes I've felt very alone in my belief that she could—or should even try.* Would the Miss Alabama Pageant system ever choose a winner with a physical handicap? *For three years we wrestled with that question.* Could a deaf girl who dreamed of becoming Miss America ever actually win the crown? *We are about to answer that one tonight!*

All this and more raced through my mind during the commercial break and then during Regis and Kathy Lee's time-killing chat with Miss America 1994, Kimberly Aiken. Finally the scores were tallied and the judges' decision delivered.

By this time my poor father had lost all circulation to both hands. I doubt a rescue squad equipped with the "jaws of life" and assorted explosive charges could have freed him from the grip my mom and I had on him. But he didn't seem to mind or even notice as we watched the five semifinalists introduced again for one last time.

The envelope was opened, and Regis Philbin called out, "Fourth runner-up, Miss Indiana, Tiffany Storm." The crowd cheered, and my blood pressure jumped a few more points. "Third runner-up, Miss Georgia, Andrea Krahn." The three remaining contestants stood at center stage holding hands. "Second runner-up, Miss New Jersey, Jennifer Alexis Makris."

As the cheering subsided, Regis went on to say, "Here we are now. Down to two. That leaves Miss Alabama and Miss Virginia."

Kathy Lee now said, "One of you beautiful ladies will win a $20,000 scholarship to continue your education and the other will win a $35,000 scholarship, plus the crown and the title of Miss America. In addition, your college or university will receive $25,000 for a scholarship fund from the Miss America Organization and from Waterford Crystal. Okay, Reg."

"Okay," said Regis. "This is it, everybody! Ladies and gentlemen, the winner of a $20,000 scholarship is ... Miss Virginia, Cullen Johnson. And the new Miss America 1995, Miss Alabama, Heather Whitestone!"

The crowd of 13,000 packing the Atlantic City Convention Center exploded into wall-shaking cheers. The bewildered expression on Heather's face told me she hadn't understood the announcement. It wasn't until Cullen Johnson pointed at her, mouthed the words, "It's you!" and then gave her a big congratulatory hug that Heather realized she'd won.

I never did clearly see what happened next. I could tell Heather was crying. I was crying. My mother and sisters were crying. Stacey and Melissa, Heather's two older sisters, were screaming and jumping up and down. Stacey's six-month-old daughter, Tessa, was bouncing up and down in her mother's arms for what had to be the wildest adventure ride of her young life. All of Heather's cousins and her aunts and uncles were cheering and applauding like mad. My father, in joyous celebration of Heather's victory and his own sudden freedom, was punching his still-numb arms into the air and screaming, "YES! YES! YES!"

I guess Regis and Kathy Lee must have been singing, "There she is, Miss America. ..." because Heather was now walking down the runway and waving to the crowd. But all that our family and friends could hear was the sound of wild cheering, our own and everyone else's around us.

When Heather made her turn and strolled back toward the stage, I could see her searching for the family in the crowd. I don't know why she didn't spot us immediately; we were the contingent of fools screaming *and* jumping up and down. There were thirty of us wildly waving and flashing her the familiar hand sign for "I love you." When she finally spotted us, she signed her love back to us, and we all screamed even louder.

By the time the other contestants surrounded Heather on stage to congratulate her, a Miss America security escort arrived at our seats to usher me, my parents, and my two other daughters backstage for Heather's first official press conference of her reign.

As we wove our way through the press of the crowd, my father, who'd been bugging me for years to keep a written account of everything we'd been through with Heather, turned and grinned at me. In his best I-told-you-so voice he said, "Now you're going to have to get started on the book."

CHAPTER 2

A Perfectly Normal Life

W e expected Heather to be a Valentine baby. But ten days later, on February 24, 1973, we were still awaiting her arrival. The weather was so mild that afternoon I lounged on a lawn chair, soaking in the soothing rays of the warm southern Alabama sun. Basking in the fresh air and sunshine helped me tolerate the growing discomfort of early labor.

When the contractions had begun that morning, my first reaction was to think, *Well, it's about time!* Then I'd called Bill at the store to tell him labor had started; this was our third child, so I knew all the signs. Bill had insisted on hurrying home, even though I told him it would be some time before I needed to head for the hospital. Now he and our two little girls were making the most of the springlike weather and providing me both entertainment and distraction as they "washed" the car together. Not that Stacey (who was three and a half) and Melissa (who was almost twenty-seven months) did much of the work. Mostly they shrieked and ran up and down the driveway while their dad playfully squirted them with a hose.

The joyous sound of my family's laughter gave me a special sense of happiness and contentment. I knew that before the day was over there would be a new addition to our family. I remember thinking, *Life is very good*.

Gently resting a hand on my tummy and feeling the vague outline of the baby nestled inside, I prayed a typical and simple mother's prayer: *Dear Lord, please let everything be all right today. Let this child be perfect. Help guide us and be with us as this new life begins*.

Not until about seven that evening did I tell Bill, "We better call your folks to come and take the girls. I think it's time to go to the hospital." Heather made her appearance in the world at 9:31 P.M. My very first thought when I saw her was, *She's so big!*

Stacey had weighed six pounds at birth. And Melissa at five pounds, ten ounces had seemed almost small enough to hold in the palm of one hand. So this seven-pound, four-ounce baby girl looked absolutely huge in comparison.

I wasn't surprised to have another baby daughter. All along I'd felt I was carrying a girl. I became even more certain after one of my prenatal checkups when the doctor, who was listening with a stethoscope, absentmindedly said, more to himself than to me, "Her heart sounds good and strong."

"So you think it's a girl?" I asked.

Acting a little sheepish to have been caught thinking out loud, he shrugged. "Don't hold me to it. But based on the sound of her heartbeat, if I had to guess, yes, I'd say you're probably going to have a little girl."

I had already told Bill what I suspected. So I shared what the doctor had said as well. But I knew even after that Bill still held out hope for a son. It wasn't as if I hadn't been wrong before; the entire time I'd carried Melissa I'd been absolutely certain she was going to be a boy.

So my second thought when I saw this new baby (after *She's so big!*) was: *I hope Bill won't be too disappointed*. Not that he didn't love our daughters. And not that I ever thought for a moment he wouldn't love a third little girl. But I also knew how much Bill, as a typical oldest son, always wanted to please his parents. And my father-in-law had very clearly expressed his disappointment to Bill when our second child was not a boy.

It seemed particularly important to Herb, Bill's dad, that he have a grandson to carry on the family name. But Bill and I had already made the decision that three children would be our limit.

So I knew the moment that I saw my little daughter there would never be a Herbert William Whitestone III. Three girls would have to do.

In truth, I think because of the anticipated disappointment, I accepted her birth as a bit of a challenge. Even then, a small part of me determined to do whatever it took to help Heather and her sisters prove that girls could be every bit as good as boys.

Bill and I had agreed on a girl's name, "Heather Leigh," several months earlier—after he had accompanied his dad to Scotland on a golfing excursion. They'd brought home stunning photos and postcards showing entire hillsides dressed in the purple glory of the fragrant little heather flower—so delicate to look at, yet hardy enough to survive and thrive in the rugged Scottish highlands. And as I'd looked through the other photos from Scotland, I'd also been struck by the pictures of ruddy-faced Scottish children—all of whom appeared wonderfully happy and robust. So from that time on, in my mind, I associated the name *Heather* with the flower and the children of Scotland—symbolizing both beauty and health. The perfect name for our newest beautiful baby girl.

Our family was now complete.

Both of our older girls acted thrilled when we brought Heather home from the hospital. I'd anticipated a positive reaction from Stacey, but I hadn't known what to expect from Melissa. At just a little over two years of age, I don't think she'd really understood the implications when I'd explained earlier that "Mommy is going to have another baby."

I'd told her, "You're going to be a big sister, Melissa. How do you think you will like that?"

She hadn't seemed at all sure.

"Do you think you'd like to have a little brother or a little sister?"

"No." She seemed very definite on that point. She was just as clear about what she *would* like.

"I want a pony!" she said.

"Oooh! I don't think Mommy can manage that," I'd told her. "If I can't have a pony, would you rather we have a little brother or a little sister?"

"A sister," she'd eventually conceded. So at least I was bringing home Melissa's *second* choice.

I needn't have worried about either of the older girls' responses, however. They both instantly fell in love with their baby sister. To them Heather was like a live doll in the house for all of us to play with. Whenever

25

I'd sit down to feed or rock Heather, Stacey and Melissa would sit beside me, feeding and rocking their own little baby dolls. And there was nothing they enjoyed more than actually getting to hold Heather or helping me take care of her.

Of course it wasn't easy having three girls so close together in age. Just taking them all out shopping at once proved a formidable challenge. To help me manage, Bill's Grandmother Rothweiler knitted a little red harness with white trim. It looked like a mini-halter with a small metal ring attached in back—to which I could hook a leash. This ingenious restraining system allowed Stacey some freedom of movement while giving me a measure of control. Melissa I would carry in a back carrier, and Heather I'd tote in my arms in a plastic infant carrier.

The four of us got a lot of smiles and more than our share of curious stares when we'd go gallivanting around town. But not everyone was very approving. I vividly recall the day a stranger accosted me in a grocery store to scold me for treating Stacey "like a little dog" by holding her with a leash.

If I could have found a hole, I'd have crawled into it. But when this meddlesome lady continued to berate me, I could hold my tongue no longer. "Excuse me, ma'am," I interrupted more politely than I truly felt at that moment. "But I would rather keep my three-year-old safe by my side than have her dart off in a parking lot and get run over by a car."

The woman sputtered on in reply for another minute or two. Finally, I simply walked away, completing my shopping with as much haste and dignity as I could muster under the circumstances.

But all in all, those three precious girls brought me far more joys than hassles. For as hectic as my life could be at times, I found it wonderfully satisfying and fulfilling. We were a normal family, feeling settled, building toward the future, and finally putting down roots.

This was the happiness I'd always dreamed of before I'd met and fallen in love with Bill Whitestone our freshman year on the University of Alabama campus in Tuscaloosa. When we married at the end of our sophomore year, I dropped out of school to work and support our starving student lifestyle while Bill finished up his degree. But I'd never given up my other dream of getting a teaching degree; so Bill had promised I could go back to school as soon as he became the family breadwinner.

By the time Bill graduated in the spring of 1969, I was already more than five months pregnant with Stacey. He had requested and received a one-year postponement of the military service his ROTC commitment required. We spent that year back in Bill's hometown of Dothan, where he worked for his parents at The Village Carriage House, the Whitestones' furniture store. Stacey was born there in Dothan, appropriately enough, on Labor Day, 1969.

The following summer, when it came time for Bill to begin his active duty, I was pregnant with Melissa. The army assigned us to Ft. Benning, Georgia, only a two-hour drive from Dothan. Melissa—our blonde-haired, blue-eyed, little Georgia peach—arrived that December of 1970.

Because the service seemed to suit Bill well, we talked for a time about the possibility of his making a career in the army. He received a lot of affirmation from his superiors. And with free medical care, subsidized housing, good pay, and thirty days of paid leave a year, the military life certainly had its advantages.

Fortunately for us, with the de-escalation of the war in Vietnam, Bill never got assigned overseas. He actually spent his entire tour of duty in administration at Fort Benning. However, when the army began offering "early-outs" to young officers just eighteen months into Bill's required two-year tour, he decided to forgo a military career and go home to become a partner with his folks in the retail furniture business.

So it was back to Dothan, Alabama, again. This time for good.

Back during college, when Bill had taken me home to meet his family, that very first time I'd laid eyes on his hometown, I'd been impressed with its feeling of "family." Dothan was peppered with playgrounds and churches. But what struck me most were all the ballparks. On our first drive into town on the way to Bill's home on Sioux Street, we must have passed half a dozen different ball fields—all being used.

I clearly recall that first exposure to Dothan in the late afternoon of a gorgeous spring day. Azaleas and dogwood were in full bloom. The sun hung low in the western sky, its glow filtered by a canopy of pines. And even then I heard a small inner voice or maybe just an echoed thought that said, *This would be a great place to raise a family.*

Tucked out of the way in the far southeastern corner of our beautiful state, Dothan didn't seem large enough to have many big-city problems. Yet it wasn't so small that you felt as if you were missing out on life either.

While that part of Alabama is perhaps best known for its peanut industry and cattle farming, Dothan had a rather broad economic base. With Fort Rucker located just a few miles away, there was always a strong military presence in town. I suppose that may have been one reason Dothan became a medical center for the region, as well as "the shopping hub for the Wiregrass Area." It was very much a regional center for that part of LA (that's "Lower Alabama" to outsiders), offering far more in the way of attractions, service, and opportunities than most other towns of forty-odd thousand people.

Though I'd grown up in the much bigger city of Birmingham, I fell in love with the flavor and feel of my adopted hometown. With Montgomery just an hour and a half to the northwest, any time we needed to shop for greater variety, ice skate, or take in the cultural events of a "bigger" city, the travel time was reasonable. My own family lived just a little over three hours away in Birmingham. And best of all, to my way of thinking, the beautiful white beaches of Panama City, Florida, were just two hours due south.

In fact, Dothan was widely known—to all truckers and many tourists en route to Florida's panhandle—as "Circle City." The nickname came from the big circular bypass designed to divert the heaviest Florida-bound traffic around the outskirts of town.

So for a lot of reasons, I felt very good about our move back to Dothan when Bill got out of the service. With a VA loan we were able to buy our first house, a new three-bedroom ranch home in what was considered the "boondocks" of Dothan at the time because it was outside the circle. Yet we were only four or five minutes' drive from Bill's parents' in-town home and The Village Carriage House, where Bill worked.

We were excited by the prospect of our first home and the settled feeling it gave us. And when we returned to Dothan, I was just as excited about the possibility of resuming my own education at the extension campus of Troy State University at nearby Fort Rucker.

While I don't think Bill ever understood my drive to finish up my degree and certainly didn't encourage me to go back to school, he agreeably kept the bargain we'd made after I dropped out of school to support him when we were first married. I enrolled for classes as soon as we returned to Dothan that summer. While I took night classes two or sometimes four nights a week, Bill would hurry home from the store in the afternoon to feed the girls supper, supervise their evening routine, and then put them to bed. I took a quarter off after Heather was born. Then it was back to school again, with Bill taking care of all three girls on my class nights.

So our lives were indeed full, but happy. I was in love with my husband. We had three beautiful, healthy daughters. Life was undeniably good.

One of the advantages of having three little girls so close together in age was watching their relationships develop. In a lot of ways they were more like friends than sisters. What one did, they all wanted to do.

I remember Heather's first Christmas, the second holiday season in our new home. The girls had been concerned that Santa wouldn't deliver any toys to our house since we didn't have a chimney. So I'd bought a little three-dimensional cardboard fireplace that we'd carefully constructed by folding, bending, and inserting tab A into slot B, and so on. We even placed some candles and a few Christmas knickknacks on the mock mantle above the orange-painted flames of our "open fire."

As far as the girls were concerned, I think the tree and the fireplace would have provided as much festive atmosphere as they needed. But I went overboard to decorate the entire house in an extravagant manner befitting the nickname my family gave me—"Scarlett O'Glitter."

It seemed just as difficult not to overdo the shopping because I felt I needed to buy three of everything. So even though Heather, at ten months, wasn't ready for the little bike Stacey got, or even a tricycle like Santa brought Melissa, we maintained the wheels theme by getting her one of those riding toys toddlers can either pull around or sit on.

Heather thought she was big stuff that first Christmas. And so did everyone else.

In fact, for the first eighteen months of Heather's life we marveled at how quickly she developed—crawling, walking, and talking earlier than either of the other girls. Looking back now with a little more objectivity, I guess she may not have been all that exceptional. Having two big sisters so close to her in age provided both example and inspiration. Heather *had* to develop and move fast just to keep up—or to get out of the way.

It certainly didn't take Melissa long to decide that her little sister could be just as much fun as the pony she'd originally wanted. Whereas Stacey, the oldest, seemed inclined to "mother" Heather, it was Melissa and Heather who really bonded from the start, becoming great friends and soul mates. Stacey was very much the strong leader, always the persuasive and articulate one. Melissa was the active, aggressive, athletic, and fearless tomboy of the crew. And whatever Melissa did, wherever she went, Heather tried to follow.

29

I couldn't take my eyes off them for a moment, even in our own backyard, or the two of them would plunge into the woods behind our house on some great mission of discovery. I nicknamed them "Lewis and Clark" because they were always exploring and going anywhere in search of new sights and adventures. During Heather's second summer, we had to be especially careful whenever we went to the beach, because Melissa knew no fear. When she'd go squealing and charging out into the surf, Heather would be toddling into the waves right behind her.

Fortunately, most of the time, Heather's desire to mimic her "big girl" sisters was more cute than worrisome. I wasn't sure for a time if she'd inherited the same stubborn streak Melissa had, or if she was just copying her big sister's behavior. But even at less than a year and a half Heather could stomp and pout with the best of them. She and Melissa always had the same response when I'd go into my stern mother routine and say, "You better *be moving* [pick up that toy, or whatever] by the time I count to three or *else*. . . ." Stacey, my most compliant child, would jump to it on *one*, or *two* at the latest. Melissa and Heather would never think of moving before *two*, and more often than not I'd be saying *thr* . . . before they'd begin to obey.

Heather could be a very determined (we could even say "demanding") little girl when it came to doing what her sisters did. Every night, when I'd roll Stacey's and Melissa's hair, Heather would insist I roll hers as well—even before she had enough hair to wrap all the way around a pink foam curler.

I vividly remember the way she played with all the big girls at Stacey's fifth birthday party in early September of 1974. In keeping with the party theme Stacey had chosen, I had made a "Pin the Pocket on Raggedy Ann" game to play with all the neighborhood kids we'd invited to help celebrate the occasion. At one point during the party, as I sat to the side with a few other mothers, watching and enjoying the fun, Heather walked over to me, laid her head in my lap, and simply smiled up at me. Then after a few seconds of reassuring contact, she trotted off to join the action again. She and Melissa were as excited as Stacey was with all her new toys and other presents.

That night as I tucked the girls into bed, I looked down on their tired, contented faces and thought once more how fortunate I was to have three such bright and beautiful little girls. A cold front had passed through southern Alabama that afternoon, and there was now a definite chill in the air. So before I left the girls' room I walked over to close the windows. Just as I did, such a sudden gust of cold air engulfed me that I shivered. It seemed an odd and surprising feeling.

Only later, when I recalled that happening, did I wonder if God had been warning me of things to come. If he was, it escaped me. I simply closed the windows, turned out the lights, and left my little girls dreaming of parties, presents, and happy times.

There was no way to know that the perfectly "normal" life we enjoyed was about to change.

CHAPTER 3

What's Wrong with My Baby?

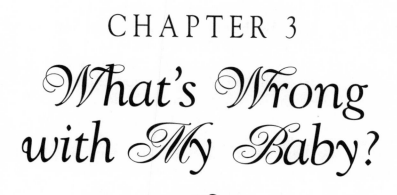

When Heather awakened with a slight fever on Saturday morning, the 14th of September, I wasn't overly concerned. She'd always been an extremely healthy baby, and I'd had enough experience with Stacey and Melissa not to get too uptight over a fretful toddler with a temperature of 101 degrees. In order to do my student teaching that fall, I'd just enrolled the two younger girls in day care. So it seemed reasonable to assume this was just some innocuous twenty-four-hour bug making the rounds among Dothan preschoolers.

So after Bill left for the store, I settled down in a chair to cuddle and comfort my restless daughter while her big sisters sat watching their favorite Saturday morning cartoons. But the longer I held Heather in my lap, the sicker she seemed to get. Unable to keep down any of the food I tried to give her, she'd become so listless by 9:30 A.M. that she seemed on the verge of semiconsciousness. Worried by this rather sudden development and the fact that her temperature had climbed to almost 103 degrees, I called our pediatrician's office to ask for a consultation. The doctor on call told me to bring her right in.

I immediately phoned our next-door neighbor, Doris, to ask if her daughter Gina, the girls' favorite baby-sitter, could stay with Stacey and Melissa. Then I called Bill at work to tell him what was going on and headed into town. By the time I carried Heather into the waiting room of the pediatric clinic, she hung limp in my arms.

As the doctor gave Heather a quick examination I described how quickly the symptoms had set in. His serious expression only confirmed what I knew: my baby was seriously ill. He seemed particularly concerned about a stiffness around Heather's neck, something I hadn't detected.

"She just had her immunization shot recently," I reported. "Could this whole thing be some sort of reaction to the DPT?"

"It could be," the doctor replied. "But I think we need to check out some other possibilities first. Right now I want you to carry Heather over to the emergency room at Flowers Hospital next door. I'll call them to say we're coming and to order a spinal tap. That should tell us what our next step needs to be."

I phoned Bill with that report, and he said he'd meet me at the hospital. With Heather in my arms, I walked quickly across the parking lot and through the doors of the hospital emergency room. One of the ER nurses ushered me into an empty room and helped me lay my motionless daughter on the examination table. A short while later the doctor arrived.

"Mrs. Whitestone," he said, "we're going to need you to help us hold your little girl down for this procedure. It's important that she be kept very still." The nurse showed me how we would clasp Heather's arms and legs, effectively pinning her to the table. We needn't have bothered. While I cringed as I watched the doctor prepare his syringe and run his finger down her back to find the spot between the vertebrae, Heather didn't so much as flinch when he inserted that monstrous needle deep into her spinal column.

The entire procedure took only a few moments. When the nurse and I released our grip, Heather still didn't move or make a sound. The doctor held up the sample for me to see. "Maybe just a little cloudiness," he observed. "But her spinal fluid is basically clear."

"That's good?"

He smiled at me and nodded. "Very good. We've got to test the fluid, but I think we can safely say from the looks of this that your daughter does not have spinal meningitis."

Meningitis! Had the pediatrician mentioned that before? If so, it hadn't sunk in. *Thank you, Lord. But what is wrong with my baby?* No one seemed to know.

By this time Bill had joined me. Together we walked back over to the pediatric clinic, carrying Heather. There the doctor confirmed the final results from the spinal tap. "At least we've ruled out meningitis," he said. But he went on to tell us he remained concerned about her general listlessness and the possibility of dehydration if she continued vomiting. "As a precaution, I think we ought to admit Heather to the hospital right away. We'll be able to keep her under observation, monitor any changes in her condition, and maybe get her fluid and energy level back up with an IV."

We hurried home and made arrangements for our baby-sitter to stay with the other girls until Bill's parents could pick them up. Then we drove around the circle to Southeast General Hospital—where our pediatricians had full privileges.

When we checked Heather into a room on the pediatric floor a little after 1:00 that afternoon, her temperature was up to 103.7 degrees. The nurses administered liquid Tylenol for the fever and started intravenous feeding. Heather was so weak and lethargic that no restraints were necessary. She slept fitfully most of the afternoon. I pulled a chair close to her bed so I could hold her hand, stroke her hair, and wipe her forehead with a cool, damp cloth. When she'd occasionally open her eyes, I'd smile and talk to her. But she never actually responded; her eyes looked glazed, as if she'd been drugged. I'd try off and on to get her to take a bottle, but she seemed too weak to care. Nothing else happened until one of our pediatricians checked on her during his rounds early Saturday evening.

"She's resting quietly. The IV should help keep her stabilized," he told us. "I suspect she has some kind of virus. If so, we can expect to see a rash appear within the next twenty-four hours or so. Then her fever should break, and we'll see a turn for the better."

I called my folks that evening to tell them we'd checked Heather into the hospital. My mother offered to drive down immediately to help with the other girls. I told her not to come—that the doctor thought it was just a virus and that Stacey and Melissa could spend the rest of the weekend with Bill's parents, Herb and Colley.

Herb dropped by the hospital to check on us all a little later that evening. And before bedtime Bill made a quick trip down to the hospital cafeteria to get me some supper. But I didn't feel much like eating.

Between the uncomfortable hospital room chairs and the nurses constantly coming in to check Heather's vitals, neither Bill nor I got much sleep that night. Heather still had a moderate fever when the pediatrician made his Sunday morning rounds. He checked carefully about her neck and midsection for a rash. "No rash yet. Probably soon," he told us. I took some comfort in his seeming lack of concern.

By noon, even with Tylenol, the fever had again risen above 102. The nurses, worried that Heather's lack of movement would result in bedsores, helped maneuver her into my lap without dislodging the IV. I held and tried to comfort her most of the afternoon, checking regularly for the first sign of a telltale rash. _Nothing!_ My beautiful little girl lay in my arms, limp as a rag doll. That afternoon, the only encouraging (if you could call it that) sign of life was that from time to time she'd give a barely audible little whine. That small noise was the first real expression of discomfort she'd made since getting ill.

I called my supervising teacher to tell her I wouldn't be at school in the morning. And when our doctor made his evening rounds, Bill and I asked why they hadn't prescribed any medication other than Tylenol. He told us he still suspected a virus, that the rash should appear "anytime now," but until he could be sure, he was reluctant to give Heather any additional medications. "They might mask other symptoms that could help us make a definite diagnosis," he said.

Monday dawned. Another one of our pediatricians came in that morning after Bill had already left to take Stacey to kindergarten and Melissa to KinderKare. When I asked what he thought might cause a fever to last this long, the doctor simply replied, "That's just the way some viruses are." But there was still no rash. And he couldn't explain that.

Heather had the basic blood work done when she'd been admitted. But now the doctor ordered a full round of additional tests. "We should have the results on these back by Thursday," he told me.

Thursday! I thought. _But this is just Monday. How long can this go on?_

I think that's when my mother's instincts began telling me, _There's something wrong here. This isn't right._ I felt even more worried a few minutes later when the medical technician who came to take blood from Heather said, his voice full of gentle concern, "We have a mighty sick little girl here."

By the time Heather's temperature escalated to 104.3 early that afternoon, I had begun to think, _If no one here knows what to do or can tell_ *us what's wrong with Heather, maybe we need to transfer her to the Children's Hospital up in Birmingham.*

By late afternoon the only change I saw was that Heather now winced in pain whenever we lifted her or shifted her position in the bed. I remember thinking, *She's not getting better, she's getting worse.* I was scared.

In the room that evening with Bill and his dad, I voiced my growing concerns about the lack of treatment and mentioned the idea of transferring Heather to Birmingham's nationally known Children's Hospital, three hours away.

Herb's response was, "These doctors are every bit as good as any you'll find in Birmingham!" Bill echoed the doctor's earlier words about not wanting to mask the symptoms with medication before they could make an accurate diagnosis.

So I dropped the transfer idea. But I was feeling very scared, lonely, and frustrated watching our little girl lie motionless and miserable in that hospital hour after hour.

When I called to update my own parents late that evening, I was almost in tears. "I'm not giving you a choice this time," my mother told me sternly. "I'll drive down in the morning. I should have been there yesterday!"

Upon awakening Tuesday morning, I noticed a slight swelling of Heather's left hand and wrist. When I called the nurses in to look, they couldn't see it; they thought I was looking too hard for a rash. When the doctor came, he dismissed my concern just as quickly as the nurses had. He noted no swelling.

But I'd spent most of the past three days holding and stroking my baby's hands. I felt sure about the swelling; I did not think it was a figment of my imagination.

Mom arrived shortly after noon. I saw the momentary look of shock and alarm on her face when she first walked into the hospital room and spotted Heather lying on that bed. She immediately tried to cover it, obviously not wanting to distress me further. But soon she was in tears.

Later Mother admitted to me how devastated she was when she'd first seen Heather: "I couldn't believe that was our Heather. I couldn't speak or control the tears that rolled down my face. I was nearly overcome with grief." More than twenty years later she still can't talk about that day without her voice cracking and tears filling her eyes.

In an odd sort of way, I found my mother's emotional response almost reassuring. After three days of worrying and feeling that my concerns were too easily dismissed by the medical people and even by my husband, I took comfort in my own mother's alarm. At least now there was someone else who clearly saw reason for serious concern. It wasn't just me anymore.

For the longest time the two of us just stood there, holding each other and crying with a shared sense of futility. There was nothing we could do for Heather other than be there. And try to comfort each other.

Tuesday proved to be another rough, restless night. Wednesday morning I thought the swelling in Heather's left hand had increased. The pediatrician humored me and examined it when he made his rounds around 8:00 A.M. Then he told me he still saw nothing there to be concerned about.

But by 9:00 Heather's hand had ballooned to nearly twice its normal size, and the skin had turned bright red. I called for the nurse immediately; there was no denying it now. The nurse contacted our pediatricians' office and two of our doctors arrived at the hospital about noon.

They examined Heather quickly and then removed her from the room for "further blood tests." When they brought her back a few minutes later, I asked if they had any idea yet what could be causing the swelling and the fever. The older of the two partners immediately replied, "It would take twelve medical books and a list as long as my arm to cover what Heather _might_ have."

I was initially so taken aback by the patronizing you-wouldn't-understand-if-I-told-you response that I didn't say anything. But as he walked out to the hall to confer further with his colleague, I began to steam. When he came back in, I asked if we could get another opinion from his senior partner, the one doctor in the practice yet to see Heather.

Suddenly he looked as angry as I felt. "Obviously you don't trust my opinion!" he snapped. Then he turned on his heel and strode out of the room. His colleague stayed and tried to calm the waters by explaining that the group's senior partner would be out of town until Friday.

When I reached Bill at the store to report what had happened, I was more upset than ever. And I got downright panicky later that afternoon as Heather's temperature skyrocketed to 104.9 and her other hand and left foot also began to swell.

I don't know that the doctors ever came back to look in on Heather again that day. I didn't see them if they did. And when I read over the nurses' records later, I didn't find the usual note, or any other indication that our pediatricians checked on Heather at all that evening.

Wednesday night was the worst yet. By far. The doctors had ordered Heather's IV removed that afternoon, perhaps because of the swelling in her arms. They didn't explain why.

Since she was no longer getting any nourishment intravenously, the nurses provided me a small syringe to try to force liquid into her mouth a few drops at a time. I may have managed to get her to swallow a few cc's, but by this time her joints were so swollen that we couldn't lift her or even turn her on the bed without her whimpering pathetically in pain.

Looking down at my little girl on that bed, I too began to cry in utter helplessness. There I was, scared to death I was going to lose my baby girl, and I couldn't even take her in my arms to comfort her without causing her more pain.

All I could do was pace—back and forth from one side of the room to the other—worrying, crying, and praying. *Please, Lord, oh please don't let her die!* I knew in my heart God was there; I believed he could hear me. But like Heather, I found no comfort in that hospital room that night. Nothing would stop the hurt. Never in my life had I felt so frightened and desperately alone.

By the time our doctor made his rounds Thursday morning the swelling had progressed noticeably farther up Heather's arms. Now even the right foot had begun to swell. She had become so sensitive to touch that we couldn't even drape a single-layer sheet over her without making her cry out in agony. When the doctor noted the changes and then left without giving any new orders, I just about lost it.

For a while I fumed and paced faster and faster across the room and back. But by 9:00 A.M. I could endure this inaction no longer. Bill tried in vain to calm me down. "I don't care what anyone thinks!" I yelled at him. "I won't stand by anymore and just watch Heather die!"

With that I marched out of the room and stormed down the hall to the nurses' station. "I want you to get on that phone right now," I screamed at the startled woman at the desk. "You call our doctors right now! And you inform them that unless they can begin some kind of treatment for Heather, or start giving us some answers in the next few hours, I'm going to remove her from this hospital and take her to Birmingham Children's Hospital, where I know someone will do something for my daughter!"

"B-b-b-ut you can't check out of this hospital without your doctor's permission," the poor flustered woman replied.

"You just watch me!" I told her as I angrily pivoted and headed back to Heather's room. I had no doubt she'd make the call.

Bill phoned the doctors' office soon after the nurse did. "Daphne means what she said," he told them. "She'll do it."

By 10 A.M. the nurses received the new orders. We were asked to sign a parental consent form giving permission for Heather to receive two injections of antibiotics. I couldn't believe I'd had to pitch a temper tantrum to make it happen, but at least something was finally being done.

I do recall thinking, *If we have to sign this, whatever they're giving her must be powerful stuff.* I don't remember anyone telling us they were giving Heather both polycillin and Gentamycin. And I certainly don't remember anyone at that time explaining the possible side effects. Maybe those were listed on the consent form; I don't know. But even if someone had explained any and all the potential dangers, I doubt we'd have made a different decision. I believed in my heart that morning that Heather was on the verge of death. Something had to be done—and soon.

Watching Heather get those two shots, one of which was administered with a needle that looked like something a veterinarian might use on a horse, gave me the first real dose of relief and encouragement I'd had in the five days since we'd arrived at the hospital. I didn't get particularly worried when Heather's temperature soared above 104 again around the middle of the day. I knew we might have to allow as much as twenty-four hours to see the full effects of the antibiotics begin to kick in.

Thankfully we didn't have to wait that long for the first signs of improvement. By late afternoon I detected a slight reduction in the swelling. By suppertime Heather even managed to swallow a few bites of rice cereal, applesauce, and mashed banana—the first "food" she'd had in almost a week.

The doctor making the rounds that evening acted pleased to see a little improvement. He said the tests that came back that afternoon indicated the presence of the Haemophilus influenza virus in her bloodstream, which could certainly explain the fever. As for the swelling of the hands and feet, the doctor said that might be attributed either to the onset of Still's disease or cellulitis. (He didn't explain either condition at the time.)

So, while grateful to finally be getting some possible answers, I couldn't help feeling cynical enough to wonder, *Why are we suddenly hearing so many diagnoses after we've been told nothing for nearly a week?*

Are they just saying this now because I made a scene and demanded action? Well, at least Heather's getting better! Thank God!

Heather received her second round of antibiotic injections that night. By Friday morning her fever dropped almost to 99 degrees, the lowest it had been in a week. While it did climb back up during the day, I had no doubts Heather had turned the corner. You could still see some swelling, but that was slowly going away. She ate more soft foods and seemed to rest much better. During that day she received two more doses of both antibiotics.

Gradually I began to relax. Saturday they took Heather off the Gentamycin, saying the polycillin should be strong enough on its own to handle the H. influenza. Later we learned that that decision also would have been influenced by the fact that Gentamycin was the more dangerous of the two drugs.

Saturday was the best day yet. Sunday turned out even better. Yet despite her obvious progress, the doctors explained they wouldn't release Heather until her temperature stabilized for at least twenty-four straight hours. While her temperature was no longer climbing so high, it still rose and fell rather sharply during the course of a day.

With Heather definitely out of any serious danger, and with my having already lost a week of school and facing the loss of my entire semester of student teaching if I missed any more days, Bill and I discussed our scheduling options. Mom decided Dad and my youngest sister and brother, who were fourteen and twelve at the time, could manage in Birmingham without her a little longer. So she stayed with Heather at the hospital during the days while I taught. I'd pick the older girls up after school every afternoon and spend a little time with them. Then Bill would run me back to the hospital to spend the evening with Heather. After she conked out for the night I'd work on my lesson plans until I dozed off. By this time I'd gotten amazingly good at sleeping in chairs, although I suppose my emotional and physical exhaustion probably had something to do with it.

As much improvement as we saw in Heather over those next few days, she was still by no means well. She came to dread those twice-daily shots so much that she'd scream at the sight of anyone in a white coat. Her little leg, where she got the injections, turned black-and-blue and looked truly awful. So most of the time she was content to lie quietly in bed or sit peacefully on Mother's, Bill's, or my lap.

At the end of that second week, Heather's temperature finally leveled out. Friday the doctors said everything was looking good. Saturday morning they told us we could take our little girl home. We were advised to continue oral antibiotics and to bring her back to their offices for a checkup in about a week. There were no other instructions. They said we could expect her leg to be sore and to have to limit her mobility for a few days. But they told us she should be running around with everything back to normal in two to three weeks.

That was good news.

I don't ever remember feeling more relieved and grateful than I did that morning walking out of Southeast General Hospital with Heather in my arms. The most horrible ordeal of my life was over at last.

Or so I thought.

CHAPTER 4
Christmas 1974

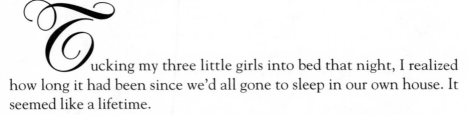

ucking my three little girls into bed that night, I realized how long it had been since we'd all gone to sleep in our own house. It seemed like a lifetime.

I thanked God for the umpteenth time that day that Heather was home again. When I tiptoed into her room to check on her one last time before I went to bed, I took a few minutes to stand over her crib and pray that God would restore her to full and complete health very soon.

The relative progress we'd seen in Heather over that second week in the hospital had been more than a little deceptive. Those first few hours home, as wonderful as it felt to have the entire family together again, had offered a sobering reminder of how far Heather still had to go. As far as we'd seen her come since she'd hung on the verge of death in that hospital room, she was still no more than a shell of the active and adventuresome little girl she'd been before. And nothing had made this glaring truth more evident than her interaction with the other girls.

Nearly ecstatic to have their baby sister home again, Stacey and Melissa had spent much of the afternoon and early evening bringing Heather her favorite toys, chattering to her constantly, and repeatedly attempting to get her to play. While she smiled occasionally in appreciation of her sisters' special attention, Heather's only response was to reach out feebly to touch one of her favorite stuffed animals.

She evidenced no real life or energy. There was no spunk, no spirit in her body. No sparkle in her eyes. She seemed only partly there. I could only pray and try to believe that God would bring back that little girl I'd come to know and love those past eighteen months. *Please, Lord, make it soon!*

We knew that in Heather's current state of health we couldn't risk exposing her to a day-care setting—even if we'd have found someone who would take such a sick child. My mother had already been gone from home for two weeks; she needed to get back to her family in Birmingham. I seriously considered staying home with Heather myself, realizing that even if she returned to normal as quickly as the doctors had predicted, there would be no way for me to complete my student teaching requirement that term. But I didn't have to face that decision because our wonderful friend and next-door neighbor, Doris Blevins, who'd regularly relieved Mother during that second week in the hospital, volunteered to come over and watch Heather every day for the next couple of weeks. "I'll be glad to do it," she insisted. "If there's something I need to do at home, I'll just carry her next door. I want to help."

God bless friends like Doris. We accepted her generous offer.

Unfortunately, neither Doris nor Bill and I noticed any measurable improvement in Heather's condition over that next week. She still wasn't trying to walk, or even sitting up by herself. "She seems perfectly happy lying in the middle of the floor on her blanket for hours at a time," Doris reported.

Thursday evening I thought I detected a little swelling around Heather's knees. Friday morning it was still there. Since our pediatricians had suggested we bring her back for a one-week checkup anyway, we called for an appointment, and Bill took her in to the doctor's office that very morning.

When they returned, Bill gave me a full report. He said Heather had been seen by one of the group's younger doctors, who was now convinced the swelling was indeed a symptom of cellulitis. This doctor explained cellulitis could be a chronic condition which exhibits arthritis-like symptoms, but instead of attacking the joints themselves, it inflames the soft tissue around the joints.

According to Bill, the doctor had told him, "I've seen three or four cases of this in my practice. There's no predicting how often or where she will experience discomfort around her joints. The condition is migratory. One time you may see the swelling and redness around the knees and the next time it may affect the elbows. Aspirin treats it beautifully. And in each of the cases I've treated, the problem has gone away completely by the time the patient is in his or her teens."

When Bill expressed our concern about Heather's continued lethargy and the fact she was neither mobile nor talking again, the doctor had assured him, "This infection Heather had won't go away as quickly as a normal virus or cold would." He restated the opinion that her lack of mobility wasn't surprising considering the number of injections she'd received in her leg. He wanted to keep Heather on the oral antibiotics for another couple weeks, by which time he fully expected her to be back to normal.

I wanted to believe that report as much as Bill did. For more than two weeks I tried. Every day I looked for progress that never came. With the end of October fast approaching, my level of concern was rising rapidly. Though the bruises had long since disappeared from her leg, the active little girl who used to run and explore everywhere still wasn't walking or even sitting up without help. This extremely verbal child, who'd been regularly spouting three- to five-word sentences before she'd been sick ("I love you, Mommy," "I go play Melissa," "I want to eat," "Come here, Mommy," "I see Melissa"), still hadn't tried to utter a word since we'd brought her home.

All along, I'd been keeping Mother updated by phone concerning Heather's progress—or lack of it. Time and again Mom had said, "Daphne, honey, you ought to bring Heather up here to Birmingham and let Dr. Humphries examine her. If anybody can help her, he can."

The last week of October I finally agreed. "Call his office tomorrow," I told her. "See how soon we can get Heather in to see him."

My family had always put a lot of faith in Dr. Joseph Humphries. He'd earned it over twenty years as our family's pediatrician—for all five of us kids. I knew my parents credited him with saving the life of my brother Jimmy, who was six years my junior. When he had been two and a half years old, Jimmy had developed a very serious blood infection after contracting chicken pox. When Mom had phoned Dr. Humphries and described Jimmy's symptoms, the doctor had rushed right over to begin treatment. He actually canceled all his office appointments for the rest of the day so he could sit by my brother's bedside in our home—until he'd felt certain Jimmy was going to pull through.

But Joseph Humphries was more than a gifted and compassionate doctor who had become a valued friend of our family. He was so widely admired and respected among his peers that at the time we decided to seek his opinion on Heather he was serving as president of the pediatricians' association for the entire state of Alabama. Needless to say, I was ready to place my full trust in Dr. Humphries before he ever saw Heather.

In anticipation of our November 9 appointment in Birmingham, we wanted to get copies of Heather's complete medical records for Dr. Humphries' reference. But when Bill called our pediatricians' office to make the arrangements, our routine request was denied. After Bill explained that we were taking our daughter to a former family doctor in Birmingham for a simple consultation, one of the pediatricians told him: "If you want your daughter's records, you'll have to sue us for them."

Bill and I were absolutely flabbergasted. Then furious. We couldn't understand that response at the time. Looking back, the only conclusion I can come to is that our doctors must have been more concerned about their potential liability than they were in providing the medical information necessary for our new doctor to offer Heather the best possible medical care.

Stunned and angry at the attitude of our doctors, Bill did contact a lawyer to find out what legal recourse we had for getting Heather's medical records. He told us we might indeed have to file a malpractice suit—a long and involved procedure which could take months or even years to settle. We instructed him to start the process. As a result, we did get copies of Heather's records the following year. Once we had what we wanted, we decided to drop the suit. But in the meantime, we had to take Heather to Birmingham without any official record of her medical history.

During our initial appointment with Dr. Humphries, he informed my mother and me that he could tell just by observing Heather that she'd recently suffered a "massive infection." The doctor listened patiently and intently as I gave him the most complete account I could of everything Heather had endured. When I finished, he conducted a thorough, head-to-toe examination. Then Dr. Humphries asked me if our doctors had prescribed any special vitamin supplements or physical therapy to aid in Heather's recovery. When I said no on both counts, he acted very surprised.

Dr. Humphries told us he saw "a number of potential concerns that may need to be addressed eventually." But his most immediate and urgent concern was the danger of muscle atrophy. He said it was crucial that we get Heather's limbs loosened, strengthened, and working again as soon as possible. His solution for that seemed simple enough. He wanted us to place her in a tub of soothing warm water several times a day and begin bending her arms, legs, wrists, and elbows. "She has very little muscle movement now," he said. "Step one is to get her using her arms and legs again." He also prescribed a vitamin supplement to bolster Heather's strength and her weakened immune system, adding that he'd like us to bring her back for another evaluation in one month.

What I didn't know until some months later (and what I will be forever grateful I didn't know at the time) was what Dr. Humphries confided to my mother after our first visit. He told her he thought Heather's reactions, and what few off-balance and irregular movements she did make, were strong indications of possible brain damage. He told Mom once we dealt with her mobility problems, he would probably need to recommend a neurologist who could check out those concerns.

Because I knew none of that, I walked out of Dr. Humphries' office encouraged that something practical and specific could finally be done to address my concerns about Heather's lack of mobility. At the same time I wondered how we were going to get the job done. I didn't want to keep imposing on my neighbor Doris. And whatever arrangements were made, I knew the frequent therapy Dr. Humphries recommended, while fairly simple, would be time-consuming. I was by then into the last few weeks of my student teaching—which meant I would have full responsibility all day, every day, for my sixth-grade class. With extensive lesson plans to prepare every night, I didn't see how I was going to be able to provide all the time and intensive care Heather would obviously need over the next two or three weeks.

When I voiced that concern to my mom, she suggested a solution I would never have considered. "Why don't you let Heather stay here in Birmingham with me?"

"Oh, I don't think so," I replied. "After all she's been through, I don't really want to be separated from her."

"It would just be during the week—you could come back to Birmingham Friday night for the weekend. You'll be away from her at school every day anyway. You said yourself you don't know who you'll get to watch her. She feels at home with me. I heard Dr. Humphries' instructions myself; I can do her therapy. Dad and your sister can help me; Stephanie will think it's fun. We'll certainly be able to work with

Heather more than you will during the week. And if we have any questions or problems, Dr. Humphries will be close by."

I still didn't like the idea of being separated from Heather, but Mom's arguments made a lot of sense. "Okay," I agreed. "We'll give it a try . . . for a week."

Every night when I talked to my mother on the phone, she told me Heather's therapy seemed to be helping. But when I drove up to Birmingham Friday night with Stacey and Melissa, I couldn't believe the progress Heather had made in just one week. She was now sitting by herself and would attempt to walk when we pulled her to a standing position.

Mom thought she'd earned another week as a personal physical therapist, and I agreed. It had been a welcome relief to be able to concentrate on my lesson plans each night. Just a couple more weeks of student teaching, and I'd have my degree. Then I'd have the time and energy Heather needed.

The following weekend Heather was actually trying to walk a little on her own. Her gait was slow, wobbly, and crooked. But to all of us it seemed remarkably wonderful progress.

By the time Mom and I took Heather back to Dr. Humphries' office the first of December, she was not only sitting and walking on her own, but from time to time she'd even attempt to run. Her equilibrium remained out of whack—she tilted to the right when she walked. Consequently she moved sort of diagonally instead of in a straight line. I had no idea Dr. Humphries saw that as another possible indication of brain damage; he expressed genuine pleasure at the progress he did see. And he said he wanted us to continue with the same course of therapy until we saw him again after the first of the year, at which time he might want to run some additional tests.

At that time I took Heather home again. Doris helped again with the therapy until I wrapped up my student teaching. Heather's day-to-day progress naturally seemed a little less dramatic than when I'd been driving up to Birmingham to see her just on the weekend. Yet each day I noticed what seemed like slight but steady progress in her walking and running.

It bothered me that she still wasn't talking at all. But she'd been so sick and slipped so far, maybe she could only make real progress in one area at a time. I could only trust that when she did start to talk again, her speech would improve as quickly as her walking had.

48

By this point Heather was regularly interacting and playing again with her sisters. However, I noticed there were still times when she seemed distracted—as if she were off in a world of her own. Her old stubbornness seemed more evident than ever; sometimes when I'd call her she'd just ignore me and not come at all. But then I knew it was about time for the terrible twos to kick in. And, with everything Heather had been through in the past few months, I guess I exercised extra patience when she didn't respond as quickly as I would have liked.

As the 1974 holiday season approached, I think I appreciated a special symbolism. This year as we prepared to celebrate the miracle of Christ's birth, I was also thanking God for the miracle of rebirth for Heather. Every day seemed to bring her a little bit closer to the healthy little girl she'd been just four months before. After everything we'd endured, I determined we would indeed be a grateful family that Christmas.

What a celebration we were to have! We took the girls to Bill's parents for the Whitestones' traditional Christmas Eve feast. The girls opened their first round of gifts there.

Then it was back to our house, just in time to welcome my mom and dad who'd driven down with Stephanie and Michael to spend the night and celebrate Christmas morning in Dothan with our family. Our house was full—of people, excitement, and anticipation—that evening.

Somehow Santa made his way in through our cardboard fireplace once again. So the next morning brought the traditional Christmas chaos—with torn wrapping paper, empty boxes, remnants of ribbon, new toys, and tired but hyper children stirred together in the merry mix strewn festively around the living room.

Eventually Bill and my dad migrated outdoors to play catch with my brother Michael and applaud Stacey and Melissa, who were trying out their new roller skates on the driveway. Heather sat quietly near the Christmas tree, playing contentedly with the set of brightly colored pots and pans (complete with friendly little smiley faces painted on the sides) which she'd opened earlier. Mother and Stephanie had started collecting the clutter. I decided it was time to finish preparing for the midmorning brunch, which had already become a Whitestone family Christmas Day tradition in the three years we'd lived in Dothan.

I'd done most of the work ahead of time. The festive fruit trays and special Christmas sweet rolls were ready to set out. The ham biscuits Bill liked so well could simply be heated up. But if I expected to have everything ready by the time my in-laws arrived to join us, I needed to get the breakfast buffet arranged and start the last-minute preparations—boiling water for the cheese grits and scrambling two dozen eggs in a big bowl.

Feeling a little rushed to be ready on time, I opened the cupboard to pull out my largest company-sized frying pan. Of course it sat under a big stack of other pots and pans, which I had to lift with one hand while maneuvering the frying pan with the other. I thought I had the pan I wanted free and clear, but when I slid it out the entire stack of metal pots and lids tumbled from the cupboard and hit the kitchen floor with a horrendous clang, clatter, and rattle that sounded for several long seconds like a terrible train wreck.

I literally jumped in involuntary response to the incredible racket—and I'd seen it coming.

For the first couple seconds after the ruckus died down, the house seemed abnormally quiet. Then I heard my mother's voice calling from the living room. "Daphne, I think you need to come in here."

Something in her tone made me go, even before I bothered to pick up the pans. And the troubled look on her face when I walked into the living room told me something was wrong.

"What is it?" I asked.

She nodded down at Heather, who was facing the tree with her back turned toward us, still playing peacefully on the floor. "I believe there's something wrong with Heather's hearing!"

"What are you talking about, Mother?"

"Stephanie and I nearly jumped out of our skin when you dropped those pans. But Heather didn't even look up."

"She's just playing so intently that she wasn't paying any attention," I told Mother. "She's been engrossed with those new pots and pans since she opened them."

Mother shook her head. "I'm afraid that wasn't it. I don't think she ever heard the noise."

"You must be wrong," I told her. And to prove it I moved over close behind Heather and clapped my hands. Heather neither turned nor looked up.

It can't be! I told myself. Rushing back to the kitchen, I scooped one of the pans off the floor and snatched a big wooden spoon from a drawer. In the living room again, I stepped carefully over toys and around boxes until I stood directly behind my busy little girl. Holding the pan tightly in my left hand, I banged the spoon against it with my right. *Bang.*

No response.

I smacked the pan sharply three times. BANG! BANG! BANG!
Nothing.

I gripped the pan even harder, leaned down right behind Heather, and swung again with all my might.

When Heather didn't so much as flinch, I suddenly felt as if the very life had been drained out of me. I literally sagged to that living-room floor beside my little girl, who finally noticed my presence. Looking over and noticing the spoon and pan in my hands, she smiled sweetly and went back to stirring the imaginary meal she was "cooking" in her little plastic pot.

My mother walked over and placed a reassuring hand on my shoulder before she gently pried the pan and spoon out of my hands. Then she walked slowly back into the kitchen to see what she could do to help with the brunch. I stayed slumped on the floor, emotionally paralyzed, staring at Heather through a blur of tears, asking myself (and God): *How much more are we going to have to go through?*

In the background carols played softly on the stereo. Neither Heather nor I could hear them. There was no Christmas spirit left in that house for me that day.

CHAPTER 5

Profoundly Deaf

Instead of the usual holiday afternoon activities—excited children showing smiling and nodding adults how their new toys work—the Whitestones and Grays spent much of that Christmas Day discussing what we should do about this latest development. There weren't a lot of smiles.

I wanted Heather to see Dr. Humphries again immediately. But we couldn't even reach his office until the 27th. His staff told us he wouldn't be in until the 30th. I took the first available appointment for that day and drove Heather up to Birmingham the night before.

Mother went with me again for Heather's appointment. We explained to the doctor what had happened Christmas morning. He conducted a little experiment of his own right there in his office. Then he nodded in confirmation: "She does seem to be experiencing a hearing loss. You're right about that. Let's take a good look at those ears."

Dr. Humphries' examination found both ears infected and full of fluid. He prescribed a basic antibiotic. But he also took a culture of the fluid he found in Heather's ear and asked if we'd be able to return the next day for the results.

An ear infection. What a relief!

We saw Dr. Humphries again the next day. He said, "The culture we took yesterday indicates the presence of H. influenza."

The doctor may as well have grabbed me and flung me back against the wall. *Not again! Please, Lord, not again!* The shock must have registered on my face, because Dr. Humphries immediately reassured me that the H. influenza is a very routine factor in most children's ear infections. It did not mean we were in any danger of another nightmare like we'd had in September. In fact, he thought a round or two of the antibiotics he prescribed should take care of the infection.

"Then a serious infection like this in both ears could explain why Heather's not hearing?" I was feeling encouraged again.

"Perhaps," he replied. "It certainly can't be helping." He went on to say there might be additional factors. But before we could know for sure the extent of any other problems, we needed to clear up the infection and get all that fluid out of her ears. He recommended we make an appointment with an ear, nose, and throat (ENT) specialist in Dothan who could follow up and make certain the fluid was gone.

We did that. The antibiotics did indeed take care of the infection. What fluid remained after that we treated with an over-the-counter antihistamine the ENT recommended. By the second time we saw that specialist, Heather's ears had completely cleared.

I even remember telling the doctor, "I think she's hearing better." I'd convinced myself it was true. Looking back, I'm not sure if I just wanted so badly to believe my daughter wasn't deaf, or if it was Heather's quick response to nonauditory clues that fooled me into thinking she could really hear me. (For example: If she and Melissa were playing when I called to them, Melissa would naturally look up, and Heather would almost immediately lift her own head to follow her sister's gaze.) The doctor wasn't convinced. And in my heart, as much as I wanted to see signs of improvement, I knew her hearing wasn't normal.

When I'd finished my student teaching in December, the Dothan City Schools had offered me a second-semester job. I was to take over a newly created Title I reading class at Highlands Elementary School. My only hesitation in accepting the job was knowing Heather still wasn't up to day care. But fortunately we found a local college-age girl looking for a part-time job. Estella would take care of Melissa and Heather in our own house from the time Bill left for the store around nine each morning until I could get home right after school in the afternoon.

The new schedule seemed to work perfectly for us and for Estella, who was as thrilled to find work that allowed for and paid for her night classes as I was to have finally attained my longtime dream of teaching. However, my excitement over the start of my new career was tempered by the ongoing questions concerning Heather's hearing.

Once we'd successfully treated the infection and fluids and it became clear, even to me, that at least some hearing loss remained, Dr. Humphries made another recommendation. He wanted us to bring Heather back to Birmingham to get a full auditory screening and evaluation at the Spain Clinic, the University of Alabama Birmingham's (UAB) rehabilitation center for hearing and vision. So I made those plans for my spring break week in March.

Dr. Humphries examined Heather again at that point. He acted very pleased at her progress in walking. Her gait was good. Her mobility seemed pretty much back to normal. And he felt the severe hearing loss definitely confirmed the need for the hearing tests we'd scheduled for the following couple of days. Because he did detect some minor swelling in Heather's ears—to indicate the recurrence of fluid—Dr. Humphries recommended that whatever the results of the hearing tests, we should plan to ask our local ENT to place tubes in Heather's ears. He said that simple operation should bring an end to any recurring ear infections or fluid buildup.

My mother and I both took Heather in for her auditory testing at the Spain Clinic. From time to time one of the staff would usher me back to an observation window so I could see and ask questions about what they were doing with my daughter. But most of the time was spent sitting and thinking in the waiting room while Heather went through one exercise after another with an examiner in a tiny soundproof room. Watching the constant commotion of people streaming up and down those halls, Mother and I were struck by the sheer number of children, all ages of children, from throughout the state, coming in to be treated or tested for hearing problems. And I prayed whatever problem they found with Heather, if they found a problem at all, could be quickly and easily corrected. She'd been through so much already (we all had) that I merely wanted the questions answered and the problem solved as soon as possible. For over six months it had seemed like life had been put on hold and forgotten; it was time to plug back in and start living again.

On the afternoon of the second day, the Spain Clinic staff finished up Heather's testing and called us in to a small conference room to give us a verbal report on her audiological assessment. Several people spoke briefly to review what they'd done with Heather and the findings of their particular test.

They explained how they'd conditioned Heather to respond to sounds using "visual reinforcement audiometric techniques." They'd conducted both bone conduction tests and tympanograms (tests of the eardrum) for indications of some mechanical problem in the structure of the ear itself.

The chief audiologist summed things up fairly quickly by explaining that after going through most of the tests twice on two different days, their results seemed clearly consistent and accurate. "Mrs. Whitestone, our conclusion, based on these tests, is that your daughter has suffered a severe to profound hearing loss in both ears."

"And what exactly does that mean?" I'm not sure if I was trying to understand or deny what had just been said.

"Well," the audiologist replied, "we have found that with children like Heather, who are classified as profoundly deaf. . . ."

Profoundly deaf? The sudden cold shock of those two words numbed me. Very little of the remainder of that conference registered on my mind as I tried to simultaneously deny the reality and grasp the implications of such a staggering thought. *Profoundly deaf? Heather's profoundly deaf?*

I don't know exactly at what point I did it. I may have actually interrupted what was being said. But I vaguely recall turning to my mother and repeating the words out loud to her. "Profoundly deaf? What are we going to do?"

At some point, I know I told the audiologist, "Help me understand what you're saying. We've never had anyone who was deaf in our family. I don't even know anyone who is deaf. I'm at a loss to know what you mean when you say Heather is 'profoundly deaf.' What should we expect out of a 'profoundly deaf' child? Give me a quick long-range picture."

"Well," the man began, "that's difficult to do because there are so many variables. So much depends on the child, her response and intelligence. The response of the family. The education and training she gets, and so on. But I can say this: As a profoundly deaf person, your daughter probably won't develop much verbal speech. Most children with her degree of deafness use sign language rather than speak. When it's time for her to go to school, she will probably need to attend a special school such as the Alabama School for the Deaf in Talladega. You can reasonably expect her to achieve maybe a third-grade education. So eventually you'll need to look at some sort of vocational training and. . . ."

I couldn't listen anymore. *Not now. Maybe not ever.* The limitations they were saying we'd just have to accept seemed unfathomable and absolutely unacceptable. My mother says she remembers me muttering, "Over my dead body!" Maybe I did; I honestly don't recall.

I do remember interrupting the long-range overview we were now getting by saying, "That's fine. But I can't be thinking too far down the road at this point. I need to know where to start. When I leave here today, what do I need to do first?"

They told me the written report they'd be compiling would spell some of that out. They gave me the name of a resource person in the State Department of Education who could help us get started in learning what therapy and special education programs might be available to us down in Dothan. They told me it was "imperative" that we begin some kind of speech conservation work as soon as possible in order to maintain and stimulate any remaining speech Heather might have. They also recommended we immediately begin the process of fitting Heather with a hearing aid in the hopes that amplification might enhance her therapy programs. Because they felt it crucial to begin language development as soon as possible, they suggested that we stop at the university bookstore and purchase a copy of *Signing Exact English* so we could begin to establish communication with Heather.

I don't think I said anything much to Mother as we walked across the street and down the block from the Spain Clinic to the bookstore. I was still in shock.

Walking into that store and seeing row after row of floor-to-ceiling bookshelves, I realized I didn't have the foggiest idea where to look for a book on sign language. But when I asked a clerk if they had any copies of *Signing Exact English*, she took me right to them. I flipped through one of the thick green paperbacks. It reminded me of a massive picture book, full of line drawings illustrating different hand and/or finger placements for different signs. Under each picture was the written English translation of that sign.

The letter signs for the alphabet appeared in the front of the book. The remainder of the volume amounted to a giant glossary of pictures. Thousands of pictures. Thousands of words.

As I browsed quickly through that imposing book, an entirely new thought hit me. *If Heather has to learn sign to communicate, that means we'll all need to learn sign. I will, Bill will. So will Stacey and Melissa. The same would be true of anyone who wants to communicate with Heather. My mother and father, Bill's family, my own brothers and sisters, their children (my kids' cousins) will have to learn to sign if they ever have hopes of developing any kind of relationship or even carrying on a meaningful conversation.*

I believe that was the very first implication to sink in since I'd first heard the words "profoundly deaf" in that conference room. And the enormity of the task before us suddenly seemed almost paralyzing. Fortunately the effect lasted just a few seconds.

We'll do whatever it takes, I decided as I closed the book, tucked it under my arm, and headed for the cash register. *I talk with my hands all the time anyway. This will be a cinch.*

I began learning to sign the alphabet that very night at my parents' house, practicing with Stephanie and Michael, my sister and brother. They thought it was a lot of fun. But then they also seemed to pick it up much faster than I did.

While telling myself I couldn't afford to be paralyzed by the challenge facing us, I couldn't help feeling overwhelmed by the sudden uncertainty about Heather's (and our entire family's) future and the complexity of the decisions to face—decisions I personally felt terribly unprepared and unqualified to make.

So, for a time, all I knew to do was to try to follow the advice and direction of the "experts." Since Dr. Humphries recommended getting tubes in Heather's ears, that's where we would start. But when we told the ENT specialist in Dothan what we wanted, he checked Heather again, saw no sign of recurring fluid, and said he didn't want to do an operation he felt was unnecessary. Once again we found ourselves at odds and frustrated with the medical establishment in our hometown.

When we informed Dr. Humphries that our doctor wouldn't perform the surgery, he referred us to another specialist in Birmingham, who scheduled the minor surgery at the Children's Hospital there the first week in April. By that point Heather had yet another ear infection, but the operation went ahead as scheduled. The procedure went beautifully.

During Heather's overnight hospital stay, Dr. Humphries arranged for a series of neurological tests to be conducted on Heather. The neurologist, Dr. Benton, stopped by Heather's room to give Bill and me his report before we checked out. He said he'd found no evidence of any permanent brain damage in Heather.

Brain damage? "Why would you be testing for that?"

Dr. Benton informed us that Dr. Humphries had ordered the workup because he'd had some concerns and suspicions. (My mother later told us that Dr. Humphries had been worried about brain damage when he first saw Heather in November, but there were so many other serious and treatable problems to address that he'd thought it better for Heather and for us to deal with those first. In retrospect I'm convinced he was right. I don't know how we'd have handled any more worries during those intervening months.)

Dr. Benton went on to explain that a massive infection of H. influenza such as Heather's could well have caused brain damage. At least that was one bullet we'd dodged. And he told us that Heather's hearing loss may have resulted from her treatment with Gentamycin, a powerful drug known to be ototoxic—sometimes resulting in nerve deafness such as Heather's. Because it had so many potentially serious side effects at the time, Gentamycin was usually reserved only for life-and-death situations. For the first time, we understood that Heather had probably been within twelve hours or so of death when the drugs were administered. We'd been that close to losing her!

Realizing what could have happened, understanding how much worse things could have been for Heather, I suppose I should have felt a sense of gratitude. I didn't.

In the beginning, at the hospital I'd prayed, "Please, Lord, just let her live!" And then, "Let her walk again." More recently I'd been praying that we'd finally know what was wrong with her hearing and what we could do about it. For eight months in all I'd been praying and hoping, believing things would be better . . . tomorrow.

Now we finally had some answers, and we needed to start looking ahead and planning what could and should be done for Heather. But I couldn't seem to get my eyes off the rearview mirror long enough to focus on the road ahead. Every day I found myself looking back, wrestling with the "what if" questions, rehashing a long list of regrets that festered and grew, first into a smoldering resentment, and then into outright anger.

The problem was knowing who to be angry with.

I remained very angry at the doctors who hadn't diagnosed or done anything until Heather had gotten so terribly sick. But being angry with people we weren't even seeing anymore felt both pointless and ultimately unsatisfying.

I was angry with Bill and his dad for not supporting my earliest contentions that we pull Heather out of Southeast General Hospital and go to Birmingham for help.

I was of course also angry with myself. If I had followed my first instincts, if I'd been stronger or quicker in voicing my concerns, if I'd done *something*, maybe Heather wouldn't be deaf.

But the easiest, biggest, and in many ways *safest* target for my wrath was God himself. If he was really the Creator and Controller of the universe like I'd always been taught, then he could have healed Heather in the hospital last fall before she reached the verge of death and needed that medicine. If he was the loving God I'd always believed in, he wouldn't have allowed a helpless little girl to suffer like Heather had. If he really cared about us, he'd be providing more of the answers and guidance we needed to know how to help Heather now.

My anger with God manifested itself in a variety of ways.

First was the sudden lack of what had been a lifelong appreciation for creation. I'd always felt closest to God and most aware of his presence when I could be out enjoying his glory amid the beauty of nature. For me, the great outdoors was an open house of worship. The woods behind our house, our yard full of pine trees and azaleas, could be his sanctuary. The beauty found in my rose garden had often turned my thoughts toward heaven. Each spring the sweet fragrance of the jasmine blooming around the patio filled the air like precious incense.

That year I'm not sure I noticed any such signs of the changing seasons. If I did, I certainly didn't stop to appreciate them. I was too mad at God.

Because of that anger, I even tried to stop talking to God.

As long as I could remember, I had talked to him. Prayer had always been a part of a very real and meaningful personal relationship with him. Certainly there had been times through the years when I'd felt and been closer to God than others. But I'd never ever stopped talking to him.

Until now.

As a mother, I'd always emphasized the importance of prayer to my children. But that spring I'd become so angry and cynical that I even quit saying bedtime prayers with my daughters. When Stacey or Melissa would say, "We need to say our prayers, Mommy," I'd say something like,

"Sure, you go ahead." But I neither volunteered to pray nor reminded them to do so.

The funny thing was, as angry as I became with God, I found I couldn't quit talking to him altogether. I guess old habits die hard. Because even during my angriest times, when I'd feel the most frustrated, frightened, or helpless, I'd catch myself inadvertently calling out to him for help and guidance. I did it when the doctors disagreed about the need for tubes in Heather's ears, when we received the devastating results of the hearing assessment, and when I ran into one roadblock after another in trying to learn what all needed to be and could be done for Heather back in Dothan.

Bill and I briefly discussed the option of moving our family where we could find more educational services and therapy options for Heather. He was understandably reluctant to leave home and give up his place in the family business after working so hard in the years since we'd moved back to Dothan. He had dreams for the store, dreams he wanted to see come to fruition.

So we decided to stay and pursue every possible option for Heather there in southeast Alabama. That's when I experienced my greatest frustration.

Because the Spain Clinic had told us how crucial it was to get Heather into some sort of speech therapy immediately, that became my first big goal. But when I went to our local speech therapists, one after another told me, "There's nothing we can do for your daughter because she's not speaking yet. When she begins speaking, bring her in. Then maybe we can help."

When I went to the audiologists to ask how to get a deaf child started talking, they said they couldn't help either. "We just test," they told me. "For speech you have to go to a speech therapist."

I knew we were at point A and that we ultimately needed to get to point Z. What I needed to know first was how to get to points B, C, and so on. And it seemed no one could tell me. I was spinning my wheels and getting nowhere.

The more frustrated I became, the more dead ends I hit, the angrier I got at the world, at myself, and especially at God for putting me through all this grief.

Then one day late that spring I just happened to pick up the Dothan daily newspaper, something I seldom found time to do. The hour was late—well past midnight. The house was quiet, everyone else long since asleep. But I'd just finished my lesson plans and was feeling tense and tired—too keyed up yet to sleep. Maybe reading a little would help. Flipping through the pages of that paper I spotted a syndicated column by Erma Bombeck. *Just what I need,* I thought. *Something light and relaxing.*

By the time I realized this particular article was not going to be either light or relaxing, I was hooked and couldn't stop reading. The column talked about mothers. More specifically, it discussed the 100,000 women a year who become mothers of handicapped children. Then it speculated as to how God assigned them their roles.

Erma imagined a discussion between God and an angel whose job it was to record all births and assign each mother a patron saint to assist in her task. When God picks out a mother to receive a handicapped child, the angel stops and questions the wisdom of the choice.

> But God says, "Yes, there is a woman whom I will bless with a child less than perfect. She doesn't realize it yet, but she is to be envied. She will never take for granted a 'spoken word.' She will never consider a step ordinary. When her child says 'Momma' for the first time, she will be present at a miracle and know it! When she describes a tree or a sunset to her blind child, she will see it as few people ever see my creations."
>
> "And what about her patron saint?" asks the angel, his pen poised in midair.
>
> God smiles. "A mirror will suffice."

By the time I finished reading I could hardly see the words through my tears. Part of me didn't want to hear that message. I didn't feel ready to accept the challenge. So I fell asleep that night feeling very guilty.

Just a few days later, on a gorgeous spring afternoon, I took all three of my girls to a local park. Sitting on a bench beneath a towering pine tree, I watched Stacey, Melissa, and Heather out on the playground. I saw how naturally the older girls had learned to accept and treat Heather as if she were normal. Yet they'd already learned to allow for her deafness. When Melissa wanted to get Heather's attention, she didn't try to yell. She walked over and touched her sister's shoulder. When Heather looked up, Melissa motioned for her to follow. It all seemed so simple and natural.

In that moment, God seemed to speak directly to my heart. "You're seeing what needs to be done. You're seeing what Heather can do, how she can fit in.

"Enough with the self-pity! It's time for you to quit feeling sorry for yourself! You can sit there being angry forever, but that won't do you any good. And it won't help Heather or those two other little girls. It's time to get up and move on. There are decisions to be made. I've been with you. I'm here with you now. And I'll be there to help you and guide you all the way. You just have to trust me."

In that little city park I reached a crossroad. After months of anger I was ready to quit asking "why" and "what if." I was ready to quit battling with God and begin to get on with my life.

And Heather's.

CHAPTER 6

Hurdles and Blessings

ince the day we'd learned Heather was profoundly deaf, I'd been at a complete loss. We had begun the long and involved process of getting her fitted with hearing aids. But I couldn't locate any speech therapist willing or able to provide the training the Spain Clinic had recommended. My search for resources or programs in Dothan had turned up nothing. And I'd found no one who could tell me what else we might do for her.

But the talking-to God gave me in the park that day provided me with a fresh dose of determination. *There have to be answers somewhere— even if I have to find them myself! I'm a teacher. I know how to do research.*

So that's what I did. I went to libraries and began to dig. One of the very first resources I came across was the *Volta Review*, the official publication of the Alexander Graham Bell Association for the Deaf, Inc., a national nonprofit organization offering printed materials and services to parents of deaf children. I immediately subscribed. But even before my first issue arrived, I'd begun devouring library copies of back issues.

In several issues of the *Volta Review* I noticed an advertisement for something called the John Tracy Clinic out in Los Angeles, which provided a free correspondence course for parents of young deaf children. *Maybe that's what I need,* I thought. *It can't hurt.* So I immediately sent for more information.

Meanwhile Bill and I had begun to attack the problem of what could be done for Heather from a completely different angle. As a new teacher of a federally funded Title I reading program, I was well aware that the federal and state governments had an extensive list of mandates for public schools regarding special education for handicapped students. I certainly knew the basic thrust of Public Law 94–142, which requires local schools to provide "the most appropriate education in the least restrictive environment" for every child (including those with various handicaps) who resides in their district. *There must be other deaf children in Dothan. If so, there has to be something the Dothan Public Schools offers that could benefit Heather.*

When I went to the director of special education for the Dothan school system, he told me he knew of only a handful of deaf children in the district. A couple were mainstreamed with remedial assistance from the regular special ed teacher in their schools. The remainder took part in the residential program at the Alabama School for the Deaf in Talladega. I assumed the local school board helped families pay for that because there was no formal deaf-education program offered in Dothan.

"And why not?" I wanted to know.

The main problem seemed to be numbers. There just hadn't been enough demand.

When I asked, "What would it take to get a program started here?" I was referred to the State Department of Education in Montgomery.

So Bill and I made several trips to the state capital that summer, knocking on door after door, following up countless phone calls, making appointments with anyone and everyone we thought could help. "How do we go about getting a special deaf-education program established in the Dothan Public Schools?" we asked. "Can you help us?"

While Heather was only two and a half at the time, we knew how slowly bureaucracy moved. We figured if we started now, by the time Heather was ready for school, we wouldn't have to face the terrible option of sending her away to school.

The tangle of red tape seemed mind-boggling at first. But the more officials we talked to in Montgomery, the more our challenge seemed to boil down to one thing: numbers. If we could get enough deaf students in and around Dothan whose parents wanted them to be educated locally, there would be funds available for a special deaf-education unit in the Dothan City Public Schools.

"How many would be enough to qualify?" we asked.

"According to federal and state regulations—seven."

Just seven! That seemed encouraging. But first we had to locate eligible deaf children. Then we would have to persuade the parents to entrust their kids' education to a program that didn't even exist yet. We spent much of that summer on the phone, trying to make that happen. The local schools joined our efforts by tracking down leads and trying to convince families of the potential benefits of a local unit.

During the time we were lobbying in Dothan and Montgomery for the new special ed program, we also completed the eight- to ten-week process of getting Heather a hearing aid. First we needed to have a doctor take ear molds and prescribe the actual hearing aids. Then it was back to the Spain Clinic to be fitted for two-week trial runs with a variety of hearing aid brands and models. At the beginning and end of each trial, Heather's aided hearing would be tested and I'd be interviewed about any changes or improvements I might have noticed with that particular hearing aid.

None of the ear-level aids made at that time were powerful enough to make any difference in Heather's hearing. So by mid-July we had settled on and purchased a Fidelity body aid, which Heather wore strapped in place at the middle of her chest. A cord ran up under her chin, where it split and went to each ear. Heather hated it. But while she still couldn't hear a thing in her right ear, the aid did seem to slightly improve her hearing of middle frequency tones through her left ear. I'd hoped for a lot more improvement, but both the reading I'd done and the experts we worked with assured me that every little bit of hearing we could get for Heather might help significantly in the acquisition of speech.

By summer's end we had six students signed up for Dothan's prospective deaf-education unit. We had seven if we counted Heather, who, even though she wasn't three yet, could qualify for the program in a preschool, preparatory capacity. With seven kids we actually had enough to begin the unit for the upcoming 1975–76 school year. The officials in our local school administration, who'd been extremely cooperative all summer, were almost as pleased as I was to see the results of our efforts paying off so quickly.

Yet one major hurdle remained. Dothan Public Schools didn't have a qualified deaf-education instructor. Finding one on such short notice would be difficult, if not impossible. At that point I looked into the possibility of getting some deaf-education training myself. I learned only two universities in the entire state offered deaf-education degrees, and it would take me more than two years to become fully certified. While that might be an option to consider for the future (it would, after all, be over two years before Heather was officially kindergarten age), there was nothing else I could do to get the program off the ground that fall. I just had to wait and see if the school board could find someone.

Meanwhile, during the weeks and months we'd been pursuing the public education possibilities, I'd received the initial correspondence course material from the John Tracy Clinic. It proved to be everything I'd hoped for and more.

I learned that the John Tracy Clinic had been founded in 1942 by Mrs. Spencer Tracy, wife of the film star, and was named for their son, John, who was born profoundly deaf. In an introduction to the correspondence course itself, Mrs. Tracy wrote about the doctor who first informed her that her son would never be able to hear, then immediately went on to say, "But you know what *you* can do about it? John can learn to talk, he can learn to lip-read, he can go through a university, he can do almost anything a hearing person can do, but you have a job!" Mrs. Tracy also recounted her appointment with a famous neurologist "and a very wise man" who confirmed for her the initial diagnosis of her son's nerve deafness. Then he said, "Mrs. Tracy, you are blessed among women. Yours can be a very interesting life."

Mrs. Tracy admitted that, while it hadn't been the kind of blessing she would have ever prayed for, "certainly mine has been an interesting life." This correspondence course, she said, was designed to help parents of deaf children get on with the big "job" of contributing to their child's growth and development. She wrote, "We will show how you can begin to build a bridge of understanding between [your child] and his family, one which eventually will link him with the world."

Wow! This was exactly the kind of thing I'd been looking for. The more I read, the more sense it all made to me as an educator: "We have put the growth and development of the whole child first, even before lipreading, language, and speech, because communication is not a separate, unrelated skill which one can acquire. Communication is part of living, of everything we do and are. It is affected by our personalities, by our attitudes and the attitudes of other people toward us, by our feelings of security, friendliness, curiosity, and all of the other feelings and attitudes which as very young children we begin to develop and some of which we may keep for a lifetime."

I knew after only ten minutes of reading the material from the John Tracy Clinic that I'd found the foundation on which I could build. Their approach jibed with everything I'd ever learned about educational theory, human psychology, and child development. This was that first step on the journey that would get us from A to Z.

The Lord was already keeping the promise he'd made me that day in the park. Whatever happened with the deaf-education unit in the school system (and I still felt optimistic about how that had fallen into place so quickly), I could definitely feel his hand guiding me to this John Tracy Clinic course.

As it turned out, the public school program we'd worked so hard on all summer did get off the ground that autumn after all. Though they weren't able to hire an experienced deaf-education specialist at the last minute, the school system did find a special ed teacher who would meet the state department's basic requirements. And, in yet another confirmation of God's concern about the details of our lives, the only school in the system with a spare classroom for the new special ed class was Highlands Elementary—in the very building where I taught every day. It couldn't have been more convenient.

Unfortunately, everything else didn't work quite that perfectly. The special ed teacher hired for the new program committed a major gaffe when a question was raised regarding her lack of deaf-education background. According to the report I heard, which had quickly made the rounds of parents with children in the program, she'd said: "It's not as if I could teach them anything. All I have to do is give them coloring sheets."

A number of concerned parents went to school administrators after that to complain, and yet another search began for her replacement. But even this setback turned out to be a blessing. The school system found a dynamic young woman graduating from the University of Alabama that January with a special ed degree in deaf education. LaTrelle Marshall took over the program in the middle of the year and did a terrific job.

While Bill and I had provided the impetus for getting the new unit started, our involvement in it those next couple of years was fairly limited. As a two- and three-year-old, Heather could not do a lot in a classroom with children ranging up to ten or eleven years old. While she attended five days a week, we only had Heather there from 9 to 12 each morning. Then it was home again with Estella every afternoon for nap and playtime. In truth, at the beginning our prime reason for enrolling Heather in the unit was to serve as that required seventh student called for by the regulations. That way the program would be established and ready when Heather started school a couple years down the road. Until then we were content for the program to provide her with a little social interaction (though she got a lot of that through her sisters and their friends) and for the teacher to reinforce what we were already doing with Heather at home.

I realized by this time that we would soon have some crucial decisions to make about the course of Heather's training. The folks at the Spain Clinic in Birmingham had assumed we'd teach her to sign. But through the *Volta Review* and other reading material, I'd learned a deep philosophical division existed among deaf educators and within the deaf community itself. On one side were those advocating the teaching and establishment of sign language as the accepted and universal language for the deaf culture. On the other side were those who argued that only the development of oral speech could adequately bridge the gap between the deaf and hearing worlds.

I soon found myself leaning toward the oral-deaf arguments. If Heather was going to live her life in the hearing world, her family's world, it would make sense to pursue oral speech. That seemed her best chance of relating and communicating with others in the hearing world.

While I knew sign might also play an important role in Heather's ability to communicate, I was troubled by my early experience with it. When I'd taken home the *Signing Exact English* (SEE) book recommended by the Spain Clinic and began using a few basic signs with Heather, she quit trying to vocalize altogether. She'd no longer attempt even the simple baby sounds she'd regressed to after her illness: *ba-ba-ba-ba-ba* and *ma-ma-ma-ma-ma*.

So I'd put the sign language book away and concentrated my training efforts on the lessons in the John Tracy course. They seemed to offer a strong developmental foundation that would help whether we eventually concentrated on oral speech or sign language.

Perhaps the single most important lesson for me in the Tracy material was to begin to see natural learning activities and communication building exercises in everyday life. There were thousands of practical little insights, ideas, and techniques I could put into practice to help foster communication with Heather. For example, it suggested reinforcing the concept of communication by verbally responding to a child's nonverbal expression of feelings—from happiness to anger—with comments such as "I know you are happy. That's fine" or "Yes, you're mad. Maybe I can help." It offered strategies for helping a deaf child feel like an active participant in family activities. It told about simple ways to use all the other senses to supplement hearing when communicating with a deaf child. And every lesson included easy and enjoyable games that reinforced the lesson for parents while making learning a fun and natural experience for the child.

Heather's training soon became an everyday part of the Whitestone family lifestyle. We all took part. Stacey and Melissa were never just Heather's sisters; they were also her teachers. And Heather's instinctive drive to keep up with and mimic her sisters motivated much of her continuing development.

While she was for the most part a cheerful and cooperative little girl, Heather's loss of hearing had done nothing to decrease the streak of occasional stubbornness she'd exhibited since birth. Sometimes she could be so bullheaded in her refusal to cooperate that I had to resort to a little treachery to bring her around. Knowing that the desire to imitate her sisters could sometimes be even stronger than her stubbornness, I would actually involve my older daughters in the plot. Often, when Heather refused to cooperate in something, I'd explain to Stacey and Melissa that we were going to play a little pretend game. I'd make an elaborate show of asking them to do what I wanted Heather to do. They, like Heather, would refuse—for a very short time. Then I'd scold them vociferously and they'd quickly obey, which would often prompt Heather to do likewise. Stacey and Melissa thought it great fun when I gave them occasional license to be naughty and disobey Mommy—even if it was just playacting. And they always got a special kick out of it whenever our little ruse worked.

I very quickly realized how fortunate I was that Heather was a third child. How much harder my challenge would have been without Stacey' and Melissa's help.

I had yet another reminder of how much we had to be grateful for during a visit that year to a clinic in Montgomery to observe a procedure called "verbal toning." It was believed that by attaching little sensors to the hands and other sensitive skin surfaces of a deaf person that he or she could feel the varied vibrations created by sounds of different words or voices and begin to sense and appreciate sound in a new way.

At that clinic I observed a little deaf boy who was also blind and retarded. Watching him I couldn't help but wonder what could be going on in his head, in a very limited brain that could never know the stimulation of either sight or sound. Watching his mother I first thought, _What a terrible tragedy! What a burden for her to be saddled with!_ Then I learned she'd adopted this little boy with the full knowledge of his multiple handicaps. And I thought, _What a miracle that God could give anyone that kind of love! I don't know if I could do that._

I went home so convicted! I vowed never again to feel sorry for my lot in life. And for a long time after that, whenever I looked into the sparkling green eyes of my bright and beautiful little girl, I reminded myself again: _We have so much to be grateful for._

Yet another meaningful event took place that spring. It began when Bill's mother, Colley, mentioned that the hearing impaired daughter of one of her longtime friends was living in Dothan. Sidney had gotten a public school education right there in Dothan and had been mainstreamed all the way through.

That was enough to interest me. And when Bill's sister-in-law Gloria told me she'd gone to school with Sidney and told me more about the girl, I made arrangements to invite her over to our home one evening.

Sidney told Bill and me a lot about her life experience. She'd left Dothan some years earlier to attend college. But after getting married, to a hearing man, they were now back in Dothan to begin their new life together.

She told us how grateful she was she could communicate orally. We found her voice clear and fairly easy to understand with only a moderate amount of the nasal tone common in deaf people's speech. She encouraged us to pursue our goal of oral speech for Heather. And then she told us if we wanted the best possible advice from deaf-education experts, she heartily recommended the speech and hearing clinic at Florida State University's Regional Rehabilitation Center down in Tallahassee. "I still go to them when I need a hearing checkup or evaluations," she said. "Dr. Haas is the director of the rehab center. You really ought to talk with him about what all can be done for Heather."

I didn't clearly see God's hand in it at the time I called Tallahassee to ask about making an appointment. But that simple recommendation from that young lady was about to become one of the most significant developments ever in Heather's life.

CHAPTER 7

Say Drink!

The Florida State program impressed me from the very first visit. Dr. Bill Haas seemed quite familiar with the John Tracy material and affirmed what we'd been doing with it. His staff conducted a thorough auditory evaluation of Heather with results nearly identical to the tests done at the Spain Clinic the year before. They also confirmed the merit and accuracy of her current hearing aid prescription. We were on the right track there as well.

After that, and after I voiced my two levels of frustration—(1) not being able to find a local speech therapist willing to take Heather before she could speak and (2) my uncertainty on which language development route (oral speech or sign) would be best to pursue for Heather—Dr. Haas said, "I think we can help you on both scores." Then he told me about FSU's summer family workshop for deaf children, their parents, and their siblings.

Bill didn't think he could afford the time away from his work at the store. But I signed up with all three of the girls. For six weeks that summer of 1976, my three young daughters and I lived in a motel room near the Florida State University campus, and we all "went to school" every weekday morning.

During my orientation at FSU that summer, I told the interviewer we needed all the help we could get with language development. And that was indeed the major focus of that summer's workshop—at least for Heather. All morning, every morning the staff kept all three girls engaged in Heather's speech therapy. Because Stacey and Melissa enjoyed the activities as much as their little sister did, their FSU experience reinforced the "family and everyday life as therapy" concept first fostered in the Tracy correspondence course we'd been using for almost a year. Even our homework assignments became group projects. We'd all go back to our motel room in the afternoon and continue our learning. For example, one day we searched through stacks of old magazines, cut out pictures of animals, and pasted them on index cards. We used these homemade flash cards to teach Heather the animals' names and the sounds they made.

While most of the "work" itself could be fun for the girls, there was also a lot of free time. We'd swim in the motel pool almost every afternoon or go shopping and sightseeing around Tallahassee. Some weekends, Bill would make the three-hour drive down, and we went back to Dothan a couple times. So for the girls it must have seemed a lot like a long family vacation.

For me it was another big answer to my prayers—just what I needed at just the right time.

While Heather and her sisters went through their speech therapy every morning, the FSU staff was working with me as well. Sometimes they'd take me into a room where we could sit and watch the girls' therapy through a two-way mirror. They'd explain what was happening and why. They showed me how I might adapt that particular learning activity at home or make that technique a regular part of our family interaction with Heather. Other times the staff would talk about what I as a parent could expect from a profoundly deaf daughter in the years ahead.

But the family speech therapy being modeled for all of us wasn't the only benefit that summer. Early in our time at FSU, Dr. Haas took me aside and told me that if I wanted to make the best possible decisions regarding Heather's future education, I needed to make informed decisions. He thought it crucial for me to not only understand, but to be exposed to all the basic methods currently being used in the field of deaf education.

I knew of course about the controversy between the oral language and sign language camps. But Dr. Haas explained there were other divisions within those two groups—he enumerated five different philosophies.

Among the proponents of sign language he listed three major groups.

First were those who advocated the exclusive use of sign and didn't encourage those who were hearing impaired to attempt audible speech at all. The practitioners of this philosophy were further divided into those who favored American Sign Language (ASL) and those favoring Signing Exact English (SEE). That exclusive sign approach didn't appeal to me much at all.

The second major group consisted of those who proclaimed and taught the benefits of an approach which had been recently termed "total communication." At the time I first heard about it, TC (as it is popularly called) advocated the right of a deaf child to learn to use all forms of communication available in language development. That meant every deaf child should have the opportunity to learn a range of both oral and sign communication skills including speech, signs, gestures, finger spelling, lipreading, reading, and writing. They were also encouraged to use whatever residual hearing they might have. What it amounted to in practice most of the time was a simultaneous use of both speech and sign—a seemingly logical and simple compromise between the oral versus manual language that had been going on in deaf education since the 1700s. I could see the appeal of TC. Why not use every possible advantage?

The third "sign" approach Dr. Haas told me about was another relatively new technique, roughly ten years old at the time, called "cued speech." As opposed to ASL or SEE where signs are used to represent concepts, phrases, words, or specific letters of the alphabet, cued speech is a phonemically based hand supplement to lipreading. This supplement was developed because lipreading, while a logical and natural skill for deaf people to develop, can be incredibly complicated. So many different English words look almost exactly alike on the lips. For example, the simple little word *met* could be lip-read at least sixty different ways, including *mitt, bet, but, bit, pet, putt, pit,* and so on. Thus the object in cued speech is to use eight basic hand shapes in combination with four positions around the face to represent various groups of consonant and vowel sounds. The intent is for the lip-reader to use the added "cues" to see/hear precisely every syllable that a hearing person hears.

I immediately saw two major drawbacks in this approach. It wasn't widely used at the time. And more important, since I'd never been very good in phonics myself, I couldn't imagine ever becoming comfortable with a communication system that required me to talk and gesture phonetically at the same time.

Among proponents of oral language development among the deaf, Dr. Haas listed two primary subgroups, both of which avoid the use of formal sign language. The first oral group calls for a multisensory approach (vision, residual hearing, and, in some cases, touch) to help children understand and produce speech. Lipreading falls into this category.

The second oral approach is often referred to as the auditory/verbal method. (Both the unisensory method, developed in Pennsylvania, and acoupedics, developed in Denver, Colorado, fall under this heading.) Many auditory/verbal advocates believe that visual cues, such as signs and even lip movements, detract from a child's ability to learn to use what hearing he has. In order to teach as much reliance on hearing as possible, they usually cover their mouths while training deaf children. Practitioners of this method believe that the majority of deaf children can acquire enough auditory skills by school age that they can be educated with hearing children.

This approach, like cued speech, was not very widespread. While the philosophical goal, enabling a deaf child to be educationally mainstreamed and learn to live in the hearing world, certainly appealed to me, I had a lot of unanswered questions about this approach.

When he'd spelled out the five basic options, I pressed Dr. Haas to tell me which one he thought would be best to pursue with Heather. He didn't want to answer that.

"Every one of these methods has its 'stars,' success stories that will prove to you how well it works," he said. "But the one universal factor you find behind every 'star' is a parent who believes in that approach and supports the child 110 percent. The most critical key to Heather's success is going to be your commitment—to her and to the communication/learning method you choose for her. Without that commitment, without your support, you could go any one of these ways and Heather will have a terrible struggle just to achieve an 'average' level of academic development. With your commitment she might well become a star example for any of the five approaches. So I recommend you learn all you can in order to decide which approach is going to make you feel most comfortable. Because the ultimate success of that choice is going to depend on you."

I had very mixed feelings after that discussion. I felt very encouraged by Dr. Haas's belief that I could play such a crucial and determining role in Heather's life. At the same time, the kind of responsibility he described certainly sobered me. *What if I made the wrong decision for her? What if I couldn't give that 110 percent he talked about?*

I could only pray that God would continue to lead me to make the right choices.

Step one toward making an informed decision was to get some firsthand exposure to the various options. So Dr. Haas arranged for me to visit three different programs operating in the Tallahassee area.

When I observed a classroom where all instruction was done totally in sign, I experienced one overwhelming reaction. I felt completely left out—as if I'd walked into a silent and alien world. If I felt left out, what must those kids feel when they walked out of their classroom into the hearing world? I watched the teacher and the class with fascination. Everything seemed orderly; everyone appeared to be on task. But the only clue I had as to what subject was being taught came from reading what was written on the chalkboard. I'd have felt more in tune with what was going on if I'd walked into any elementary school classroom in Peking. While I wouldn't have understood any more Chinese than I did sign language, at least I would have known who was talking to whom and been able to infer some meaning from the tone of their voices.

That one visit convinced me I could never be comfortable choosing a communication method for Heather that didn't include some oral aspect.

When I observed a TC classroom, I understood more of what was happening. But the speech being used seemed very sporadic; much of the communication relied totally on sign. So I still felt I was missing out on a lot.

The last observation I did while we were in Florida that summer was with a public special ed teacher. She relied on lipreading to work on a vocabulary development activity with hearing impaired youngsters who received the supplemental instruction as part of a mainstream educational experience. Of the three classrooms I observed, I felt most tuned in to this one, because I could understand the instructor's spoken words. I could also understand much of what the children were saying, though their speech wasn't very clear at times.

Because all the approaches I'd observed had their drawbacks, I still didn't feel ready to make up my mind. Before we left FSU at the end of the workshop that summer, Dr. Haas encouraged me to make my decision soon. Timing was going to be critical, particularly if we opted for an oral approach. While basic proficiency in signing could always be acquired later if we changed our minds, the foundation for oral language

77

development would need to be laid immediately. By four or five years of age it might be too late.

Based on my own reading research, I had pretty much ruled out cued speech. And because the only place I could observe it at that time was in the area around Galludet University in Washington where it originated, I decided not to try to see it in action. That left only one other method to investigate—the auditory verbal approach.

I learned that Doreen Pollack, who developed the auditory verbal program she called *acoupedics*, was the director of speech and hearing services at Porter Memorial Hospital in Denver. We had previously scheduled our family vacation to visit my sister Deborah and her family in Colorado that August. *What a coincidence! Or was it?*

I called Porter Memorial for information and to set up an appointment. They sent me a brochure, and the list of their claims for the program read like a list of my own goals for Heather:

> It enables the child to learn to use his residual hearing to acquire the auditory information available to the normal hearing child . . . encourages his educational and intellectual development . . . helps avoid the emotional problems due to the devastating isolation of silence.
>
> He can learn to speak clearly and with natural voice quality.
>
> He can communicate without an interpreter. His speech and language abilities are learned as hearing children learn them, rather than through manual methods.
>
> He may be able to attend regular schools for the normal hearing as opposed to special schooling.
>
> He has a much better chance to lead a more normal, independent life, without social or vocational restrictions.

I remember thinking, *It sounds almost too good to be true! But if it is true. . . .*

Our visit to Porter Memorial Hospital in Denver turned out to be the most exciting and encouraging development yet. Bill and I received a full tour of the facilities, observed a number of different therapy sessions, talked with the staff who explained the acoupedic approach, and even had the opportunity to meet Doreen Pollack. But what impressed us most were the hearing impaired kids themselves. We met and talked with several—all different ages. And what seemed so amazing to me was that we actually did *talk* with them. They understood us. What seemed even more remarkable, *we* understood *them*! Naturally some spoke more clearly than others. But we communicated easily with them all, without signs and without special instruction or training.

I knew then, without a doubt: *This is what I want for Heather!*

I was full of questions. How do we start? Where do we go? What do we do?

Doreen Pollack's staff assured us that what we'd been doing already with Heather was a good start. They provided us with more information on the acoupedic approach and encouraged us, saying there was a lot we could do as parents to work with Heather. They also recommended we get Heather into professional therapy with a speech and hearing expert trained in acoupedic methods. But they didn't have the name of a single trained therapist in the entire state of Alabama they could recommend.

While that did indeed seem to be a major problem, I had been so impressed by what I saw in Denver that I refused to be discouraged or deterred. Those children I'd met and talked with at Porter Memorial Hospital had given me a vision of Heather's future. What they had was what I wanted for my daughter. *Someday, somehow, Heather is going to be able to speak and communicate like that!*

The first order of business was to find a therapist, any therapist, let alone an acoupedic practitioner, who could offer professional help for Heather's speech. Again I contacted everyone I could think to call in our part of the state. The search finally paid off when I found Judy Harper, a young speech therapist right there in Dothan. She listened to my description of our situation and agreed without hesitation to take Heather. Judy admitted she'd had limited experience working with deaf children, and she had no other deaf clients when we began going to her. But she was a warm, compassionate, and committed professional who wasn't too proud to say, "I'm willing to learn."

Building on the progress Heather had made in her speech therapy during the summer at FSU, working from the sample acoupedic materials I'd picked up in Denver and from my description and explanation of the method as I'd observed it, and then drawing from her own speech therapy training and experience, Judy took on the challenge. She started simply by encouraging Heather's vocalization of typical baby sounds such as *b-b-b-b-b* and *d-d-d-d-d*. From there she progressed to animal sounds—*baa* and *moo*—and then on to stimulating some initial attempts at actual speech.

Because we didn't have any pets at the time, one of the things that made therapy at Judy's house so appealing was the opportunity to see and play with the Harpers' miniature dachshund, Stash. Heather just loved that little dog.

In fact, one of the first encouraging milestones in her therapy came one afternoon after school when Heather suddenly started babbling on to me about something. I couldn't understand anything until I clearly heard the word *dog*, and I knew she was talking about something Stash had done that morning at Judy's. While it may not seem like much, I was thrilled. Because, though Heather might have said a recognizable word from time to time when prompted in therapy, this was her very first "success" in normal, spontaneous "conversation." For us, that little "dog" was a major breakthrough. We were on the right track.

So two mornings a week Bill would drive Heather to her 8 A.M. therapy with Judy. At the end of each session Judy would tell Bill what they'd worked on and suggest homework activities we could use to reinforce the lesson. Then at 9:00, on his way to the store, Bill would drop her off at Highlands at the deaf-education class.

We explained to LaTrelle Marshall, Heather's deaf-ed instructor, that we'd decided to pursue an acoupedic approach. We explained the basic concept, emphasizing the importance of the rule the folks in Denver had said was of utmost importance: No signing with Heather. If she was going to learn to use what hearing she had, we needed to teach her to rely on auditory stimulation. Though she knew very little about acoupedics, LaTrelle was supportive of our desires and willing to cooperate. "But you realize Heather's just one of seven children in the class," she said. "And while I will try to be careful not to use sign with her, I will need to be using sign regularly with the other children."

"Of course," we told her. "We understand that." We didn't think that would be any problem.

We soon learned we were wrong.

The factor we hadn't counted on was Heather herself. She was bright enough to realize the other children in her class were communicating with sign. And she began learning it on her own.

In other circumstances we might have been both pleased and proud about our little girl's precociousness. Instead, we were concerned.

The more sign Heather began to pick up at school, the more she wanted to use it at home, and the less she tried to vocalize. After months of hard work just trying to get speech started, she was suddenly going mute on us again.

I will never forget the day Heather ran into the kitchen all hot and sweaty. She tugged at my arm to get my attention. When I turned around, she gave me the sign for "drink."

I saw she was thirsty. But I prompted her, "Say *drink*."

She signed again.

"No, Heather," I told her. "No signs. Say *drink*!"

I recognized the you're-not-gonna-make-me look in Heather's eyes even before she adamantly shook her head and angrily signed again.

"If you want a drink, you have to use words. Say *drink*!"

Heather just stood there, gnawing angrily at her lip, trying to stare me down.

"Sorry. No drink then!" And I turned back to whatever it was I'd been doing.

When I heard her stomp out of the room, I felt like the meanest mother in history. My heart was chiding me: *How could you do that? Your daughter was thirsty, and you wouldn't let her have a drink. Why make such a big deal out of a little thing like that?* I did some serious soul-searching those next few minutes before I convinced myself: *If she's going to learn to speak, you're going to have to be consistent. It's gonna take commitment; you can't give in.*

It wasn't long before Heather tiptoed back into the kitchen and tugged at my arm again. Pointing at the refrigerator she said something I loosely translated to mean "drink."

That was good enough. "You want a drink? Good. Thank you for asking. Let's see what we have that you would like." Heather grinned happily, and I knew our big little confrontation was over.

I think I realized even then that the course we'd chosen was going to be hard—maybe the hardest of the five options we'd learned about at FSU. I just had to cling to Dr. Haas's advice (that we had to do what we felt best for Heather) and to the assurance that God was still leading.

What I couldn't have known then was that this would not be the last time (far from it) I'd struggle with doubts—my own and those of others—about our choices regarding Heather's education.

CHAPTER 8

Decisions, Decisions

When I called Dr. Haas to describe our dilemma, he concurred with our decision to pull her out of the classroom. "Since you're committed to the acoupedic approach, you don't have any real choice," he said. "Heather needs consistency. Leaving her in the public school program and exposing her to sign language at this point in her life will confuse her and hinder her verbal language development."

He recommended we enroll her in a regular preschool program to give her more social interaction and expose her to auditory stimulation in a classroom environment. So that's what we did.

With Judy Harper's help, we also pursued a more complete and informed acoupedic approach. Soon after she'd begun working with Heather, Judy had agreed to provide speech therapy to yet another deaf child—a one-year-old little girl by the name of Julie Coleman. Over the course of the next few months, what I shared with Judy about acoupedic techniques, she passed along to Debbie Coleman, little Julie's mother. By that following summer both Judy and Debbie were convinced enough to go out to Denver with me for an in-depth, week-long session of acoupedic training. Debbie and I soon understood the basics, but we really needed Judy's expertise in some of the more in-depth sessions. We all came home feeling more knowledgeable about the acoupedic approach and excited about applying what we'd learned.

The merits of the acoupedic approach seemed so obvious to me. The only question was how well and how quickly Heather would respond.

One thing Heather had going for her was an outgoing and aggressive personality. When I think of her as a four- or five-year-old, I can't help but remember our next-door neighbor. On warm evenings after supper Emory liked to sit in a lawn chair on his carport to read a book or his afternoon newspaper. Because Emory's lot sloped down from the street while ours was quite level, Heather would wheel her little yellow riding car over to his drive. She would pedal furiously downhill, and when she'd built up so much speed her little legs couldn't keep up with the pedals, she'd raise her feet and coast. At the bottom of the driveway, which was only forty or fifty feet long, she'd jerk the little steering wheel to the right, go skidding into the carport, and finally come to a halt by ramming full speed into Emory's lawn chair. He laughed when he told us, "The first time she did it, I was sitting there reading, completely engrossed in my book, and *wham!* It nearly scared the stew out of me! Heather just laughed and laughed. Then she went back up the driveway and did it again. I saw her coming that time—charging down that hill like a little Sherman tank."

That became a regular routine for Heather and Emory after that. Every time she came to a crashing halt he'd jump and act surprised, and Heather would laugh and do it all over again.

Our neighbor's description of Heather looking "like a little Sherman tank" inspired one of her earliest nicknames. From then on, whenever I witnessed other examples of Heather's full-speed-ahead personality, I just called her "Sherm."

That kind of aggressive, adventuresome spirit would serve her well in life—as well as in her new and sometimes tedious therapy. There was, however, another very obvious side of her personality that made therapy and life with Heather an interesting challenge.

Heather could be such a willful, stubborn little girl that I sometimes told people, "She went straight from the terrible twos to the frustrating fours!" As Judy quickly learned during therapy, when Heather made up her mind she didn't want to do something, you were in for a battle of wills. Fortunately we'd found a very patient therapist who believed once we harnessed that stubbornness it could be transformed into determination. And she would need determination to carry her through in the long run.

But that would take long and concerted effort on the part of the entire family, including Heather's sisters, who clearly considered themselves partners in her therapy process. I remember more than one occasion when the older girls and I would walk in at the end of a therapy session at Judy's to have Melissa, who was just six or seven at the time, inquire: "And how did we do in therapy today?"

Some days Judy would smile at us and nod in satisfaction as she reported, "We had a good day today, Melissa." Other times she'd shake her head and respond, "You see who's sitting over in the corner, don't you?"

Time-out was a common consequence when Heather refused to follow instructions or cooperate. One day Judy told me that her little dachshund, who loved Heather as much as she loved him, had followed Heather over to the time-out corner and sat down beside her chair looking up at her. "It was so funny I had to work hard not to laugh," Judy said. "I don't know what in the world she was saying. She hadn't wanted to talk to me at all. But there she was, giving Stash what for—wagging her finger and scolding him for all she was worth."

In those early days, one of the main goals of acoupedic training was to teach Heather to use what hearing she had. To get Heather to attend to sound and get used to listening. Judy would hold one hand in front of her mouth to hide her lips and ask Heather, "Where's the red crayon? Good! Now where's the blue crayon? No, listen! Blue! Very good!"

Sometimes Judy would play a tape recording of a common sound and ask Heather to pick the match from a set of pictures spread out on the table. A ringing phone. A barking dog. A car horn. Eventually she would ask Heather to repeat the word. Phone. Dog. Car.

A lot of therapy consisted of fun and games. Literally. Board games such as "Candyland" gave constant opportunity for listening and language. "Heather's turn!" "My turn." "Yellow!" "Uh, oh. Go back!"

Some activities were little more than practicing following directions. Eventually Judy could stand behind Heather and say, "Pick up a green crayon and draw two circles at the bottom of the page."

Behind-the-back training became a fundamental aspect of our acoupedic approach. Like the hand-over-mouth technique, it exercised and developed what little hearing Heather had left.

Speech therapy was hard work for all of us. Every night I'd go over the homework Judy gave—mostly repeating the exercises she did with

Heather in therapy. All day, every day, I repeated words and asked Heather to indicate she heard what I said, or I'd ask her to say the words after me. The repetition seemed endless. I had to constantly remind myself what I'd heard in the training session out in Denver. "If a hearing child has to hear a word twenty or thirty or one hundred times before she understands it enough to use it in conversation, a hearing impaired child may need to have it repeated hundreds and hundreds of times."

Progress often seemed slow. But there was enough to keep us all motivated and committed to our course. Every new word Heather picked up and used in context seemed a significant triumph.

I remember how encouraged we all were when she finally seemed to understand her name and repeated a word that at least approximated "Heather." But then for what seemed the longest time she thought everyone's name must be Heather. She'd point to Melissa or Stacey or me and say "Heather." We had to keep telling her, "No, no. I'm 'Mama.' That's Stacey and Melissa."

The concept finally registered. But she had a terrible time saying Melissa's name. It always came out sounding like "Monty." So that became Melissa's nickname for years.

I'll never forget another highlight in Heather's speech development. It came one night when I was putting the girls to bed. When I tucked Heather in and said, "I love you," she smiled sweetly up at me and said, "Wuv oo."

A warm fuzzy feeling only a mother could understand flooded through me. It had been over two years since I'd last heard those words from my little girl. I gave her an extra big hug that night before I turned out the light.

The long-range goal we had set was to have Heather talking some, but listening well enough to cope in public school kindergarten when her age group began school the next year—in the fall of 1978.

We experienced what seemed like a major setback in the spring of that year when Judy Harper's husband got transferred and they made plans to leave Dothan. But we were reassured to find out Diane Steensland would be taking over the practice. Diane, an associate of Judy's, had learned the acoupedic method from observing her work with Heather and Julie Coleman. She had already developed a warm relationship with Heather when she'd covered for some of Judy's sessions. So we felt good about her.

Still we were going to miss Judy. Not only had she been the one speech therapist we could find willing to work with a deaf child who didn't speak, but she'd been so committed to Heather and our family that she'd given up a week of her own time to go out to Denver with me for the acoupedic training. In less than two years she'd become much more than Heather's therapist. She'd shared our dream and become our friend.

As a good-bye gift we framed a small picture of a bird along with a photo of Heather and a note that read: "When God created the world, he placed the bird upon it so that man might hear the greatness of his love. To parents of a deaf child, this same thrill comes when they hear that child *say,* 'I love you.' Thank you!—Daphne & Bill Whitestone."

The summer before kindergarten, I knew Heather still had a long way to go with her speech. And it was that summer, when she was five and a half, that I came up with an idea I thought might help. I don't remember what triggered the thought to begin with; God must have given it to me because it just hit me one day. Since both Judy and Diane sometimes used music as part of Heather's listening therapy, I wondered if enrolling Heather in a dance class might teach her to hear the changing pitch and tone of music. Maybe that would help her understand the changing pitch, tone, and inflection in spoken language so we could avoid the flat, monotone voice quality common to many deaf people's speech.

It seemed kind of a radical idea at the time, even to me. But Diane, our new therapist, agreed it was worth a try.

The trouble was finding a dance instructor willing to go along with the experiment. Searching through the phone book, I discovered there were only four dance studios. And the response was the same at the first two I called.

"Hello, my name is Daphne Whitestone, and I'm calling to see about enrolling my daughter in your ballet class."

"That's wonderful. We're taking registration now for our fall classes. What's your daughter's name?"

"Heather."

"And how old is Heather?"

"She's five. She'll be starting kindergarten this year."

"Has she had any dance classes before now?"

"No. This would be her first."

"That'll be fine. We have several openings left in our beginner's troupe."

"There is a problem I should tell you about. Heather is profoundly deaf."

I then had to wonder about the hearing of the person on the other end of the line. A sudden, awkward silence lasted for several seconds. "Well . . . uh . . . we'll need to think about that. I . . . uh . . . don't know how my instructor would feel about that. Let me talk to our 'beginning ballet' teacher and get back to you. Can I have your number and your name again?"

Neither ever returned my call.

So I called the third name on my list: the Dothan School of Dance. I went through the same basic conversation with the director, Tracy Mitchell. Until I got to the part where I told her, "Heather is profoundly deaf."

"I don't think that will be a serious problem," she said. "Let's give it a try and see how it goes. You'll need to stop by for a registration form. And we'll look forward to having Heather in our dance class."

What a heartening response to find someone so open-minded she didn't seem to have any reservations about giving a deaf child a chance! I didn't even bother calling the last name on my list. I just hurried over to Tracy's studio and signed Heather up.

Looking back, I can see why the idea of enrolling a deaf child in ballet classes might seem like a foolish idea to some dance teachers. I suspect that some of my friends and even a few of our relatives shook their heads and wondered if I was being very realistic about Heather's handicap at that point. But I was willing to try anything that might improve the chances Heather could someday live a normal life in the hearing world.

I realized it would take some time before we learned whether or not the experiment would actually help her speech. But I knew after the first week that the tuition would be worth every penny, because Heather absolutely loved to dance.

She really bonded with her beginning ballet instructor, Patti Rutland Richards. While Patti was just a young apprentice teacher with Dothan School of Dance, she was gifted with a natural ability to teach small children. Heather thought her dance classes, in contrast with speech therapy, which involved a lot of hard work, were pure fun.

Heather was soon twirling and dancing everywhere she went. Through the house. Out in the yard. Down the aisles of the grocery store. I couldn't help smiling as I watched her. In her own mind Heather had become a prima ballerina overnight.

The second important development in our lives that year was the beginning of Heather's public school education. For months Bill and

I discussed how we should handle it—whether or not we should go in ahead of time to explain about Heather's deafness and to discuss our concerns and expectations, in essence asking the principal and kindergarten teacher to give special consideration to Heather.

But having just experienced the closed-minded response of some dance instructors to the idea of working with a deaf child, and having been a teacher long enough to have witnessed the danger of self-fulfilling prophecy, I felt reluctant to "warn" the school officials and have them anticipating problems that might never arise. So we didn't even talk to the principal or Heather's kindergarten teacher ahead of time. We decided it would be best to take Heather in the first day, explain then that she was deaf, and figure we could deal with any problems that came up—when and if any did.

That turned out to be one of the worst decisions I'd ever made in my life.

Fortunately Heather's kindergarten teacher that year had a wonderful, sweet, and loving nature. Unfortunately she was extremely soft-spoken and hard for Heather to understand. More significantly, she was a young, fresh-out-of-school teacher who not only faced all the usual first-year challenges and adjustments to teaching, but faced the imposing task of integrating a deaf child into the normal, hearing environment of your typical kindergarten classroom.

It wasn't fair. To the teacher. To the school. Or to Heather.

But I didn't realize there were any serious problems until we'd gotten halfway through the year. In hindsight, I can see why the school didn't come to me earlier. The fact that I hadn't been more open and up-front with them about Heather's deafness, combined with the fact that we'd opted to mainstream her instead of enrolling her in Dothan's deaf-education program we'd helped begin three years before, might have led them to conclude we were in a state of denial. At the very least we probably seemed unrealistic. So it's not surprising if they felt awkward and uncertain about how to approach us.

Therefore the call I received that January came as a complete surprise. I was teaching at Girard Middle School that year when I was summoned out of my classroom to the front office. The principal of Girard Elementary School, located just across the street, was on the phone for me. I'd known Joanne for several years; she'd been Stacey's teacher one year. So I could tell by the sound of her voice she was distressed.

"I'm sorry to have to call you like this, Daphne," she began. "But we had a little incident here today, and I had to paddle Heather." She went on to describe how Heather had pitched an all-out screaming, crying, stomping fit in the bathroom. The teacher had called the principal, who couldn't get Heather to stop either—until she swatted her bottom. Joanne continued, "I want you to know how badly I feel about this; I hated doing it. But I just didn't feel I had any choice. We simply can't allow her to pitch that kind of temper tantrum anymore."

Anymore? "You mean this has happened before?" I asked.

"Well . . . yes. A number of times."

"I think you and I and Glenda [Heather's teacher] need to have a talk," I told her. "What about today right after school?"

In our meeting that day I got the full report. Heather had not been attending well in class all year. When it was time to work on papers at the table, she would want to wander off and play in the block center. But the much bigger problem was the physical confrontation when the teacher tried to get her back on task with the other children. Her temper tantrums were wreaking havoc on the entire classroom.

Again Joanne expressed her regrets for paddling Heather. "I felt so awful. After I did, Heather looked up at me with those expressive green eyes of hers, and I imagined a door closing inside her."

I quickly reassured Joanne that I understood what she'd done and why. I certainly didn't think she'd needed to worry that she'd done any serious damage to Heather's psyche. I thought I knew my daughter better than that.

Then I turned to Heather's teacher and said, "I feel as if I'm the one who owes you an apology. I should have done a better job of communicating with you about what you should expect out of Heather. And I want you to understand that the behavior you have just described to me is not the kind of behavior I would allow out of Heather in my house."

Throughout our training, first at FSU, then out in Denver, whenever the subject of disciplining deaf children was discussed, our advisors had given us one simple rule of thumb: "If you won't allow a certain behavior from a hearing child, don't allow it from your deaf child! Just make absolutely certain your child understands what it is you expect and why she is being disciplined."

So that's pretty much what I told Heather's teacher and principal. "If you don't let the other children do something, don't let Heather do it either. Should you need to paddle her again, you have my permission. But please let me know if you're having any problems. I should have said all of this to you before; I'm sorry I didn't. I want you to know I don't hold you, or the school, accountable for seeing that Heather accomplishes everything at the same rate all the other kids do. I know that because of her hearing problem she will need extra work. And I'm willing to supplement what you do in class by working with her at home. I want you to see me as part of the team."

I went home that day satisfied that we'd reached an understanding but a little frustrated that it had taken us so long to come to it. I didn't blame the school officials. In their good-hearted attempt to be compassionate and patient with Heather, they'd merely tried to make allowances for her deafness.

In a way, the reaction of the principal and the teacher reminded me of an encounter I'd had in a store just months before. I'd been walking down an aisle, pushing my shopping cart, when I realized Heather was no longer by my side. She'd stopped to grab a bag of candy off one of the bottom shelves. When I'd told her to put it back, she had just stood there and stared at me, her eyes full of defiance. When I told her again, "Put it back!" and started toward her to enforce the order, she launched into a crying, foot-stomping temper tantrum. I took a firm hold of her arm and told her, "Stop it right now!"

Heather's volume only increased. So I spun her around and firmly swatted her on the behind. Then I looked her in the face again and said, "Now stop. And put the candy back."

About that time a very indignant lady stormed over to me. "I've got a mind to turn you in for child abuse," she began. "That poor child is deaf. How dare you hit her knowing she can't hear a word you're saying and doesn't understand—"

"I beg to differ, ma'am," I interrupted her. "But Heather happens to be a very bright child. She knows exactly what I said to her. And she understands very well what I expected of her. She was merely being defiant and pitching a fit." I would like to have added, *Maybe you would allow your children to disobey and pitch temper tantrums, but I won't. So mind your own business.* Instead I just walked away, embarrassed at the scene we'd created and angry at the woman for butting in.

I was not angry at the principal and teacher, even though their attitude had been much the same as the nosy lady in the store: *Because your daughter's deaf, we can't expect her to behave like a "normal" child.*

If anyone was at fault this time, it was me—for not anticipating the problem and communicating my expectations from the beginning of the year.

Things got a lot better at school after that conference. But the damage had already been done. Or maybe the improvement just wasn't enough to avoid a conflict when it came time a few weeks later to discuss Heather's placement for the following year.

During a special parent-teacher conference with the principal in attendance, I learned that the school's recommendation was that Heather not be moved up to first grade the next fall.

"We don't think Heather's emotionally ready."

"She just doesn't have the language development necessary for first-grade work."

"It's just too difficult for a teacher to understand her speech."

They said they were willing to try her in kindergarten again. But what they really wanted me to do was pull her out of a regular classroom altogether and put her back in the deaf-education unit. And I didn't want to do either.

So I did what I'd done before when I'd been at the end of my rope and needed help. I prayed for guidance, then called Dr. Haas down at Florida State University. "We've got a problem with Heather and the schools here. I don't know what to do."

CHAPTER 9

Dance and Lady Di

When I explained that the school didn't want to move Heather on to a regular first-grade class the next year, Dr. Haas wanted to know the reasoning. I said, "The main problem they keep coming back to is Heather's language deficiency." I told him I didn't know how to respond to that concern because I'd been encouraged by her progress in speech therapy over the past year.

"Why don't you bring Heather down, and we'll run some tests?" Dr. Haas suggested. "Maybe we can offer some recommendations that will help in your discussion with the school officials."

I made the appointment and soon after, Heather and I drove to Tallahassee for yet another battery of tests. The FSU staff put Heather through one language, speech, hearing, and psychological activity after another. With my blessing, because there had seemed to be some question on the part of school officials about how realistic my expectations for Heather might be, they even administered a nonverbal IQ test.

The results—some discouraging, others heartening—were certainly enlightening.

One of the examiners' comments on Heather's psychological report jumped out at me: "The mother reports that she is able to understand ninety percent of Heather's speech. However, during evaluation, it was somewhat difficult to understand Heather's speech and her attempts at verbalization were limited."

Maybe I don't have an accurate reading on Heather's speech development after all.

The overall assessment estimated Heather's basic working vocabulary at 225–250 words. Given her deafness and the fact she'd only been in speech therapy a couple of years, I thought that sounded encouraging. Then I learned the average vocabulary for a six-year-old child was approximately 2,500 words—roughly ten times Heather's vocabulary. The speech evaluation portion of the testing found both Heather's receptive communication skills (listening) and her expressive communication skills (speech) computed out to the twenty-eight-month level.

She really is way behind her classmates in language development.

The upside was that the twenty-eight-month level of achievement almost equaled the time we'd had her in formal speech therapy. If we figured her language age actually began when she started therapy at three and a half, she was right about on target. At least she was making steady progress. So I took some comfort from the statement in the summary report: "The results of this test are not considered to be representative of Heather's language *potential,* but rather serve as a guide for the development of management objectives." And then they offered a list of several specific suggestions for Heather's continued language development.

At least they see reason for hope.

They suggested an increased concentration on expanding Heather's vocabulary. Among other recommendations, they thought we needed to work more on conversational dialogue skills. They also felt there needed to be special attention given to improve Heather's syntax.

We've got a long way to go there; I haven't even worried about sentence structure up to now.

In the beginning I'd taken to heart the consistent advice I'd received from the Tracy Clinic, FSU, and my acoupedic training—not to worry at all about sentence structure, that our most important goal was to get Heather vocalizing and using words. But somewhere along the line I'd failed to make the appropriate transition and begin encouraging proper sentences. I saw that now when I read the sample sentences they'd recorded from Heather's speech. Sentences such as: "School

Heather cry" and "Heather feel sick." Because the meaning seemed obvious to me, I would just subconsciously translate those words so that in my mind I was hearing Heather say, "I was sad and cried at school today" and "I'm not feeling very well this morning."

When I really thought about it, I realized I regularly "translated" and elaborated on Heather's words that way. For example, she loved to look at books with pictures of dancers. And when she saw a photograph of a ballerina she would point to it and say simply "pretty." She wouldn't even attempt the word *ballerina*, yet I would hear in my mind (and sometimes respond out loud to Heather), "The ballerina is pretty."

It's no wonder I've been overestimating her language development!

The results of Heather's nonverbal intelligence test were more encouraging. That report summary stated: "These results place Heather in the superior range of nonverbal intelligence. . . . This IQ indicates that Heather is an intellectually gifted child."

Also very heartening were the overall recommendations regarding Heather's educational placement.

"In summary," the report concluded, "Heather appears to be an intellectually gifted deaf child. It is important that Heather be provided with the best special education facilities possible so that her high intelligence may be used as an asset in her educational and emotional growth. It appears that Heather has done a remarkable job in adjusting to her sensory handicap, and her superior intelligence may be used to help her overcome the difficulties faced by a deaf child in developing speech and language."

The very first conclusion regarding Heather's ongoing education was this: "It is recommended that Heather be placed in a regular classroom with individualized tutorial instruction for language and reading." The report suggested ideas for curriculum planning and encouraged the creation of socialization experiences with other children in group settings. And it offered this strong warning/comment: "It is essential that training in language, speech, and reading permeate all activities and all content subjects during the elementary years. If Heather does not learn speech and language at this level, it is unlikely that she will acquire these skills later."

We've got our work cut out for us here; this is crucial.

With this FSU report backing us up, Dr. Haas actually drove to Dothan and went with me to meet with the school system's special education director to present our carefully thought-out plan. Diane, Heather's therapist, and I would make a concerted effort that spring and summer to greatly increase Heather's vocabulary. And if the school would place her in first grade that next fall, with her age group, then I would take a leave of absence from teaching that next year and devote my primary time and energies to providing that "individualized tutorial instruction for language and reading" she obviously needed to catch up with the other children her age.

The school agreed. I cashed in my retirement account to help meet our family living expenses and made plans to become Heather's *official* tutor.

Having learned our lesson with a hands-off strategy the year before, I interacted with the principal and heartily approved of her choice of a first-grade teacher for Heather. Dorothy Wages was an experienced teacher, a warm, motherly figure with a nurturing manner. I met with Dot before school started that fall to tell her all about Heather. We scheduled a weekly Friday afternoon conference. In those meetings Dot would report on progress and problems she'd noticed since our previous meeting and fill me in on her lesson plans for the coming week. We found that when I could orient Heather the night before—to let her know what the teacher would be covering and expecting the next day—she had a much easier time following along in class.

Dot did a great job of working with us. She made a point, when they had a spelling test, to sit right in front of Heather when she read out the words, instead of walking around the class as she might ordinarily do.

She was also good about making sure Heather wore the Phonic Ear trainer—a miniature amplification system we got to augment the hearing aids in a classroom setting. The teacher wore a little transmitter-powerpack attached to a small microphone that broadcast her voice to the receiver-powerpack Heather wore, which in turn relayed the boosted signal to Heather's hearing aids.

Our combination of improved technology, regular communication, and hard work paid off for all concerned. Heather enjoyed school. We didn't frustrate the teacher. There were none of the behavior problems we'd experienced in kindergarten. And my evening job tutoring Heather left time during the day for me to finish up the graduate program I'd been plugging away at in night school for the past couple years. I'd pursued my master's degree in reading, in part because I'd been working in a Title I reading program when I'd begun grad school, but also because extra training in that specialty could be put to good use in working with Heather. Everything I read and every expert I talked to had told me that deaf children have special challenges to overcome in order to acquire any language and reading skills.

So far that had been true. But Heather was doing well enough in school now to make all A's and B's on her report card. And the follow-up testing we did down at FSU again that spring of her first-grade year showed steady (if slow) progress in terms of language development. I felt more convinced than ever that we were on the right track. So when we encountered no real debate about whether to pass Heather to the second grade, I decided to go back to teaching in a classroom again.

Heather's second-grade teacher, Jeannette Sutherland, proved to be another good match. For one thing, like the experienced elementary school teacher she was, she just naturally talked slowly, clearly enunciating her words—which is just what Heather needed. She also emphasized the "we are family" concept with her students. "In this room we are going to look after each other—like family," she told her students. Her emphasis on kindness and consideration showed itself among her students in a variety of ways—one of which was their sensitivity to Heather.

On more than one occasion, when children from other classes made fun of Heather on the playground, her classmates quickly came to her defense and then told Mrs. Sutherland what had happened. In the classroom, when the noise level began to rise, Heather would put her hands to the side of her head and announce in her loudest voice, "Hurt my ears! Hurt my ears!" And the kids around her would invariably apologize and quickly shush the rest of the class.

"The kids are great natural interpreters for Heather," Jeannette would tell me. "Frequently, by the time I noticed the puzzled look on Heather's face and realized she hadn't understood my instructions, one of the children sitting beside her would already be saying, 'What Mrs. Sutherland means is. . . .' And Heather would respond, 'Oh, okay' and begin the task. It works the same way when I fail to understand Heather," she laughed. "One of the other children can usually translate without any problem."

All along we'd found that her peers often had an easier time understanding Heather than adults did. As illustration of that point, Jeannette Sutherland told me another story, an anecdote indicative of yet another reason why we appreciated Heather's second-grade teacher. She made a genuine effort to treat Heather like any other child in the room.

"I often sent students out of the classroom on little errands for me," Jeannette remembered. "One day when Heather raised her hand to volunteer, I thought, *Why not?* I made sure she understood what I wanted and let her go. It took her longer than I'd expected, but when she returned a few minutes later she had the book, or whatever it was I'd wanted, and a rather proud, self-satisfied smile on her face.

"That afternoon after school one of my colleagues accosted me in the hall. 'Did you realize you sent that little Whitestone girl to my class to give me that message this morning?'

"'Of course! What about it?'

"'But she's deaf!'

"'I know that!' I laughed.

"'It took me the longest time to figure out what she wanted.'

"'But you did, didn't you?'

"The teacher smiled and nodded her head. 'Only because that child refused to leave until she got what you wanted. She just kept right on talking and talking until I finally understood. I'll say this, she was one determined little girl.'"

I tutored Heather again that year, much as we had done during first grade, finding out what the class assignments would be ahead of time so we could discuss the subject the night before and then reinforcing the lessons by helping with follow-up homework the night after. The big difference from first grade was that when I finally finished up Heather's work each night and got her to bed, I had to begin my own preparations to teach my middle-school classes the next day.

Despite our long hours of daily work, that year in second grade turned out a lot better for Heather socially than it was academically. She consistently brought home A's and B's again on her report card. But when she took the standardized achievement test administered to all second graders in the spring, it confirmed the serious discrepancy between Heather's language/reading abilities and those of her classmates.

This time I didn't fight the recommendation to hold Heather back. I realized she was lagging farther and farther behind her age-group in language development. I only prayed that another year in the second grade would give her the time and opportunity she needed to start catching up.

Fortunately for Heather, she still had her dance, because the rest of her daily life—at least during the school year—consisted almost entirely of hard work and long hours of speech therapy and schoolwork. Any recognizable progress in those areas came slowly and at a great price.

Dancing was different. For Heather it was pure joy. I think one reason she enjoyed her dance class was because students seldom had to speak or answer questions out loud, so she didn't feel so different. She fit into the crowd and felt just like everyone else out on the dance floor. She believed she could dance just as well as anyone else in her class—maybe better.

I knew there were still some people who had a hard time understanding how or why a deaf child would be taking ballet. I vividly recall a conversation I overheard early one Saturday morning during a dress rehearsal for a recital. Sitting by myself in a row of seats out in the auditorium, watching Heather's little troupe practice their numbers, I caught just enough of something said behind me that I began to listen carefully. I didn't turn around to look, but two mothers I didn't know, who evidently also had daughters up on stage, were talking about Heather. "She's deaf, you know. Can't hear a thing. I don't know what she's doing in dance class anyway; it's a shame Tracy let her in. I just know she's going to mess up tonight and ruin the whole program."

I had a thing or two I wanted to say to those ladies. But for once I simply bit my tongue and let it go. Even if I hadn't been convinced that the dance training helped improve the inflection in Heather's voice (and both Diane and I thought it did), by this time no one could have said anything to make me pull Heather out of her ballet. I saw how much it meant to her. And I felt it invaluable for her to have something that was all hers. Something she didn't do because it was expected or required. Something she did purely for love.

Dance performances also gave Heather a welcome chance to shine in public. My family—my parents, Stephanie, and Michael—would drive all the way down from Birmingham for her recitals. They always made such a fuss over her afterwards that I'm sure Heather thought she'd been the star of the show. I felt that affirmation was good for her.

Another one of the joys Heather got out of her ballet I didn't fully understand until her teacher Jeannette Sutherland told me this story. She said during group time in class one day she asked the children to tell one thing they did when they wanted to irritate their brothers or sisters. According to Jeannette, when Heather's turn came, she walked to the front of her class and got this incredibly mischievous grin on her face. Then she explained that if she wanted to make her sisters Stacey and Melissa really mad, she waited until they were watching their favorite Saturday morning cartoons, then she'd begin dancing back and forth across the room. She demonstrated with a little twirl and laughingly told her classmates: "I go front TV, they get mad and yell."

As Jeannette related the story I couldn't help but laugh. I'd seen Heather pull that stunt many times, though I'd never realized she'd done it to deliberately aggravate her sisters. I'd always thought she was just so engrossed in her dance routines that she was oblivious to what her sisters were doing, or to their words when they would yell at her: "Get out of the way, Heather! Who do you think you are, anyway? Miss America or something?"

The truth was, Heather's infatuation with dance was good for more than what it provided in the way of self-esteem or as a surefire means of irritating big sisters. I used it as a motive for language development as well—checking out every book I could find that had anything at all to do with dance or ballet. We'd use them for reading practice and discussion exercises because Heather never seemed to tire of reading or talking about dance.

About this time we gained another great motivational interest with the media coverage of the royal romance between Prince Charles and Lady Diana Spencer. Heather so fell in love with Lady Di that I could hardly get through a checkout line at the grocery store without Heather demanding I buy any and every magazine with Diana's picture on the cover. So it was at Heather's insistence that on July 29, 1981, like millions of Anglophiles and hopeless romantics the world over, my three daughters and I got out of bed at the unprecedented hour of 4 A.M. to watch the televised coverage of the royal wedding.

While we all enjoyed the pomp and pageantry, Heather seemed particularly enthralled. She usually wasn't one to watch a lot of television. But she sat right in front of the set for hours that morning taking in the entire spectacle.

For months, even years afterward, Heather's fascination with the royal couple, especially Princess Di, served as an interest point around which we structured hours and hours of reading, language development, and speech therapy. We bought a picture book of the wedding, and we cut out magazine articles and photos to make into a special Princess Di scrapbook for Heather. Together we'd pore over the material and I'd ask: "Who is that in the picture? Princess Di. What is that on her head? A crown. Look closely. Is it a crown or is it a tiara? Look at Princess Di's pretty dress. Can you say 'polka-dot dress'? What is Princess Di doing in this picture?"

Sometimes I'd even use her interest in Princess Di to inspire written exercises. Heather's writing needed a lot of work. It tended to be very fragmented because she habitually omitted articles, prepositions, and pronouns just as she did in her speech. That gave her writing almost a shorthand kind of feel. Because language remained a major struggle, we used anything we could find to make it interesting.

Heather had Jeannette Sutherland again that second year in the second grade. We thought that if Heather had to make friends with an entirely new group of kids, at least her teacher would be familiar. Some things we handled differently, however. For instance, we pulled her out of the classroom for more individualized instruction in reading and language with Beth Dowling, a new deaf-education specialist.

That year Heather's math scores continued to be high. And she did pretty well in subjects like science, because she had a good memory for facts. But when she took the standardized tests again at the end of the year, Heather actually scored lower on the reading segment than she had the year before. While no one wanted to hold Heather back for yet another year in the second grade, I was becoming more and more concerned about her lack of progress in the area of language.

I didn't know it then, but so were a growing number of educators in the Dothan public school system.

CHAPTER 10

Determination and Doubts

❧

Girard Elementary, or "Little Girard" as it was called throughout Dothan, housed only kindergarten, first, and second grades when Heather attended there. For third grade she switched to nearby Wilson Street School, which meant I needed to orient an entirely new administration and staff concerning Heather and our goals and expectations for her.

About this time I started picking up on clues that I had made something of a reputation for myself throughout the school system.

Evidently some people labeled me a very difficult and demanding parent. If I was, I certainly didn't mean to be.

Whenever I had dealings with the school, I tried to be on my best behavior. As a teacher myself, I always wanted to see things from Heather's teacher's perspective and to take the standard school policy into consideration. Was I really *demanding* and *difficult*? Sometimes, maybe, I don't know. I'd rather have called myself *determined*. I was undoubtedly that—*determined* to see Heather got every possible chance to succeed in school, even if that meant stepping on toes or sometimes being misunderstood.

I realized some people thought I expected too much of Heather and pushed her too hard. And I found out later some people in the school system believed me so unrealistic that they were actually saying, "Daphne has her own agenda. It's a shame, but she doesn't even have her daughter's best interests at heart."

What they didn't know and didn't see—because they weren't working with her day after day, night after night—was how much Heather pushed herself. They didn't understand the incredible inner drive Heather had to be like everyone else—especially like her big sisters. All of her life Heather wanted nothing more than to live up to their standards, to bring home the same straight-A report cards, to attain the same high level of achievement and success Bill and I had come to expect from Stacey and Melissa.

By that third-grade year it had become very clear, even to Heather, that she was falling far short on that score. And what bothered me most about that was that it was beginning to bother Heather.

That fall of 1982 I just happened to be appointed the teacher representative from my school to attend a special enrichment workshop on "learning styles." Dr. Walter Barbe, a nationally noted educator and an editor with the children's *Highlights* magazine, came to Dothan to lead the seminar. I was so intrigued by his discussion of the differences between students with "visual," "auditory," "kinesthetic," or a "mixed-modality" learning style (and so impressed when he instantly picked me out of the group as a classic example of a "visual learner") that I went up between sessions to talk to him about Heather.

I gave Dr. Barbe a quick rundown on Heather's history and explained that our biggest continuing frustration was the language and reading problem. I'd become particularly irritated with the schools lately because they insisted on keeping Heather in the Houghton-Mifflin reading series we used in the Dothan system—even though our latest FSU assessments had recommended we move her from such a phonetic-based reading program into a "meaning-based" curriculum.

In complaining about this to Dr. Barbe, hoping a man with his impressive credentials and obvious understanding of learning styles might lend support to my case, I said, "Everybody knows a deaf person can't learn phonics!"

Dr. Barbe looked at me for a moment and then brought me up short by responding: "If your daughter doesn't learn phonics, how else can you ever expect her to read well?"

He'd obviously missed the point. "Dr. Barbe," I said. "Maybe you didn't hear what I said: Heather is profoundly deaf."

Dr. Barbe smiled kindly and shook his head. "No, you're not hearing what *I* said. You can learn to 'listen' with your other modes. What makes you think that the only way a child can learn phonics is by hearing them through the auditory mode? There are reading programs that utilize other modes to enhance phonetic concepts."

He mentioned several reading systems—including two I was familiar with, the *Beka* and *Alphatime* programs—which he thought most effective with nonauditory learners.

I felt chastised. I'd been guilty of doing what always upset me when I saw others do it with Heather—automatically assuming she couldn't learn something simply because she couldn't hear well enough.

Finally, I decided the Beka curriculum, with its visual approach and the memorization of rhymes to introduce phonetic sounds, would work better for Heather. I asked if we could include that reading program in Heather's individualized education plan. But because the Beka texts include clearly stated Christian principles, introduce moral concepts, and even use biblical references, I was told they were not appropriate for use in the Dothan Public Schools. Not even as part of the one-on-one supplementary instruction Heather received from the special ed staff outside of class? The answer was no.

Frustrated again, I refused to be deterred this time by the school system's inflexibility. I eventually learned that one of Dothan's private Christian schools used the Beka curriculum. And after extensive inquiries I found a teacher at that school who agreed to tutor Heather in reading after school using the Beka system.

The only problem was: How would we fit one more major commitment into the family schedule? Even with Bill's help sharing carpool duty, some days the logistics seemed absolutely insane. Every afternoon after school I picked up all three girls and drove to either speech therapy or now her Beka tutor. While we waited outside for Heather, I'd open the back gate of our family station wagon to create a makeshift desk and work area for the other girls to do their homework. Melissa and Stacey knew that if they were going to need my help with their schoolwork, that was the only time they could get it, because I had to devote all my time after supper to working with Heather on her speech therapy as well as her schoolwork—and now the Beka material on top of it all. Some nights we'd finish so late that I'd send Heather on to bed at 10 or

10:30 knowing I'd have to wake her up before 5 the next morning so we could go over the words for her spelling test.

On top of all the girls' academic pursuits, we had Heather's regular dance class commitment (I certainly wasn't going to drop that) plus all the other typical activities any three girls could ever get involved in—like scouts, church, and gymnastics. The only time I ever had to myself, or for preparing to teach my own students, I had to find late at night or in the wee morning hours long after the girls and Bill had gone to bed. I couldn't count the number of mornings my family found me slumped against the couch or sprawled out on the living-room floor, surrounded by my own schoolbooks or a scattering of papers I'd been grading when I'd finally nodded off to sleep.

Exhausting and hectic as our life was, it wasn't without its many rewards. Summers especially offered welcome relief from the everyday pressures of school—for me as well as the girls. Panama City Beach remained a favorite weekend destination. The girls enjoyed sailing out in the Gulf with Bill on the used catamaran he bought. Another annual highlight for me was the cross-country trip the girls and I made every August out to Denver to visit my sister and her family. Since Deborah also had three daughters who were roughly the same ages as mine, our kids always had a ball together. All year long Stacey, Melissa, and Heather would look forward to the next time they could join their Colorado cousins—Christy, Kim, and Holly—for such memorable summer adventures as hiking in the Rocky Mountains or rafting down white-water rivers.

But I also found real excitement and encouragement in some of the quieter moments of our strenuous daily routine. Like many parents with handicapped children, I learned that sometimes the smallest things could provide the biggest inspiration. I recall the first time Heather finally, clearly, articulated her full name: "Heather Whitestone." For six long years, nearly every day, we'd asked again and again: "What's your name? Where do you live? What is your phone number?" For six long years my worst nightmare had been fearing that if she was ever lost, no one would be able to understand who she was. So when she finally got "Whitestone" down, complete with those two tricky "t" sounds in the middle, we all celebrated.

Unfortunately, the slow steady progress we continued to make with Diane Steensland in speech therapy, and what improvement I thought I saw in Heather's Beka reading series, evidently didn't translate into Heather's regular classroom work.

Heather continued to bring home A's and B's on report cards, even in reading and English, which I first took as a sign of encouragement. Finally, however, we realized that those grades weren't a true reflection of Heather's mastery of the material. All they really proved was just how easily an extremely bright deaf girl could bamboozle the public education system. Heather had become so adept at reading body language and picking up on other visual clues that when a teacher gave her any sort of preprinted workbook exercise she'd work her way slowly from question to question, watching the teacher's reaction to her every move. A smile or a nod meant she was on the right track; anything else meant she probably needed to look more carefully at one of the other answers. Her excellent memory also helped; but she managed to memorize countless facts without ever seeing how they fit together or ever understanding the various shades of meanings in the words she learned.

Fourth grade, the 1983–84 school year, brought a major turning point in all our lives. That's about the time in most kids' lives when they are beginning to experience meaningful friendships and draw more of their identity from their interaction with peers, and less from their parents. At ten and eleven years of age, some little girls are becoming aware of, and starting to pair off with, boys. That happened with Heather's friend Claudia, who'd been her closest and dearest friend since second grade. So Heather began to feel a little left out, a little more different from the other kids than she'd ever felt before. At the same time this is also about the stage in child development when kids begin to gain a new measure of self-awareness. So all these factors came into play for Heather at approximately the same time.

I still vividly recall the stab of pain that went through my heart the day Heather came home from her fourth-grade class crying.

"What's wrong, honey?" I naturally wanted to know.

"Other kids not like me. Not be friends," she sobbed. "Because Heather different. I deaf."

For years I'd known a day like this was coming. But I still didn't feel prepared.

I wished I could give her the whole child psychology lecture and convince her it would be all right, that someday it wouldn't matter. That ten- and eleven-year-old kids can be incredibly hurtful and mean. That we'd get through this like we'd gotten through all the other challenges life had thrown at us. But I knew none of that would ease the loneliness and pain she was feeling.

"You know, Heather," I told her, "every one of us is different. Every person in your class is different. And God didn't make any of us perfect; the only perfect person in the history of the world was Jesus. Everyone else—all of us—have handicaps. Some are more obvious than others—like your deafness. Like a person who is blind. Or someone who has a crippled leg and can't run. But many of us have handicaps people can't see. Maybe we're shy or afraid. Maybe we're selfish or hateful and mean toward others. Or maybe we just don't feel very good about ourselves. And if there are some people in your class who don't like you and don't want to be your friend, just because you are deaf, then maybe that's their handicap. If it is, I think that's a lot bigger handicap than not being able to hear like other people."

I don't know that my speech helped a lot that day. I could only hope that in time Heather would understand what I'd said. In the meantime I just had to pray that God would comfort and assure Heather of her self-worth through his love for her.

One very positive thing we had going for us that year was that Heather's fourth-grade teacher, Mary Ann Hornsby, was a longtime friend of mine. She not only loved Heather, I think she actually valued and accepted my input. But Mary Ann's sensitivity wasn't enough to alter the fact that Heather no longer seemed like a very happy girl.

Perhaps the cumulative effect of all those long days of work, month after month, year after year, was finally taking its toll on her spirit. Maybe she was discouraged because she was working on a first-grade book in the Beka series at the same time she and I were struggling so hard to keep up with the fourth-grade reader she was using at school. Or, just maybe, the way everything was adding up, Heather was simply realizing for the first time how far behind her classmates she'd fallen—how "different" that made her. Whatever the causes, I could sense the effect. Heather's frustration level was rising fast.

To add to that concern, the school had started pressuring us once more. Wasn't it about time we considered the deaf-education program again? Beth Dowling, the new deaf-education specialist, was a proponent of "cued speech" and felt every bit as strongly about her chosen method as I did about acoupedics. I liked and respected Beth; she'd respected our wishes by not using sign when she worked with Heather outside of class. But I knew she felt strongly that she could help Heather if we'd just change our minds about mainstreaming and let her try cued speech as part of Heather's daily therapy in the deaf-education unit.

I was determined to hold my ground. But I suddenly felt assaulted from all sides.

Everything came to a head the day Heather came home from school with a book I assumed she'd found in the library. (Later I wondered if someone had deliberately given it to her, but that didn't occur to me then.)

"You got a new library book today, Heather?" We always talked about what she was reading; it made for a very natural, conversational, language-development exercise.

Heather eagerly showed me her book—a picture story about a little girl. "She like me," Heather pointed. "She deaf, too."

"It's the story of a deaf girl?"

"Yes. She dance like me."

"I see. There she is practicing her ballet." She was like Heather; I could see why she seemed so excited about this book.

Heather turned the page. "But she go special school. Just deaf children."

I nodded my understanding. "She goes to a special deaf school, does she?"

Heather nodded. Then she looked up and said to me, "Heather need go special school."

"Oh, no, Heather," I said matter-of-factly. "You don't have to go to a special deaf school. You can go to a regular school and live at home with Melissa and Stacey and Dad and me. I'd miss you if you had to go away to a special school."

I thought I saw a little disappointment in Heather's eyes. And on some level, maybe just subconsciously, I think that scared me.

From the very beginning I'd been told by everyone that an acoupedic approach would be the hardest and slowest way to go. For eight long, difficult years I'd been heartened by Heather's own bulldog stubbornness and determination to learn to speak. If she was ready to give up on the acoupedic approach, I knew there was no way to go on.

As much as I still believed we'd done the right thing, as certain as I'd been that God had been leading us—from Dr. Humphries to FSU, to Doreen Pollack in Denver, and even to Dr. Barbe's learning modality workshop—I was suddenly consumed by doubt.

Even Heather now thinks she needs to go to a special school. What if I've been wrong all along?

CHAPTER 11

A
Special School

Once again I called Bill Haas at Florida State University. Since he'd already made a couple trips to Dothan to meet with school officials, he told me, "I think I've done all I can personally. But my friend Gladys may have some ideas. Let me check with her and get back to you."

I'd met Gladys Crawford, an oral-deaf advocate. She was formerly a deaf-education coordinator with the state of Florida's Department of Education, and also the mother of a hearing impaired son. When Dr. Haas briefed her on Heather's situation, she told him she thought our first step in determining whether or not to change the course of Heather's schooling should be to get a thorough evaluation from a program specializing in oral-deaf education. She recommended we take Heather to the Central Institute for the Deaf (CID), a world-renowned school in St. Louis, Missouri.

When Bill Haas called back to pass along Gladys's advice, he assured us: "You can count on a fair and forthright assessment from CID. They're so widely respected they don't have to solicit students. They'll be completely honest with you about Heather. If they feel her learning deficit is too great to overcome with an oral-deaf education and that her educational programs and goals need to be changed, they will tell you. While their school is not an acoupedic program, they are oral/deaf specialists who know what is available in oral-deaf education. I agree with Gladys; they are the best folks to tell you what Heather needs at this point in her educational development."

I called CID immediately and made arrangements with the school's director, Dr. Jean Moog, for us to take Heather to St. Louis for evaluation. "What we're really looking for is your assessment and recommendations regarding our daughter's future education. And we're not really interested in enrolling our daughter in a special school," I explained. "But just out of curiosity, how much does it cost to send a child to your school?"

She told me the yearly tuition was approximately $5,500 a year, with another $4,000 per year room and board. So for resident students the total came to $9,500 a year. I remember hanging up the phone, shaking my head in shock, and telling one of my teaching colleagues: "There's certainly no way we could ever afford that!"

That was Bill's reaction as well. "We could never pay that, Daphne. I don't have any problem taking Heather to St. Louis for the testing. But if they recommend enrolling her in their program, there's just no way we can do it! No way!"

While *I* understood that, I don't think *Heather* did. Even though we explained that the purpose of our trip was to test her to help us know what to do about her education, Heather got it in her mind that we were going to see a "special school," like in the book. "Heather go special school," she insisted. Nothing we said to the contrary seemed to sink in. And she got so excited on the drive to St. Louis in the family station wagon that Bill and I decided to let it drop until later.

We found the CID "campus" in downtown St. Louis with no trouble—its main four-story brick building is located across the street from part of the Barnes Hospital medical complex. The entire family, the three girls included, got a quick preliminary tour before the testing began the first morning.

As a professional educator, I have to admit that I was impressed by what I saw. Everything seemed so carefully and thoughtfully planned out. The classes were small—many had only three or four students per instructor. Each student had his or her own individualized educational plan. A child working in a third-grade reading book who was strong in math might be in a fifth-grade arithmetic class. They gave remedial help where needed, while challenging students in areas where they could be challenged. And CID didn't seem locked into any particular curriculum; they drew on a multitude of resources to find the best approach for each student.

From that first exposure I began thinking, *If I ever had to send a child off to a residential school, this would be the kind of place I'd choose.* But I still hoped the testing would provide us with recommendations that would somehow enable us to continue with the acoupedic approach and meet Heather's needs back in Dothan.

But those hopes were soon dashed. When one staff member escorted Heather away to begin testing, another took Stacey and Melissa off to participate in some other activities. Bill and I were then ushered into a tiny observation cubicle next to Heather's testing room. In all the testing we'd been through over the years, this was the first time I'd ever been able to observe the entire procedure. So what I saw at first fascinated, then distressed me.

The audiological testing was what I'd expected and seen before. And the results were consistent with earlier tests. No surprise there.

What Bill and I couldn't believe were the results of various verbal and language tests administered to Heather. I might not have believed it if I hadn't been sitting there watching through that two-way mirror. As Heather gave one incorrect response after another I felt my heart sink lower and lower. At one point when I glanced over at Bill, he had his face in his hands and was sadly shaking his head. There was no denying it—Heather was clearly deficient in her educational development.

How deficient? We'll know that tomorrow when they give us a report.

I think the low point for me was when the examiner showed Heather a picture of bacon strips and she called them "pig." I wanted to console myself by saying, *Well, that's where bacon comes from, isn't it?* But I knew we had some serious problems when my eleven-year-old daughter didn't know the word "bacon," wasn't able to tell the examiner that the sun set in the "west," and couldn't correctly answer any number of other simple questions you'd expect a child her age to know.

The longer I sat and watched those tests, the closer and closer the walls of that little observation cubicle seemed to be. With my entire world caving in, I began asking myself: *What are we going to do now? Do we go back to Dothan and start over? Will we have to put Heather in a regular deaf-education class and begin teaching her to sign?* I couldn't help wondering, *Why have we wasted these past eight years? Is it too late to make up the lost ground now? Have I been unkind to my little girl by expecting too much? How much damage has been done?*

That night in our motel room, Bill and I were still in shock. But Heather acted like a kid at Christmas; she was so excited by everything she'd seen at CID. She'd made up her mind: "I go school here. Heather like special school." Her sisters were almost as excited for her, telling her all about the rooftop playground they'd enjoyed that afternoon and the games they'd played with some of the interns and older students in the school.

While the girls carried on their animated conversation and watched TV, Bill and I sat in a daze on the edge of our bed. We asked each other, "What now?" But neither of us could think of a good answer.

I lay awake most of the night, feeling much like a condemned prisoner dreading the dawn. Tomorrow, when the testing was finished, we would be called in for an official consultation. But I already knew what the verdict was going to be.

Before that, there were a few more tests and a more extensive tour of the facilities. We visited the older resident-students' dorm across the street. We ate lunch with the students in the cafeteria. And we observed a physical education class in which two youngsters gave us a remarkable demonstration of fitness by scampering up a rope into the rafters of the gymnasium. It was in the phys ed department that I was struck by the realization: *They don't treat these kids like they're handicapped here. They really challenge them.* That too impressed me.

What made the most lasting impression, however, were the youngest students at CID. Two- and three-year-old boys and girls, some of whom lived together in dorm nurseries right in the main CID building, attended class, received therapy, and learned to speak by reading lips. Despite the obvious love given these tiny children by the committed CID staff, I couldn't help but imagine the heartache of parents who had to send such little children off to school. *I don't think I could have done that,* I thought. *But maybe I should have. Maybe we wouldn't be in the predicament we are today if I hadn't been so adamant about keeping Heather at home.*

I was also impressed that every class, whether it was reading, science, or even math, and every activity—from lunch to chores in the resident dorms—was viewed as a language development laboratory. If a math teacher asked a student, "What is 6 times 7?" the student could not simply answer, "42." He couldn't even respond, "The answer 42." He had to say, "The answer is forty-two." At lunch students were not allowed to ask for "salt and pepper!" They had to say, "Please pass the salt and pepper."

Every possible opportunity was taken to assist and enable students to speak clearly, with correct syntax, and in complete sentences. Not only the teachers but the houseparents in the dorms and all the other staff people reinforced this language emphasis. I could see how that would make a significant difference in speech development, and I wished I'd started insisting on that with Heather much earlier in her educational career. *I've made so many mistakes!*

The time for our dreaded conference in the director's office finally arrived. Those staff members who'd conducted the actual testing were there to report. The audiologist had found nothing new, but she did have one unexpected recommendation. Because Heather's best hearing sensitivity and speech perception came through her left ear and she preferred listening with that ear to listening with both, the CID audiologist recommended the use of amplification in her left ear only. We needed only one hearing aid.

The other test results clearly indicated a serious deficiency in verbal scores and communication ability. Perhaps most discouraging were the results of one expressive-language test designed to measure the complexity of language usage: Heather scored in the first percentile when compared with normal hearing *five-year-olds.* What that meant is that 99 percent of the normal hearing kindergartners who had been evaluated with this same procedure had scored better than she did. *No wonder she's frustrated in a fourth-grade classroom! No wonder she'd been feeling left out and different!*

I winced as I heard the report on Heather's written language, which included these sample sentences:

> They found an animals in old another earth.
> They are bad outside, no food, missy and dirty.
> They leave away the old earth.
> Aimals love him because they helpful but they readly love outside.
> A duck swim the water, a grass was green.

When the rest of the staff completed their reports and promised a written summary, they left us with the director, Jean Moog, for a final summary of the findings. She confirmed what we already knew—that while Heather's nonverbal intellectual abilities were "within the superior range," her verbal abilities showed a significant deficit. She was reading at a second-grade level and her overall achievement level was "third grade, fourth month." But, even though her language skills were within the normal range for a hearing impaired child her age, "they are significantly delayed in comparison to normal hearing five-year-olds."

She went on to say that because Heather's language, reading, and achievement levels were behind her present grade placement in a mainstream setting, "a change in Heather's educational program is strongly recommended."

Here it comes.

Bill interrupted. "Watching those tests yesterday made us wonder if she'll ever catch up. She seemed so far behind!"

"No, no," Jean Moog responded. "You must not think that!"

I felt a faint hope stir in my heart. "Are you saying she does have oral speech capability?"

"Yes," she answered without hesitation.

"You're not recommending we switch her to cued speech or to sign language?"

"Oh, no!" she responded just as quickly.

This was more than I'd dared hope. "But what about the deficiency in her language and her achievement scores? What do we do? How can we make that up?"

The CID director assured us that her staff would include a number of detailed recommendations in their written report of Heather's assessment, which we would be receiving in a few weeks. But she also said she thought what Heather needed most was intensive language development in a program that emphasized language and speech twenty-four hours a day. She added that she believed it crucial for Heather to be grouped with other children similar to her in their language skills. She told us she considered Heather a strong candidate for placement at Central Institute for the Deaf and felt very confident that CID's program could provide Heather with the educational benefits and setting she needed to make up lost ground. Given time, she thought they could prepare Heather academically to be successfully mainstreamed again.

Bill and I explained that we didn't have the financial resources to send Heather to CID. We both had good jobs and worked hard. But we had two other daughters to support. And there was just no way we could pay $9,500 a year for Heather's education.

Dr. Moog informed us that while it was a little late to be making such arrangements for the upcoming fall term, she thought she might be able to make some calls about possible scholarships for which

Heather might qualify. Those scholarships could amount to three or four thousand dollars.

She suggested we might also check to see if our local school district would provide some funding for Heather. She told us CID had some students whose state department of education paid their full tuition because they couldn't provide the educational services those students needed in their home district.

But Director Moog also told us timing was critical. If we were at all interested in Heather attending CID in the fall, we needed to be filling out an official application as soon as possible.

Bill still didn't think it was possible. But my own hopes, nearly destroyed during that first day of testing, had been resurrected by the other things I'd seen and learned at CID. Maybe, just maybe, there was a chance to reach the goal we'd worked so hard to attain over the past eight years. Maybe Heather could achieve a mainstream education and experience success in the oral, hearing world. Whatever that took, even if it meant sending Heather away to school, I was now ready to consider.

If I hadn't been, I think Heather herself would have convinced me. She'd definitely made up her mind. "That where I go school," she told us all the way home. "Need special school. I like school. People are nice. Feel home there."

When Bill expressed his doubts about the possibility, she begged him: "Please, Daddy! Please! I need go there!"

Melissa and Stacey sided with their sister. "It's a good school," they said. And I think Bill sensed from my reluctance to back him up that my mind was changing on the subject.

By the end of our long drive back to Dothan, Bill had agreed to use his, and his father's, political connections to check on the possibility of any funds from the State Department of Education in Montgomery. "We'll see. . . ." was all he would say.

But that was enough for Heather. She began telling all her friends, "I going special school next year." As far as she was concerned, there was no doubt.

The initial contacts we made at the state level and locally sounded encouraging. We showed CID's recommendations to several officials, and there was some talk that a combination of state and local funds might be made available. Nothing was final, but things looked encouraging enough that we made the commitment to enroll Heather at CID for the upcoming fall semester.

Then in July we learned the local school district had received word that the state would not be making any money available. And while there were funds designated for special education for students residing in the Dothan Public School district, it seemed no local officials wanted to set a precedent of paying for an out-of-state program such as CID's.

At that point we talked again with Dr. Haas's friend Gladys. She informed us of our parental rights under Public Law 94–142, which states that a school district must provide an appropriate educational program for every child in the district. She advised us to take the official written recommendations CID gave us to our local school district and ask if they would be able to provide a program that met those requirements. If they could, great; Heather would get the kind of program we wanted and needed for her. If they said they couldn't meet the recommendations, we'd have legal grounds to ask them for financial assistance to enroll Heather in CID.

But over the next few weeks we couldn't get anyone to say they could or could not provide a program for Heather that would meet the recommended requirements. We met once with school officials in late July. They wanted more time to study the recommendations and wouldn't commit to anything. Feeling like we were being given the royal runaround, Bill and I first got frustrated, then upset.

The summer was slipping away, and still no answer to our question. By August, Bill was so angry at the local school officials that he agreed we should send Heather to CID and then demand a due-process hearing or do whatever else we had to do to force the local schools to help pay for it.

Those last weeks of the summer were consumed with preparations to send our eleven-year-old daughter off to school for a year. I actually enjoyed shopping with Heather for things like curtains and clothes and such personal items as shampoo, soap, and toothpaste. Melissa, Stacey, and my sister Stephanie had great fun helping Heather decide what toys and stuffed animals she should take. (CID encouraged kids to bring things that would help them feel at home.) I think some of Heather's incredible excitement rubbed off on all of us and even helped counteract my own natural apprehensions.

The older girls didn't make the trip to St. Louis with us that fall. We barely had room for Heather with all the belongings we packed into that station wagon.

Despite all the weeks of frantic planning, shopping, and packing, as our car rolled north, I couldn't help feeling terribly unprepared for what was about to happen. I kept thinking, *Most parents have seventeen or eighteen years before they have to send a child off to school.* I'd only had eleven. There was so much to say yet, so much I didn't know how to say.

And the mileposts whizzed by outside my window.

Bill and I tried to warn Heather about homesickness. We assured her it would pass, that we'd write, she could call us anytime she needed to, and she could look forward to coming home at Thanksgiving. I knew she knew all that. But we had to say it all, as much to reassure ourselves as Heather.

She virtually bubbled over with excitement and vulnerable innocence at the prospect of this new life adventure. I, on the other hand, had to fight to contain my own emotions. *How am I going to leave my little girl? Who is going to hold her hand and wipe her forehead with a cold damp cloth when she gets sick in the night? Who will she find to talk to and give her a hug when some friend hurts her feelings?*

Somewhere outside Paducah, Kentucky, an explosion in the engine compartment interrupted my thoughts and fears. As Bill whipped the car onto the shoulder and hit the brakes, a huge cloud of smoke rolled out from under the hood, completely obscuring our vision. "I think we just blew a radiator hose," he said as we hurriedly climbed out of the car.

I'd barely slid out and shut my door before I realized Heather had already jumped the ditch and clambered to the top of a nearby embankment. There she stood hugging Pooh Bear, her favorite stuffed animal, and waving us to get away from the car.

"I thought car would blow up," she explained later. We laughed and teased her about leaving her poor parents to fend for themselves by a car she thought ready to explode. That little excitement seemed well worth the price of a radiator hose, because it gave us something to talk and laugh about for the rest of the trip. I for one had needed the distraction.

All too soon we were in St. Louis, unloading the station wagon and getting Heather situated in her room. There was a helpful orientation time for the parents of all new students—where staff members and parents who'd been through the process before reassured us that our children would be well cared for and would probably have an easier time making the adjustment than we would. That certainly seemed true in Heather's case.

Somehow I managed to hold back my tears as we said our goodbyes. But I think Heather sensed a need to reassure us. "I fine. I happy.

Do not worry!" she told us. But as I walked out of the dorm to our car I felt as if a vital part of me had been ripped out.

Surprisingly, I think Bill had an even harder time than I did. At least twice, maybe three times, he made some excuse to go back and remind Heather of one more thing, or ask one more question of Theresa, the dorm mother. They must have thought they'd never get rid of us.

It wasn't until Bill got in the car and we began to drive away that the dam finally broke and my tears poured out. Ten minutes later, when I began to regain some control, Bill lost it. That was one of the few times I'd ever seen Bill so emotional about anything.

For the next few hours, I suspect the people driving past us must have assumed we were having one rip-roaring fight. We took turns crying; when one of us finally stopped the other one would begin all over again.

As much as we knew we had to do it, we loved our little girl too much to let her go without feeling an almost unbearable loss. And to make it worse, coming to the point where we actually had to send her away to school seemed to me a very personal defeat. Because it meant that, as much as I'd thought I'd known what was best for Heather, as hard as I'd worked with Heather for eight years, as much as I loved her, I hadn't been able to give my daughter everything she needed.

I had to let her go.

CHAPTER 12

A Change in Spirits

I'd expected to miss Heather. And I did. But the real adjustment to her absence from our daily family life wouldn't take place for several weeks. Stacey, Melissa, and I were too consumed with the usual details of a new school year. And Bill and I devoted any spare waking minutes we could find to preparation for the "due process" hearing scheduled for the last week in September. The school board had finally informed us of that hearing date before we'd left with Heather. But by then we had been too busy getting Heather ready to give it much thought. So now, having returned from St. Louis, we had to begin gathering all our documentation and lining up our arguments as quickly as possible.

Gladys Crawford had warned me, "You need to realize, Daphne, you could be jeopardizing your career by pursuing this hearing. You'll be going up against your own employers, and they won't like it."

"I don't think they'd dare try to fire me over this," I told her. "But if they do, we'll cross that bridge when we come to it. No matter what happens, I have to do what I think is right for Heather."

"Okay. I'm with you then," Gladys told me as she agreed to come to Dothan to serve as an expert witness on our behalf. "I just felt I needed to warn you."

I anxiously awaited our hearing. I wanted to get it over with, to have our case decided. I worried whether or not the state-supplied hearing officer would find in our favor. But I guess I was just being naive in that I never expected it to be the horribly unpleasant experience it turned out to be.

The hearing began at 9:00 A.M. on September 26 in a school board meeting room. In the presence of the hearing officer, Dr. Ronald Evelsizer (a university professor of special education who'd been assigned this duty by the Alabama Department of Education), and a court stenographer, Bill and I faced a whole panel of school officials across a conference table. Bill made an opening statement and then I, because education was my field of expertise, began to present our case. We wanted to show two things: first, what Heather needed for her education based on the requirements of the acoupedic approach we had chosen for her and the recommendations of FSU and CID; and second, that Dothan City Public Schools had been unwilling and/or unable to provide an educational program that would meet Heather's special needs.

It quickly became clear, both in their cross-examination of us and our witnesses, as well as in the testimony of their own expert witnesses, that the school officials in that room had a multipronged strategy of their own. First they wanted to argue that they already had a program in place that could meet Heather's educational needs. Then they wanted to portray us as uncooperative parents who would neither comply with their special education program nor take the advice of their special education experts who had been "telling us for years that Heather was having serious problems." And finally they were arguing that we had yanked Heather out of the local system and sent her off to school in St. Louis without giving them a fair chance to respond to the latest recommendations from CID.

All day long we went back and forth. Most of our witnesses were sharply cross-examined. At one point after Gladys had testified about a program in Florida, one of the school officials actually questioned the relevance of her testimony by saying, "That may be true in Florida, but this is Alabama." Gladys responded something to the effect that she'd assumed Alabama schools were as concerned as Florida schools about meeting the educational needs of all their children. But we could only hope the mediator wasn't as provincial as the local officials.

Diane Steensland, Heather's private speech therapist, received the roughest treatment. In questioning her presence at the hearing and then her professional qualifications as a speech-language pathologist, one school official became so sarcastic that Diane stood up and walked out of the room. The mediator followed, and by promising he would insist on a change in the tone of questioning, persuaded her to return and complete her testimony.

I heard later that several of the school's witnesses, which included all but one of Heather's former classroom teachers as well as some administrators and special education personnel, had been gathered together weeks ahead of time to be coached about what they should say and what kind of questions they should expect to be asked at the hearing. While I didn't know that at the time, I did know I felt both hurt and betrayed to have so many people I considered (and still do consider) my friends—colleagues who'd played an important part in the team approach I'd tried to take toward Heather's education—used to help the school officials paint a portrait of me as an unrealistic, difficult, unreasonable, and demanding mother who obviously had ulterior motives and "her own agenda."

At one point I argued that if the school system had always been as concerned about Heather's academic deficiency as they claimed, then that concern should have been reflected in Heather's progress reports. But when I pointed to the consistent A's and B's on her report cards, they had no response. Time and again the special ed experts cited my reluctance to follow their suggestions for putting Heather in the system's cued-speech deaf-ed program as evidence of my stubborn refusal to cooperate.

As the day wore on, I felt emotionally battered by what seemed a very personal attack on me, not only as an educator, but as a mother.

After everything was finally said and done, and the hearing ended at nine that night, I stood slowly and approached the assistant superintendent of schools. Only half in jest I asked, "Dr. Sasser, will I still have a job tomorrow?"

"Of course you will, Daphne!" he laughed. "So I suggest you hurry home now; you're going to have an early morning tomorrow."

In the aftermath of that due-process hearing, I really began to feel the impact of Heather's absence in our family's life. For so long I'd set my daily plans around Heather's schedule—her therapy, the hours of daily work on her school assignments. And for the month we prepared for the hearing I had continued to spend every possible minute trying to do something for Heather.

Suddenly now, as I waited for an official decision to be rendered, I found myself for the first time in eight years with nothing to do with, for, or about Heather, her therapy, or her education. There seemed to be a huge, gaping hole in my life.

Whenever I walked into the room she'd shared for so long with Melissa, I'd feel a stab of loneliness and loss. But there was no predicting what else might trigger a thought or a memory that would then unleash similar feelings. One evening scanning through the newspaper I read something or maybe heard something outside that prompted an immediate flashback to a time three or four years earlier when Stacey and Heather had had a rather ordinary sibling squabble. Stacey had gotten so angry with her little sister that she'd picked Heather up, carried her out of the house, dumped her unceremoniously in the yard, then raced back in and locked the door from the inside. Heather, who always did have a temper, had been so enraged at this indignity she began pounding on the door. Furious when her sister didn't open up, she actually kicked out a small pane of glass in the French doors leading out to the backyard patio and unlocked the door. I almost laughed to remember the horrified looks of guilt and remorse on the faces of all three girls when Bill and I returned home a short while later. Then, just as quickly, tears filled my eyes as I realized how much I missed my daughter.

The only thing that made the loss bearable was the firm belief that we had done the right thing in sending Heather to St. Louis. That and Heather's continuing excitement and obvious happiness every time we talked to her. The staff at CID expressed amazement at Heather's ability to converse over the telephone. While other students (some of whom had less hearing loss than Heather did) had to rely on TDY devices to type out messages for relay over the phone lines, Heather could just pick up the receiver, dial home, and begin talking. Those long hard years of acoupedic work were paying off.

We eventually received the official eleven-page final report on the due process hearing results around the middle of October. I tore the envelope open and scanned quickly through the pages until I got to the "Decision" heading on page ten. It said:

> Based on evidence presented, it is the decision of this hearing officer that:
>
> 1. Dothan City Schools is responsible for providing an appropriate education for Heather Whitestone at no cost to her parents.

2. The least restrictive environment for Heather Whitestone is a self-contained special class with children of similar needs and communication modality, with regular classroom participation limited to library, music, physical education, and lunch.

3. The Dothan City Schools is responsible for placement in the least restrictive environment consistent with the needs of Heather Whitestone.

There was a section right before the "Decision" paragraph which talked about Heather fitting the definition of a handicapped child as defined in Public Law 94–142. And a paragraph afterward talking about the rights of either party involved in the hearing to appeal the findings and conclusions of the hearing officer. And ten more pages summarizing the factual findings of the hearing in paragraph after paragraph of educational gobbledygook and legal mumbo jumbo. Bill and I reread the "decision" again and again. We agreed with everything said there; so we guessed that was good. But nowhere in the entire eleven pages could we find anything that explained what the "decision" meant in practical terms or said in whose favor the hearing officer had ruled.

We called Gladys Crawford and read the pertinent section to her. "That's great!" she responded. "The part where he said Heather needed to be in 'a self-contained special class with children of similar needs and communication modality' seems to be the key. He's talking about an oral-deaf program, which is something Dothan doesn't have and can't hope to offer Heather anytime soon. He's finding in your favor."

"But what happens now?"

Gladys replied, "The school system will almost certainly appeal the decision. The entire report and all the documented evidence will be reviewed by a judge at the state level. His decision will be absolutely final."

"How long will that take?" we wanted to know.

"I don't know," Gladys answered. "Several weeks anyway. Maybe months."

Great! More waiting and uncertainty.

"At least you should feel encouraged knowing you won the first round," Gladys consoled us.

Yet our case might still be overturned. All we could do was wait and hope and pray.

We flew Heather home for Thanksgiving. What a reunion that was! I'm not sure Heather ever quit talking all weekend. Aunts, uncles, cousins, and grandparents all wanted to see her. And of course Stacey (tenth grade) and Melissa (eighth) had to fill their sister in on all the latest happenings at school and with friends in the neighborhood. But Heather spent most of that first visit home excitedly describing the details of her new life at CID.

I listened with rapt attention and a mixture of reactions. Remembering the frustrated and unhappy fourth grader she'd become the year before, I was thrilled at her obvious contentment. At the same time I couldn't help feeling a tinge of something—maybe jealousy, resentment, or at least regret—to realize I had no real part in this whole exciting new phase of my daughter's life. Still I remained convinced we'd done the right thing by sending her to CID. The changes I saw in Heather's spirits in just three months were a dramatic and positive confirmation of that.

She told us about her classes and her friends, and about dorm life and her favorite teachers. I think her older sisters must have felt a tad jealous. To them it sounded glamorous—like some extended summer camp adventure. All of us listened and asked questions and laughed at Heather's stories.

The funniest story she told involved an audio-trainer, the microphone and amplification transmitter that every CID instructor wore. Because these devices have impressive range and to avoid confusion, each teacher's unit was set to a different frequency. That meant each classroom had a set of receivers tuned to that teacher's trainer; and the students had to take off their receivers at the end of each class before moving to another room and picking up another receiver tuned to that teacher's audio-trainer frequency.

Heather laughingly recalled the day one of her male teachers assigned a few minutes of desk work and excused himself from the classroom. He'd been gone only a short while when Grace Lee, Heather's Korean-Canadian roommate, lifted her eyes from her work and looked toward the windows with a funny expression on her face. "I hear rain," she said, obviously puzzled to see clear skies outside. Heather and the other student in the class, a boy about Heather's age, looked at each other and grinned.

"What's so funny?" Grace asked. "Do you hear the rain?"

"That is not rain," the boy told her as he and Heather began to snicker.

"Then what. . . ."

Just then all three of the students heard a clearly amplified flushing sound. "Oh!" Grace exclaimed as she finally understood. They all began to laugh.

A couple of minutes later the instructor returned to the room. "I thought I heard rain," Grace greeted him as he walked through the doorway. "Then I hear flushing sound."

With a horrified look the teacher glanced down at his belt to confirm that he had indeed forgotten to turn off the trainer before he went to the bathroom. "The teacher so embarrassed!" Heather told us. "His face turn bright red!" We all laughed for a long time over that one.

Heather came home again at Christmas for a longer, more satisfying visit. She mentioned how much she missed her weekly dance lessons (we hadn't been able to get that for her at CID), but her happiness at school clearly outweighed any regrets she had on that score. I knew how much dancing had meant to her for so many years, and her willingness to sacrifice it said volumes to me about her adjustment to her new school.

But then the regular progress reports we received from CID and my occasional phone conversations with Heather's dorm parents Theresa and Ferdie had already assured me of that. She had to be happy to be making the kind of academic progress she'd made in a few short months.

What pleased me just as much as the classroom education Heather seemed to be getting in St. Louis was something I hadn't anticipated, something I may not have been as sensitive to as I should have been before: Heather's social development.

For the first time in her life Heather felt as if she belonged—that she was just like all the other students in her classes. She not only felt accepted by her peers, but by all reports she was very popular. And it was wonderful to see what that did for Heather's self-esteem.

Theresa, the dorm mother, reported that Heather was a sweet and cooperative child. But she did laughingly add that Heather had a way of making it known when she didn't want to do some chore. I said that didn't surprise me; she'd been opinionated and stubborn all her life. Theresa told me Heather seemed to get along well with everyone. And she also remarked on Heather's spiritual sensitivity and devotion; she said there were several times when she'd walked into Heather's room to find her reading her Bible. I told Theresa that didn't surprise me either, that Bill and I had often jested that if we could ever find a convent with its own ballet school Heather would probably be content to live out her entire life as "the dancing nun."

127

The CID staff affectionately referred to Heather as their "Southern Belle" because they said she had such a distinctive southern accent. I had to laugh at that one because in all our years of speech therapy I'd never once thought about her having any kind of accent at all.

Some of the folks in St. Louis seemed quite surprised when Heather became best friends with Bola, one of CID's international students and the daughter of a doctor from Kenya. I had to shrug off their stereotyped assumption that it was somehow unexpected and extraordinary that Heather, simply because she hailed from Southern Alabama, would ever find a kindred spirit in a black African girl her own age. The truth is, I think Heather, like a lot of kids who grow up in rural and small-town South, had more and closer interracial relationships than do most kids growing up in the North. In fact, I saw the cross-cultural friendships Heather developed with Bola, Grace Lee, and her Mexican friend Blanca as a truly enriching aspect of what was a very cosmopolitan education there at CID.

One day in March the mail contained an official-looking envelope bearing a Montgomery postmark. The judge reviewing the Dothan City Schools' appeal of the hearing findings had finally ruled. He said that because the schools already provided a deaf-education program for students in the district, that they would not be required under Public Law 94–142 to provide Heather's tuition to attend Central Institute for the Deaf in St. Louis, Missouri.

That was it. We'd lost on appeal.

I felt sick with disappointment. And more than a little angry. All those months of waiting and hoping, and now it was over.

But the good thing about not getting the bad news until March, when Heather's first year at CID was nearly over, was that we realized that by tightening our belt a few notches, and with the help of CID's scholarships, we'd actually survived the year financially. It had taken most of my take-home pay as a teacher. But we'd made it. And the year had obviously been so positive for Heather that both Bill and I knew we had to send her back to St. Louis again the next year.

Heather attended CID three years in all. The last two seemed a lot easier than the first. For one thing we knew what to expect; in fact, we were among those parents asked to share our advice and experiences during orientation for new students and their parents. I was surprised and pleased that Bill actually opened up and shared how emotionally hard it had been for him to leave Heather that first semester.

There she is ... Miss America!

Top: As a baby, Heather was like a live doll in the house for all of us to play with.

Middle: Heather at 14 months—just four months before her deadly illness.

Bottom: Christmas 1974—the day I discovered Heather was deaf.

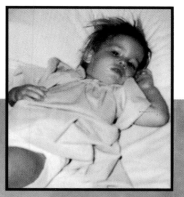

September 1974—at 18 months, Heather lay seriously ill in the hospital. Twenty years later—almost to the day—she was crowned Miss America.

The Whitestone family was now complete: Stacey (5), Melissa (4), and Heather (2).

At age 10, Heather already showed signs of pageant-winning beauty.

Top: On weekends, Heather enjoyed sailing with her dad.

Middle: One of the hardest choices I ever made was to send Heather to the Central Institute for the Deaf (CID) at age 11. But she soon made many friends.

Bottom: Heather graduated from CID at age 14. Here she is with her gym coach, Jim Marko, who taught her the sport of orienteering.

Heather's schoolwork and dance didn't leave much time for a social life, but she did attend the senior prom.

Top: Heather as Princess Leia, age 8, with her sisters, Stacey (left) and Melissa (right).

Middle: Heather, age 12, dressed as her fairy-tale heroine, Princess Diana.

Bottom: Heather at age 12, dressed up for a Society for Creative Anachronism event.

For her 21st birthday, Heather wanted a "dress-up dinner" with family and friends.

Heather always enjoyed
dressing up.

Top: Heather and her first dance teacher, Patti Richards. From the moment I enrolled her in ballet lessons at age 6, Heather loved dancing.

Middle: Some mothers were sure that Heather would "ruin" the dance recital because she was deaf. Heather proved them wrong.

Bottom and inset: Heather the dancer at age 10. She spun and twirled everywhere she went.

In the Briarwood Ballet, Heather gained a new vision of how to use her dance to worship God.

The road to Miss Alabama was long and grueling. At one point, Heather entered four pageants in five months. Here, Heather as Miss Cullman Area 1993.

Top: Shelby County Junior Miss 1991

Bottom: Miss Point Mallard 1992

Middle: Miss Jacksonville State University 1992

Heather was first runner-up for Miss Alabama two years in a row. Here, Heather with Miss Alabama 1992, Kim Wimmer.

*God's timing was perfect—after
two years as first runner-up,
Heather finally wins Miss
Alabama 1994.*

When Heather became Miss America, she gave me her Miss Alabama crown.

Top: Because of her deafness, Heather could not hear the dramatic announcement: "And the new Miss America 1995, Miss Alabama, Heather Whitestone!"

Right: What a week! The Miss America Organization puts on an exciting and well-run pageant. At the Friday night States Parade, the buzz was in the air—Heather was the favorite.

Below: The five finalists: from left, Miss Georgia, Andrea Krahn; Miss Alabama, Heather Whitestone; Miss New Jersey, Jennifer Alexis Makris; Miss Virginia, Cullen Johnson; and Miss Indiana, Tiffany Storm.

Below: Family and friends shared one of the most thrilling moments in Heather's life. From left, my mom, June Gray; my dad, Jim Gray; Bill Whitestone, Heather's father; Stacey Vera, my oldest daughter; me; and Melissa Gomillion, my middle daughter.

I am proud to be "Miss America's Mom."

I continued to appreciate the wide range of enrichment opportunities CID gave its students. Heather's gym teacher, Jim Marco, made a real effort to challenge the kids and give them new opportunities to push themselves and grow. He was the one who introduced Heather to the sport of orienteering.

I have to admit I felt a measure of motherly concern when I first heard Heather talk about being dropped off in the wilderness with only a map and a compass to find her way through a series of intermediate checkpoints to a predetermined finish line some distance away. But when I talked to Jim, he assured me that everything was carefully timed over a known terrain so that no students would be lost for very long before someone would find them. And Heather's enthusiasm for this unusual sport overrode any remaining qualms I might have had.

Heather had always been good with maps. From the time she was seven or eight, she had served as my navigator on our long drives out to Colorado every summer. That map-reading experience plus an uncanny sense of direction made her a whiz at orienteering. Her second year in the sport at CID she actually won a state championship trophy for her age-group. She was so proud!

As was her entire family.

What made us all feel even better was that each year Heather spent at CID, she made two years of academic progress. The test results confirmed what I knew just from listening to her conversation. The language intensive educational strategy employed at CID really worked. Heather's language skills literally multiplied.

We had known from the start that three years was all the time Heather would have at CID. The school didn't take students older than 14. The thinking was that if they were to achieve the ultimate goal of preparing their oral-deaf students to be able to achieve and succeed in a mainstream educational setting, the job had to be done by the end of junior high school.

Any longer was probably too late.

Thankfully, because of her remarkable academic progress, we and the school's staff had determined by that spring of 1987 that Heather's training at CID had done all we'd hoped for and more. She was ready to return to Dothan to begin high school that next fall with the same class of kids she'd started kindergarten with eight years before.

For me that sounded like a dream come true. And all those sacrifices we'd had to make to send Heather to CID seemed well worth it.

Even Heather, though she enjoyed her last year in St. Louis as much as she had her first, was looking forward to coming home that summer for good. I remember one warm spring evening she evidently got so excited just thinking about it that she called me long distance to tell me she could hardly wait for the school year to end. "It will be so wonderful!" she exclaimed. "I will be home next year, and we will all be a family again!"

She sounded so excited I didn't have the heart to burst her bubble by telling her what I was thinking. _Oh, Heather, honey. I wish it could be that simple._

I didn't know how to tell her that what she was hoping for might not be possible.

CHAPTER 13

Marital Trouble

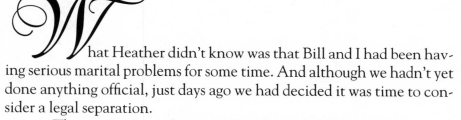

What Heather didn't know was that Bill and I had been having serious marital problems for some time. And although we hadn't yet done anything official, just days ago we had decided it was time to consider a legal separation.

There were several reasons Heather didn't know. While many of the problems could be traced back to the beginning and early years of our marriage, things hadn't escalated to open and obvious conflict until about the time Heather left home and went to CID. She hadn't been home very much during those three years. When Heather was home, because we wanted that time to be special for her, both Bill and I worked hard to keep most of our conflicts hidden. Besides, Heather's hearing impairment not only limited what she could hear of arguments in other rooms, but also made it difficult for her to pick up on the subtle (and sometimes not so subtle) tone and emotion behind the words she did hear. Heather simply didn't realize what would have been obvious if she'd not been deaf.

Stacey and Melissa certainly knew there were problems. But because they were as protective of their sister as Bill and I were, they hadn't talked with Heather about any of the unhappiness at home. As far as I knew, they had never breathed a word.

Bill and I had broken the news to our parents that we'd decided to separate. But I don't think anyone else outside the immediate family realized our marriage was in crisis. We'd kept up such a good front that only my very closest friends knew there were any marital troubles at all. In part because I was raised with the attitude that family business should be private business, I was reluctant (and still am) to air our troubles in public.

I'd read and talked with enough people to know the statistics: For parents of children with any kind of handicap the divorce rate is multiplied. But I was then, and remain today, very reluctant to point to that as the root of our marital problems.

Bill has said he feels I devoted so much of my time and energy to Heather and her sisters over the years that there wasn't much left for him or our marriage. As anyone with children knows, parenthood can be terribly time-consuming. And if only one partner is actively involved, it's tough to meet everyone's needs. So I have to admit there may be some truth in Bill's statement; there were occasions when I didn't make Bill or our relationship the priority they needed to be.

At the same time, however, Heather's handicap had also served to bind us together as a couple. In fact, if Heather's special needs hadn't given us something to focus on together for so many years, there were some very basic marital issues—communication, division of roles, mutual submission, and respect—which might have reached the critical crisis point even earlier in our relationship.

Bill had been unhappy for years. But I hadn't sensed any serious problems until the year or so before Heather left for CID when Bill ran in and lost two political races for state representative from Dothan. I worried when he became despondent after the second loss, but I failed to understand the depths of his discouragement. Perhaps I wasn't as sensitive as I should have been to his feelings. Suddenly, a lot of arguments centered on his increasingly pessimistic attitudes and my suggestions (that seemed like nagging to Bill) about how he might better deal with this setback and get on with life.

Looking back, I can see how, even earlier in our marriage, we'd established a pattern that too often allowed us to go our separate ways. Most of the time just the three girls and I took those long family vacations to Colorado every summer to visit my sister and her family. And as much as I enjoyed the beach, I eventually quit going to Panama City with Bill, opting to stay home and get caught up on school or housework on the weekends he took the girls sailing. I had my own hobbies and crafts the girls and I did together. I had my own career and my own friends from work and around the neighborhood. So by that spring of 1987, Bill and I didn't share many interests or even socialize much as a couple.

I never once remember questioning Bill's faithfulness to me. But without ever making a conscious decision to do so, we had gradually come to lead very separate and independent lives. And those differences had become more obvious than ever during Heather's years at CID. More than once on a Friday evening when I'd call the store to find out when Bill would be home for supper his mom would say, "Didn't you know? Bill left early this afternoon to go down to Panama City for the weekend."

When I tried to ask him what was wrong, Bill talked about feeling tired of our ongoing financial pressures and the constant responsibilities of life. I suggested we get some counseling to help us deal with those issues together and improve our marriage relationship. His response was, "I don't need any counseling. The only problems in our marriage are with you, Daphne."

So the tensions and differences continued to fester and build until one of us would explode. We had so many bitter arguments that Stacey and Melissa began telling us, "If you can't be decent to each other, maybe you ought to think about getting a divorce."

I can't say the thought had never crossed my mind, but because I valued family and believed that God's idea of marriage calls for a lifetime commitment, I would quickly dismiss the possibility. I told myself: *You're a strong person, Daphne. You can take the conflict. Surely things will get better.* But finally, after realizing that our ongoing marital problems were beginning to have a serious negative impact on our daughters, I went to Bill and said, "We just can't go on like this."

His response was, "I agree."

In a surprisingly amicable discussion, we agreed to a legal separation and informed Stacey and Melissa about our plans. Then Heather called so excited about coming home and being a part of the family again.

Her words so pierced my heart that the moment I hung up from talking to Heather, I picked up the receiver again and called Bill, who was up in New England on a business trip. "We can't do this to Heather!" I said. I told him about her call from St. Louis, how excited she was about coming home and having us all be a family again. "You and I are just going to have to work out our problems. I think we owe it to Heather to try," I told him.

He too was moved by Heather's words. "You're right," he agreed. "We'll work it out."

That spring, Bill and I went with Melissa, Stacey, my parents, and my sister Stephanie to St. Louis for Heather's graduation from CID. Watching my beautiful teenage daughter walk proudly across that stage was a shocking reminder of just how fast time was passing. Only three years ago I'd sent Heather off to school as a little girl; she was coming home a young woman. Just three years ago her assessment tests had indicated she was functioning at the second-grade level. Now Heather would return to Dothan and enter a regular public high school next fall. To our family that seemed like a miracle worth celebrating.

So much had happened, so many things had changed, that despite our best efforts Heather wasn't really coming home to the same family.

Her sisters had grown as much as she had. They'd been pursuing their own dreams, living their own lives. Melissa, who'd always been Heather's bosom buddy, was now a popular student and track star with her own interests and new set of friends. Stacey was graduating from high school that spring with plans to leave later that summer for Colorado Springs to begin the Air Force Academy Prep School, the first big step to attending the Air Force Academy itself the next year in pursuit of her longtime dream of becoming an astronaut.

So we all knew things would be different for our family. It was 1987, and we could not go back to 1984. And yet we all shared some of Heather's excitement at her return. Finally, she could again follow in her sisters' footsteps.

I worried as much that summer about Heather's upcoming freshman year as I did about sending Stacey off to school in Colorado. There were so many adjustments to be made. CID had a personalized program and classes of three or four students, all hearing impaired. In contrast, Dothan's Northview High School was one of the largest high school campuses in Alabama at the time with more than 2,500 students.

But I was amazed at how well prepared Heather was to cope in a mainstream educational setting. The study skills CID had taught her served Heather well. Because language and vocabulary would always be a challenge, we'd been advised to purchase personal copies of each of Heather's textbooks. The first time she read new material, she could circle any and all words she didn't understand or know how to pronounce. Then she could look up each of those words in a dictionary and actually write in—beside or above the word in the book—a definition she understood. At that point Heather would be able to read back through the material once again with a fuller understanding of what it said.

Another valuable technique she'd learned was to keep an ever-present stack of index cards on hand to make flash/study cards for any words or terms she didn't know. Heather's memory was so good that once she'd isolated and learned new words she would then be able to use and understand them forever afterwards.

Yet another invaluable learning technique emphasized at CID was one which I'd tried to instill in Heather from an early age: Never hesitate to ask for help when you don't understand. The fact that she had learned this lesson well helped immensely in making a surprisingly easy adjustment to high school work. Her teachers at Northview were more than willing to help when they saw she wanted to understand. So while Heather worked very hard and spent long hours every night to keep up with her class work, she began pulling A's and B's from the very beginning of her high school career.

As it turned out, the most difficult event the Whitestones faced that fall involved our oldest daughter, not Heather. Around the end of October we received word that Stacey had fallen head over heels in love with someone at the Air Force Academy Prep School in Colorado Springs. And because marriage was strictly forbidden by Air Force regulation for cadets or cadet candidates, Stacey had decided she wanted to drop out of school to pursue this romance.

Bill insisted that I fly to Colorado, talk some sense into our daughter, and put an end to this "foolish relationship." But I never made that trip because Stacey quickly convinced me that her mind was already made up; she fully intended to marry Tom. So as concerned as I was about the suddenness of Stacey's decision, and as many reservations as I had about the significant age difference between the two of them, I decided not to take such a rigid stance that I might permanently damage my relationship with my oldest daughter and the man she wanted to marry. I shared my reservations with Stacey and Tom. I also told them what Stacey already knew, that I could never condone their living together without being married. So if she'd truly made up her mind to drop out of school for Tom, I saw only two options. If they decided to get married right away in Colorado, we'd fly out for the ceremony. Or she would be welcome to come home, give things a little time, and plan a wedding in Dothan.

I felt grateful when Stacey chose the latter option. But Bill remained furious—at me now as well as at Stacey. He refused to pay a cent toward Stacey's wedding expenses. So out of my paycheck I covered the cost of the small Christmas-holiday wedding that Stacey and I hastily planned together. But I'll be forever grateful that I was able to maintain a loving relationship with my oldest daughter by doing so. And I'm glad to say that as the years have passed I've come to love and appreciate my son-in-law Tom for being a devoted and loving husband to Stacey and a wonderful, committed father to my first two grandchildren, Shane and Tessa.

As much as Heather enjoyed her role as bridesmaid (Melissa was maid of honor) in Stacey's wedding, and as grateful as she was to be at home again in a regular high school, I think the most important highlight of her ninth-grade year at Northview High School may have been the opportunity to resume her dance training.

Heather had tried to keep up a dance routine as much as possible on her own during the years at CID. I'd been so impressed by her self-discipline that we'd paid her tuition in a summer dance program when she'd been home between school years. But when Heather got back into ballet on a consistent basis for the first time in three years, I began to realize the depth of her commitment to dance. For the first six or seven years I'd seen her ballet as therapy, an enjoyable physical outlet, and a point of interest we could capitalize on to help build Heather's language and reading interests. Now I was beginning to see Heather's love for ballet in terms of a serious dedication to the art.

As a girl when Heather had talked about growing up to be a ballet dancer someday, I'd listened and smiled and nodded like mothers do. But now, when my high school daughter told me she wanted to be a professional ballet dancer, I knew it was no longer just a little girl's fanciful dream.

I also knew no matter how much talent Heather had, how much she loved to dance, and how committed she thought she was, becoming a professional ballet dancer would not be an easy dream to achieve—even if she hadn't been deaf. But I'd never been one to discourage any of my daughters' dreams—no matter how lofty and improbable.

Well, except once. When she was in junior high Stacey had gotten her heart set on the role of Leisl in a school production of _The Sound of Music_. She fancied herself a wonderful singer. Stacey did, in fact, have all the poise, confidence, and volume the role would have required. The trouble was, she'd inherited my voice and musical aptitude. And while

I love to belt out a lively tune in the shower, I may be the only woman in history whose attempts to sing along with the car radio prompt her deaf daughter to cover her ears with her hands and say, "Please don't do that, Mother. Your singing is hurting my ears."

Because I realized how much Stacey sounded like me and I didn't want her to be embarrassed, I did discourage her from pursuing this dream of singing on stage. But I'd always encouraged her other dreams. When she'd decided to use her organizational skills to help found a new government club at Northview, I had backed her. When she'd decided to run for youth governor of Alabama, I had encouraged her to go for it. When she won, I was there to see her sworn in. I even went with her to Baltimore for the national meeting of all fifty youth governors. And I could not have been more proud than I was when she was selected as one of twelve special youth ambassadors to go from the United States to France the summer after her senior year. And when the Air Force Academy Prep School refused to admit her at first because they said she was "overqualified," I encouraged her decision to pick up the phone and call the school's administration office to ask that they reconsider and accept her application (which they did).

In the same way, when Melissa had wanted to try out for cheerleader, I had encouraged her. I cheered her on at her track meets. I helped her plan her participation in Northview High School's annual beauty walk, and when the big night came I thought my blonde sophomore beauty clearly outshone all the competition. And that year when Melissa decided she wanted to go to Russia the upcoming summer on a student ambassador program, I helped her fill out all the necessary applications.

So when Heather told me she wanted to become a professional ballet dancer, I wasn't about to discourage her. One day when I went with her to purchase a new pair of ballet slippers, I listened as Heather conversed with the lady who owned the small shop. Seeing Heather looking at the ballet pictures on her wall, the woman pointed out one of those dancers as her own daughter. "She wants to be a professional dancer someday," the woman announced proudly.

"So do I," Heather told her.

"Then you ought to see about going to ASFA," the woman said.

"Where?" Heather asked.

"Alabama School of Fine Arts," the woman explained. "It's a public high school up in Birmingham with a special emphasis on the performing arts. They have a wonderful dance program. That's where my daughter goes. If you want to become a professional dancer, you really should look into ASFA."

Heather asked her dance teacher what she knew about the Alabama School of Fine Arts. She said she'd heard a lot of good reports.

Although I was a professional educator, I'd never heard of the school. So I asked a few questions and learned it was very much like what is called a magnet school in some places. While it was indeed a public school, not everyone could go there. There were strict entrance requirements and talent qualifications. Heather sent for information. And because everything we learned sounded so impressive, she decided we should visit ASFA.

The caliber of the program impressed me. Some of its students, who come from all over the state, actually live on campus and take a normal high school curriculum with the addition of an intensive program in one of the performing arts like drama, music, or dance. While I wasn't very excited about the prospect of Heather going off to another residential school after only one year back from CID, she could possibly live with my parents and commute downtown to ASFA.

Though ASFA had never had any deaf students, everyone we talked to there treated Heather's interest in the school with consideration and respect. However, the director of the school, Dr. Nelson, was very straightforward. "You know, Heather," he said, "of all the fine arts careers, professional ballet may be the hardest to break into."

His words didn't phase Heather a bit. "I love ballet," she told him. "I realize that it will require a lot of work. But I'm used to working hard. And I want to be a ballet dancer."

I think Dr. Nelson was impressed by the obvious determination in Heather's response. I know I was.

He told Heather her academic record at Northview indicated she could meet the school's academic requirements. But she would still need to prove she could qualify for the school's rigorous dance program. "Unfortunately the auditions for next fall's program have already been completed," he said. Reading the disappointment on Heather's face, he hastened to add, "However, we are offering an extended summer workshop in dance this July at the University of Alabama in Tuscaloosa. That would be a valuable program for you to take anyway, and during that workshop our instructors would have a chance to evaluate your dancing and decide whether or not they thought you were a good candidate for ASFA next fall."

I thanked Dr. Nelson for his time, told him we'd consider the workshop idea, and headed home. I think Heather had made up her mind. Once again she'd found the school she needed to pursue her dreams. While I was willing to keep the option open, I realized she hadn't been accepted yet. And the cost of that special summer workshop in dance was $1,000.

In addition to the question of Heather's future plans, there was a lot more marital tension at home. Things had gotten so bad between Bill and me before and after Stacey's wedding that even Heather had picked up on the problems. She and her dad even had a few arguments of their own. I think Bill was taking out some of his frustrations with me on Heather because he sarcastically called her "Little Daphne" a number of times.

Sadly, that sort of sarcasm, like most vocal subtlety, was completely lost on Heather. Genuinely confused, she would respond angrily, "Why did you call me Daphne? I am Heather. My name is Heather!"

When I learned by way of the grapevine early that spring that Bill had been out apartment hunting, I figured he'd decided to give up on our marriage. Since I'd heard a number of horror stories about women coming home from work one day to discover near-empty houses and learn their husbands had moved out with virtually everything they owned, I got worried. I went to a lawyer, explained the situation, and asked what I could do to insure a fair and equitable division of belongings if Bill and I did indeed separate and divorce. The lawyer suggested that by serving papers on Bill before he moved, nothing could be removed from the house without mutual agreement. So that's what I did.

I think Bill was surprised. I know he wasn't happy. He accused me of planning to divorce him, to move out of town and take his daughters away from him. I promised him I'd never do that. I'd never even considered it. I had a home in Dothan. I'd been teaching there for twelve years. I had friends there. I had no reason to ever move.

Bill soon found an apartment not far away. And when it came time for him to actually move out, everything seemed relatively pleasant and agreeable again. I told him to take anything he wanted from the house. I even encouraged the girls to go over to his new apartment to help him arrange his linen closet, put a tablecloth on his table, and apply a few other such homey touches.

I don't know what happened over the next few weeks and months to sour the situation; maybe it was just the inevitable result of a twenty-one-year marriage coming to an unhappy end. At one point I went to Bill and said if he thought there was any hope for our marriage I'd be willing to give it another try. He told me he wouldn't take me back "if you were the last woman left on the face of the earth." And as much as I hate to admit it, things got even uglier after that.

Bill told Melissa and Heather that he could no longer afford to pay his half of Melissa's trip to Russia or Heather's summer dance workshop. He tried to tell them they'd just have to learn that such disappointments were an unfortunate side effect of divorce. Fortunately, my school principal had learned from one of my friends that Melissa's plans were in jeopardy, and unbeknownst to me, but with the full support of all the teachers and students, he donated enough from one of his annual school fundraisers to make her trip possible—if she could do an assembly for the students once she returned. And when I came up with $500 for Heather's dance workshop, my parents insisted on paying the other half.

Bill soon got into the dating scene and took great delight in telling me all about his exploits. He told Melissa he was going to make my life in Dothan unbearable. And it wasn't long before I learned just what that meant. A couple of friends informed me of some rumors going around town that were so degrading I wouldn't repeat them in print. When I confronted Bill, he shocked me by admitting he had been saying what I had heard.

"Forget the fact that you and I have been married for more than twenty years," I told him. "Just tell me this: Why would you hurt your own daughters by trying to destroy their mother's reputation with such disgusting lies?"

He shrugged and said he'd done it to keep other people from thinking the problems we had were his fault.

The divorce finally went through in June of 1988, just days after our twenty-first wedding anniversary. Among Bill's demands was a stipulation that I give up the name Whitestone and take back my maiden name. He never wanted there to be more than one Mrs. H. William Whitestone, Jr., and he evidently thought he already had a likely new candidate for the position who was going to be everything I'd ever been and much more.

But by that point I'd been Daphne Whitestone for more than half my life, and I wouldn't have considered being anyone else. And I certainly wasn't going to change my name without first getting my daughters' reactions. All three girls told me it wouldn't bother them; Stacey said she had already taken her husband's name, and Melissa and Heather expected to do the same when they got married. So I acceded to Bill's wishes, signed the divorce papers, and became Daphne Gray once again.

By that point I felt absolved of the vow I'd made Bill to stay in Dothan. When Heather impressed the workshop leaders enough to be accepted for the fall semester at ASFA, I immediately drove up to Birmingham to apply for jobs. My assistant superintendent, Mr. Sasser wrote me a wonderful letter of recommendation, but he warned me that I might be too late to find a teaching position for that year. I figured, nothing ventured, nothing gained.

Again God seemed to open doors when I didn't know where to turn. I learned of a newly organized school district that was still looking to fill a math position. I arranged an interview, and the following weekend back in Dothan I received the wonderful news that I had a new job with Hoover City Schools come September.

After Melissa got home from Russia, I told her that I'd make whatever arrangements needed to be made so she could stay in Dothan with her father, her grandparents, or whoever she wished to finish out her senior year at Northview High. "I can't stay in Dothan any longer," I said.

Melissa surprised me by deciding to move with Heather and me. So I put the house up for sale and headed to Birmingham to begin a new stage of life together with my two daughters. And—as things turned out—with a whole lot of other people.

CHAPTER 14

A Sense of Humor

Since I couldn't afford a house payment *and* rent, my parents suggested we move in with them. "Okay," I agreed, "just until I sell the house in Dothan and get back on my feet financially."

While I don't know how else we could have afforded to make the move back to Birmingham that year, my folks' generosity made for a rather sudden and difficult change in lifestyle. My sister Stephanie and her four-year-old son, Trey, were already living with Mom and Dad between apartment leases. So Heather, Melissa, and I took the last of the three bedrooms with its one bed (fortunately king-sized) and a single closet (which wasn't). When it came time to retire every evening, I think my poor girls must have felt like the Waltons, "Good night, Granddad! Good night, Grandma. Night, Mom. Good night, Aunt Steph. Sleep tight, Trey. Don't let the bedbugs bite. Good night, Melissa. Night, Heather. Good night, John-Boy."

I figured my parents deserved sainthood for taking us all on in what should have been their quiet retirement years. I could only hope

143

we wouldn't drive them crazy before they got those well-deserved stars in their crowns.

What I didn't see then was how God in his infinite wisdom was looking out for Heather, Melissa, and me. I didn't yet understand how much we would have to depend on family in what was going to be perhaps the most difficult year of our lives.

With Heather adjusting to the rigorous demands of her new program at the Alabama School of Fine Arts, Melissa wanting to hit the ground running for her senior year in a different school in a strange new city, and me starting a new job teaching middle school math in a brand new school district, just figuring out the logistics of our combined daily routines proved a nightmare. Eventually we developed a workable and relatively efficient strategy for getting all three of us where we were supposed to be and back home each day.

Melissa drove herself to Berry High School in our ancient, full-sized family station wagon, which had become (by default mostly) the kids' car. I'd leave my folks' house in south suburban Birmingham each morning shortly after 6:30 to drive Heather to ASFA, which was located on the northwest side of downtown Birmingham—close to the civic center, right near where I–65, I–20 and I–59 all intersect. If I dropped Heather off early enough, I could avoid the worst of the morning downtown rush hour and get right back on the less-congested outbound interstate for the drive to my school in Hoover, a town southeast of Birmingham.

Evenings were even more complicated. Melissa would drive herself home after school, but I'd have to time my own getaway to the minute in order to race downtown, meet Heather on the street in front of ASFA at precisely 4:30 when she walked out of her daily afternoon dance workout, and try to escape downtown Birmingham before the evening rush hour clogged the streets. As little as five minutes' delay in getting Heather could mean an added forty minutes in our commute back home.

However, transportation wasn't the only problem. An even bigger daily challenge was Heather's schoolwork. The fact that ASFA had never had a deaf student before, and didn't even have the typical special education support all local school systems offer, turned out to be a critical factor. While Heather's teachers tried to be considerate and accommodating, they didn't have a clue as to how to enable a hearing impaired student to better meet the strenuous academic and physical demands of their curriculum.

144

Heather actually relished the opportunity to train for three hours and more every day under the exacting eyes of her widely experienced and respected dance instructor, Sonja Arova. In addition to the ninety-minute ballet class incorporated into the regular school day, Sonja required an additional workout every day after school. Perhaps because she'd missed dancing so much during her CID years, or maybe because she sensed how much improvement could result from such intensive effort, Heather seemed to find a real sense of joy—almost rapture—in what was a physically exhausting daily workout routine.

So, except to the degree that it drained her of energy she could have committed to other areas of life and study, Heather's dancing caused her no problem. According to all the feedback we got from Sonja, Heather showed talent, commitment, and steady improvement as a dancer.

Things didn't go so well in other classes. And only part of the problem could be chalked up to ASFA's lack of experience with hearing impaired students. Perhaps the biggest obstacle concerned the audiotrainer Heather had to use in every class. All her teachers gladly cooperated by wearing the mike/transmitter portion of the device. The problem was that when Heather turned on her receiver, the sounds of her teachers' voices were regularly interrupted by the CB transmissions of truckers passing through the spaghetti-junction of expressways only a stone's throw away from ASFA's building. The constant static and chatter proved to be far more than an annoying distraction. Hearing conversation in a busy classroom setting posed a challenge to Heather under the best of circumstances. But trying to follow a science lecture or understand the fine details of an English assignment while some good ol' boys' "Breaker! Breaker!" or "Ten-four, good buddy" echoed in her ear greatly frustrated Heather. We tuned and retuned that audio-trainer, but no matter what frequency we tried, trucker talk would punctuate or drown out most of her teachers. That made classroom learning nearly impossible.

The only solution we came up with was to begin taping every one of Heather's classes. Then as soon as we got home each evening, while Heather began her algebra assignment (she seldom if ever needed assistance in any of her math courses), I'd begin transcribing that day's class tapes for all her other subjects. As soon as I'd finish one tape, I'd pass my handwritten transcript to Heather. Then she could begin reading the lecture or following whatever instructions that instructor had given while I went on to the tape of the next class. A lot of nights

Stephanie, or Mother, or both would help me with the transcribing. Still, it was usually 10 or 11 o'clock before we finished providing Heather with access to all the information she needed to complete her homework and feel prepared for the next day's classes. And only then could I begin grading papers or doing my own lesson plans.

For Heather, it was like completing two days' worth of work every day. The effort paid off with consistent A's and B's on her report card. But combined with her grueling dance schedule, her academic success took its toll on Heather, emotionally and physically. It took its toll on me as well.

In fact, I don't think either of us would have survived that year without the consistently supportive efforts of my family.

The long evening hours spent helping Heather with her studies weren't the only contribution either. Within weeks of the time we moved into my parents' house, my dad—bless his insightful heart— pointed out something in Heather I'd never noticed.

"That girl needs a better sense of humor," he said. "She doesn't know when somebody is teasing her!" To a world-class kidder like my father, who believes anyone who can't take a joke and laugh at herself has a real social handicap, this was a serious shortcoming. So from that day on, as long as we lived with my folks, he took as one of his primary missions in life to personally exercise and develop Heather's sense of humor.

The root problem proved to be not so much a personality quirk as it was Heather's hearing deficiency. She'd honed her listening and communication skills to such a fine point that I often forgot she was deaf. The truth was, while she'd learned to read lips and to use what little residual hearing she did have to know *what* words were being said, her aided hearing was so weak and distorted that she seldom understood *how* something was said. She'd never learned to audibly distinguish or differentiate between irony, sarcasm, or satire. Virtually everything she heard was taken literally. And since she couldn't detect the teasing tone in someone's voice, she never knew when she (or anyone else) was being kidded.

For example, late in the evening when she'd take out a carton of ice cream to get a bedtime snack, Dad might say something like, "You're eating me out of house and home, girl. And look how fat you're getting! Before you know it I'm going to have to call in a contractor to widen all the doorways around here." Heather's response, because she took him seriously, would be to put the ice cream back in the freezer and flee the room. She just didn't understand verbal give-and-take.

146

Not only would Heather get frustrated when she didn't understand what was going on, but she would also assume that people who were laughing about something she hadn't understood must be laughing at her. So Dad took a head-on strategy. He teased Heather unmercifully as a regular part of their interaction. He'd poke, prod, jab, and tickle her until she learned to retaliate in kind and they'd both laugh. "Jim, she's a young lady!" Mother would often exclaim. "You're not teaching her to be ladylike."

"She needs to learn how to play and laugh," Dad insisted. He thought such playful physical roughhousing a valuable prerequisite for playful verbal jabs and banter. He determined to show her life wasn't all serious.

Heather didn't know how to take her grandfather at first. There were times when he'd say something in mock anger or jest, only to have her burst into tears and run out of the room. "Look what you've done now," Mom would scold. "You've gone too far."

Dad would shake his head. "It's a tough world out there, June. If Heather doesn't learn how to take a little teasing, how is she ever going to be strong enough to survive?"

He was right. And his efforts soon paid off. My father and my youngest daughter gradually developed a very special bond—punctuated by frequent laughter and underlined by a deep enjoyment and affection for each other.

I also came to appreciate and reap the benefits of this new side of Heather's personality. I was soon able to tease her in ways I never would have considered before.

Sometimes I'd catch myself forgetting her hearing limitations and try to tell her something when she was in another room. Or we'd be carrying on a conversation and I'd casually turn to do something while continuing to talk where she couldn't read my lips. I'd pretend to be exasperated when she didn't understand. "Are you deaf or something?" I'd say. (You should have seen the shocked looks I got from some of Heather's friends when I pulled this in their presence.) But Heather would laughingly reply, "As a matter of fact, I am deaf. And I wish you wouldn't forget it."

Thanks in large part to my dad, Heather slowly but surely developed a very keen sense of humor that has enriched all of our lives. But she certainly wasn't the only one to enjoy surprising benefits from the time we lived with my parents.

147

I didn't realize how emotionally vulnerable the girls and I were in the wake of our recent family trauma. But the familiar and reassuring stability of my parents' marriage and home applied a soothing balm for all our troubled spirits.

Having just experienced the bitter end of my marriage, I'd walked away from a home I hadn't been able to sell and a life I hadn't wanted to leave behind. I'd uprooted my girls, left my dearest friends three hours away, and started a new job in a new place while living in a cramped bedroom with two teenage daughters who themselves had to face their own variation of all these issues. I was under unspeakable stress, which I certainly felt but hadn't yet stopped to understand.

My physical health was nearly destroyed. I'd lost more than twenty-five pounds since the ordeal of our separation and divorce began. I felt unable to eat or sleep with any regularity.

I hated the person I saw myself becoming: an emotionally shaky woman whose out-of-control emotions left her feeling scared and vulnerable, and an increasingly bitter woman whose relationships were threatened by the vindictiveness I harbored toward my ex-husband. I told myself, *You're not a hysterical, bitter person.* At least I never had been. Had I? Because I no longer knew myself, my self-confidence was shot.

While the divorce had given Bill a new lease on life, I seemed to have the same life and problems I'd always had—but without any of his help in coping with it, and with my financial base suddenly cut in half. Because my only contact with Bill came through my girls now, I'm afraid they felt, or at least witnessed, the brunt of my negative feelings. And I couldn't understand why they didn't have the same resentments I did.

This constant low-grade tension I now experienced with Heather and Melissa seemed to boil over every time they returned from Dothan after a weekend visit. I know they felt torn and trapped in the middle. When they came home from Bill's and I'd ask, "How was your visit? Where did your dad take you? What did you do?" they felt I was trying to pry information about Bill out of them. On some subconscious level I must have been upset that they had a good time. So we'd usually have at least one major blowup the first day or two they were home.

After a while I tried just not asking about their visits with Bill. But then they accused me of not caring. I couldn't win. And it didn't help that I felt like the only loser in the bargain.

Always before I'd been a regular part of every aspect of my girls' lives. Now there was this big chunk of their lives I could have nothing to do with. We couldn't even seem to talk about it without fireworks. I felt shut out and robbed of the closeness we'd always shared. And that only added to the bitterness I felt, increasing the tensions, and escalating the conflicts between us in what seemed like a vicious, uncontrollable cycle.

Not that everything was bad. Living together in one bedroom did help us maintain an inevitable physical closeness that bonded us together in the common effort for daily survival. And each of the girls experienced her own memorable highlights from that school year.

One of Heather's high points came when ASFA students were selected to dance in the big annual production of *The Nutcracker* performed professionally by Birmingham's prestigious Alabama Ballet Company.

Heather danced as a candy cane. While hers was hardly a feature role, it seemed a significant enough part that she experienced both excitement and pride in abundance that holiday season.

Sitting in that huge audience, watching my daughter dance on stage for the first time with a professional ballet company, I couldn't help flashing back to three years earlier. When Heather had come home from CID for Christmas the very first year, my parents, Stephanie, and I had taken all three girls to the Alabama Ballet Company's production of *The Nutcracker*. I remembered how much I'd enjoyed watching Heather's mesmerized reaction. She had literally sat on the edge of her seat, gripping the balcony railing, never taking her eyes off the dancers for a moment. That she seemed so obviously enthralled made me wonder how much of the orchestra music she could actually hear. I'd understood then that Heather had a very special gift; even though she could only hear a small part of what the rest of the audience heard, her love of music and dance was so great that it allowed her to imagine the rest and enjoy the whole thing.

Driving back to my parents' home that evening, Heather had been so excited she had talked nonstop about the performers and the dancers. "Someday I will do that. I will dance in *The Nutcracker* with the Alabama Ballet," she declared.

Mostly I just listened, enjoying her excitement and dreams. But when I stopped at an intersection with enough streetlights for her to see my lips, I turned to her and said, "Won't that be great, Heather? One day we'll all come to watch you dance as Clara in *The Nutcracker*."

And now here she was. It didn't matter to me that she wasn't Clara. I couldn't have been any prouder or happier for her if she had been.

Another memorable highlight for Heather came that year on her sixteenth birthday. But to understand what made it so special, you first need a little background. For as long as I could remember, Heather has had a very close and meaningful personal relationship with God. But she found her deafness to be a real limitation when it came to group worship. She could seldom understand what was going on in church. I couldn't take notes fast enough for her to keep up with the sermon. Even when we sat down in front so she could read lips more easily, she knew she was missing much that was said. And that really bothered her.

That's why television, believe it or not, played a significant part in Heather's spiritual life. Because cameras zero in for a lot of close-ups of the speakers' faces, she got a lot more spiritual input and inspiration from televised services than she could in a local congregation. So she and I regularly watched a number of television preachers. One of her favorites was the weekly telecast from Robert Schuller's church in Southern California. I think part of his appeal for Heather (and also for me) was the frequent emphasis on overcoming and on the great possibilities resulting from faith. But another reason Heather watched every week was because Dr. Schuller's program was among the first to use closed captioning. Finally, Heather could follow along with every part of the service.

Shortly after they got married, Stacey and Tom had moved to Southern California, where they attended and actually did volunteer work for a time at the Crystal Cathedral. One day Stacey happened to tell a staff person she'd met about Heather—how her sister really appreciated the closed-captioned broadcasts every week, how much Heather thought of Dr. Schuller, and how she would love to tell Dr. Schuller what his ministry had meant to our family.

The staff person listened and said, "Why don't you write Dr. Schuller a letter and tell him what you just told me? Maybe he could call or write your sister a letter."

"You think he would?" Stacey asked.

"It wouldn't hurt to ask!"

So that's what Stacey did. And I received a call from Dr. Schuller's secretary a week or so ahead of Heather's birthday. She said they'd been so moved by Stacey's letter that Dr. Schuller wanted to try to call Heather to wish her a happy birthday. His schedule looked pretty full for February 24; he would be on the road. But if he could squeeze it in, he would try to slip away to a phone. So I gave her a time when I knew we could be home. But I didn't tell Heather because I wanted it to be a surprise and I didn't want to disappoint her if things didn't work out.

I knew exactly what her reaction would be if the call did come. She wouldn't believe it. She'd think it was another one of her grandfather's pranks. So I made some special provisions ahead of time.

When the appointed hour came, the phone rang. I quickly answered, confirmed who it was, and called Heather to the phone. "It's for you," I told her.

"Who is it?" she asked me as I handed her the receiver.

"Someone who wants to speak to you on this special day," I told her.

She held the phone to her ear and said hello. I watched, delighted, as she got a very puzzled look on her face at the sound of a man's voice singing "Happy Birthday." When he finished the chorus, she asked, "Who is this?"

A sudden skepticism spread across her face. "It is not. No, who is this really?" she asked. "Is this Granddaddy? Did my grandfather ask you to call me?"

At about that time I held up my previously prepared sign that said, "Yes, Heather, it really is Robert Schuller!"

Her eyes got big as the realization dawned on her. "You are Robert Schuller?" I think she finally began to recognize his voice. "Really? You are. Mom, it really is Robert Schuller."

I laughed and mouthed the words, "I know."

"I watch your program every week," she told him. "Why are you calling me?"

He told her about Stacey's letter. They talked for a few more minutes until he had to go. But Heather was as high as a kite all day. She wanted to call and tell everyone she knew that Robert Schuller had called her personally to sing "Happy Birthday." "I just can't believe it!" she kept saying. And neither could I. When I phoned Stacey to tell her about it, I asked her, "As long as you're out there in Southern California anyway, do you think maybe you could persuade Robert Redford to call on my birthday?" She laughingly promised to work on it.

Another couple of months passed. I knew Heather and I had a serious decision to make that spring. For months I'd dreaded bringing it up because I knew how much the dance program at ASFA meant to her. And I had been convinced, if she wanted to pursue a career in dance, there wasn't a better place in Alabama for her to be. But I simply didn't see how either of us could continue to meet the academic demands there. I'd just recently completed the sale of our house down in Dothan, so it was time to think about moving out of my parents' home and finding a place of our own. With Melissa following in Stacey's footsteps by attending the Air Force Academy that summer, there would be just the two of us together next fall. If I had to continue transcribing all of Heather's class lectures by myself, I didn't see how either one of us could get enough sleep to survive.

What I thought needed to happen was for Heather to transfer to nearby Berry High School. Since Melissa had gone there, Heather would be somewhat familiar with it. I'd learned the school system would provide a liaison person to make sure Heather was getting what she needed. And if she could use her audio-trainer again without hearing half the truckers in Alabama, she could understand most of what went on in class.

The day of reckoning came when Heather brought home the registration forms for the next year's class schedule. I took a deep breath, breathed a prayer for help, and said, "You know, Heather, you've had a tough year here at ASFA. I think it's been good for you, especially for your dance. And you've made terrific grades. But I don't know if we as a family can go through another year like this one."

"I know," Heather replied. "And I realize my education is more important than my dancing."

Her reaction was an answer to prayer.

We talked for a while about the options. As she discussed her dance experience, I realized she'd been learning more than I thought at ASFA. She'd come to realize that for some people dance became almost an obsession. And she had seen enough of the competitive side of things to decide, "I don't want to be that way." Her maturity and wisdom made me very proud to be her mother.

Heather assured me she would be happy to transfer to Berry, that she would in fact look forward to the opportunities and atmosphere of a regular high school again. And I assured her that we would somehow, somewhere, find a way for her to continue to develop her dance. Even though I didn't know how.

CHAPTER 15

Getting On
with Life

✌

ince ballet was not a part of the regular curriculum at Berry
High School, I knew we would have to find a private instructor. And
because Heather had reached the point in her dance training where she
required daily workouts and instruction in order to maintain her condi-
tioning and continue improving her skills, I expected the price of such
an intensive private dance program would be steep, if not prohibitive.

I had also started thinking we should get Heather back into regular speech therapy. We'd been away from Dothan and Diane Steensland's regular therapy for almost a year by this time. And while I
wouldn't say Heather's speech had regressed, I didn't think she'd really
made significant progress either. And after all those years of steady, obvious improvement in Heather's speech, it bothered me to think her language skills had peaked, or at least plateaued.

I don't know that I'd ever appreciated Diane's expertise and her
lifelong commitment to Heather any more than I did when I began pric-
ing speech therapy around Birmingham. The going rate for a basic program of private speech therapy was as much as $125 an hour. (This was

not acoupedic therapy either, because I couldn't find another acoupedicly trained speech therapist anywhere in the state.)

No way could I afford to pay for Heather to take dance *and* speech therapy—not with Melissa going off to college in the fall. While her nomination and acceptance as a cadet at the Air Force Academy in Colorado Springs provided full tuition along with room and board for four years, I realized Melissa would need some monthly financial support to cover her personal expenses. I also knew that the hidden costs (travel, wardrobe, etc.) could be considerable.

It did no good to ask Bill to help share any of these "extra" expenses. So I talked to my lawyer and decided to take Bill back to court to request an adjustment in our child support agreement. Since his monthly child support payments for Melissa were scheduled to end in December when she turned nineteen, I asked that they be continued through college. That way I could send the monthly sum on to Melissa to cover her expenses at school. My lawyer didn't think a favorable ruling likely, but she told me it wouldn't hurt to ask. It might improve the chances of a judge approving some additional support for Heather.

I was dismayed by the intense anger that surfaced as I prepared and then went back to Dothan to press my claims in court. It also frustrated me to realize how emotionally vulnerable I remained and consequently how much impact Bill still had in my life. So the legal confrontation itself proved far from pleasant.

In the end, the judge refused to require Bill to provide any support for Melissa beyond her nineteenth birthday. The court also sided with Bill in saying Heather's dance lessons could not be considered as therapy (although we'd considered them that since the beginning) and that her good grades in school proved she didn't really need more speech therapy. So I would get no help in paying for either of those. The one concession I did win came when the judge ruled that, because of the special circumstances involving her hearing impairment, Bill's monthly child support for Heather would not end at age nineteen, but must continue until she became self-sufficient. Since none of us knew what college would require for Heather, this significant decision made the financial future look a little brighter for us.

The aftermath of that court hearing brought an even more important benefit. The Lord finally began to get through to me. And I suddenly realized he'd been trying for months.

Looking back I can clearly see how God had been speaking to me through my father, who'd sat me down and had a number of heart-to-heart talks with me about how the emotional devastation of the divorce had impacted me. He warned me that my bitterness toward Bill could poison my relationships with my daughters. He told me I couldn't expect the girls to feel the same kind of pain, anger, and resentment that I did. He reminded me that Bill would always be the girls' father—which meant they would forever feel a need for his loving approval and long for some kind of a meaningful relationship with him. While I hadn't always been receptive to everything my father was saying, the validity of his logic and insights began to sink in.

God had also been working through the church the girls and I had begun attending. While I'd grown up Methodist, and in Dothan had attended the Episcopal Church where Bill grew up, the girls and I began attending a large Baptist church that met our varied needs. Lots of kids from Berry High School took part in Shade's Mountain Baptist's active youth program, so the girls soon felt at home there.

My sizable "singles" Sunday school class gave me exposure to many others who understood my pain. It seems so naive, almost clichéd, to say, "I thought I was the only one who'd ever experienced this." But for a long time after the divorce, that's exactly how I felt. I guess when you're feeling incredible personal pain you lose perspective; you think, *No one else ever went through anything this bad.*

However, through realistic discussion and honest sharing in my new Sunday school class, I began to realize I wasn't the only person walking that difficult road. There was someone (or many someones) in that Sunday school who had experienced everything I had and more. Whenever I felt alone, I could know that I never really was—that God was always there for me to lean on. So God began to use the supportive fellowship I found at Shade's Mountain to heal my heart.

The combined momentum of all these things seemed to come together after my latest court case. While I can't claim I heard an audible voice, God clearly spoke very sternly to my heart. *Okay, Daphne. The courts gave you some extra support for Heather's future. Don't you think it's time to get on with that future? How much longer are you going to wallow in your anger and resentment? How long will you let bitterness gnaw away at your soul and your relationships? Can't you see your girls need a mother? Don't you understand Heather will need your support in these coming years?*

155

It's been almost two years now; don't you think it's time to get on with your life? I'm ready to help; are you ready to trust me again?

I told him I was. I stopped blaming God and asked his forgiveness. Then I went to each of my girls to apologize. I told them God had gotten through to me. I didn't like the person I'd become since the divorce, and while I wished I could go back and change things, I couldn't. I told them I'd been unfair to expect them to feel as I did toward Bill. I'd allowed bitterness and all my other emotional reactions to have a toxic effect on my relationship with them. And with God's help, I wanted to be a better mother in the months and years to come.

I can't say God transformed me overnight. But for the first time in a long time life took on a new luster. I began deliberately rebuilding my relationships with the girls. As I did, I began to regain a little of my old confidence. I felt a little better about myself. And that was a start.

The financial pressures didn't ease any. Knowing I couldn't afford both dance and speech therapy for Heather, we had opted for dance. I'd been doing daily, if informal, speech therapy for years to augment Heather's regular therapy with Diane. While we'd lived with my folks, their home had become an intensive, twenty-four-hour-a-day language lab. Whenever Mother, Stephanie, or I heard Heather say or pronounce something wrong, we'd correct her until she said it right.

So I knew the family and I could probably provide Heather with adequate speech therapy. What we couldn't offer was the expert instruction she needed to progress to the next level as a dancer. We would have to pay for that training. As expensive as it was, my parents offered to help.

One day Stephanie told me about something called the Briarwood Ballet—a dance company that was actually a ministry of nearby Briarwood Presbyterian Church. Some of her in-laws sent their kids there.

I learned this dance program was the culmination of a longtime dream Barbara Barker, the pastor's wife, had for founding a Christian dance company dedicated to teaching and performing dance as a form of worship to God. Remembering our old family joke about Heather someday becoming "the dancing nun," I laughed and thought, *This could be perfect for Heather!* And when we checked it out, Heather and I heard many good things about the program and about Barbara as a respected dance teacher. Although all her advanced classes were full for the fall, once she saw Heather dance, Barbara made special arrangements for her to join the top group.

Heather absolutely loved the daily workouts and the frequent performances of Briarwood Ballet. Before long she gained a whole new vision of how she could use her dance as a personal offering of worship for God.

Heather also enjoyed her new school experience that year at Berry High. I worried a little that she'd be attending her third high school in three years. But the fact that Melissa had gone there the year before provided a measure of familiarity. And Heather knew a lot of Berry students from the youth group at church. So the overall adjustment went surprisingly well.

However, when our old brown station wagon had finally given up the ghost before Melissa left for Colorado, Heather and I suddenly faced another transportation dilemma: I couldn't hope to get away from my school soon enough to pick up Heather and drive her to dance. The solution proved fairly simple, if a bit unorthodox, once we unleashed our creative thinking. We decided that Heather (who had taken driver's training on the downtown streets of Birmingham while she was at ASFA) would drive me to work in the morning and take my car on to Berry High School. After school she could drive to dance and then swing back over to Hoover to pick me up around five every evening.

I took some kidding from my colleagues about being a mother carpooled by her daughter instead of the other way around. But the schedule worked. Relieved of the usual after-school chauffeur duty, I discovered I could usually get all my own papers graded and lesson plans made during my daily wait. Then after Heather picked me up, I could devote the rest of the evening to helping with her studies.

Fortunately, the academic situation was much better for Heather at Berry—primarily because the Hoover City School System provided excellent resources and special education personnel. Heather spent one hour every day with a special advisor, Lisa Armstrong, a trained and certified teacher for the hearing impaired. Part of her job was to serve as liaison between Heather and each of Heather's instructors. Lisa actually did for Heather many of the same things I'd done during the elementary years down in Dothan: finding out ahead of time what material would be covered in class each day so that Heather could be oriented and prepared; meeting with teachers to make sure Heather had understood all assignments; making sure the regular communication lines were open; anticipating and then heading off any potential troubles or misunderstanding. Lisa not only did her job well, she became a dear friend and confidante to Heather. Many were the nights I thanked God for Lisa and the decision to transfer Heather to Berry High.

Being able to use the audio-trainer again in class without the constant interruption of trucker talk made a world of difference. We still taped some of Heather's classes in case she had questions or didn't understand something that was said. But we didn't have to transcribe nearly as many of those tapes as we had the year before. So that junior year Heather earned her usual A's and B's, but without the blood, sweat, and tears we'd invested the year before at ASFA.

Good thing. Because there always seemed to be something else requiring our attention and energy.

That junior year we began to consider colleges for Heather. Despite the early predictions we'd gotten when we first learned she was deaf—that we should expect no more than a third-grade education— I'd always assumed Heather would go to college one day. Heather always assumed it too.

We quickly discounted most private schools because of cost. We did look at Birmingham Southern because of its terrific dance program; but they offered no support services for deaf students, so we ruled that out. At Lisa Armstrong's encouragement, we researched three schools in the Alabama university system that she felt offered the resources that could best meet Heather's needs—the University of Alabama-Birmingham (UAB), Montevallo State, and Jacksonville State University. I think both Heather and I leaned toward Jacksonville State because of its large popu- lation of deaf students and a widely respected support system for helping their hearing impaired collegians cope not just academically, but in every other aspect of normal college life. A visit to all three campuses that year only seemed to confirm the decision for her.

I think I was probably just as impressed as Heather the weekend we saw JSU. Not only were the folks there experienced and committed to helping their hearing impaired students succeed, they were straight- forward and honest in answering all our questions. They didn't try to gloss over the difficulties Heather could expect to face.

I especially appreciated the personable, yet straightforward, manner of Dan Miller, the director of JSU's deaf-education support pro- gram. Dan was the one who told us Heather would be at a distinct dis- advantage if she didn't know how to communicate in sign. "Because we provide a trained interpreter in every class a deaf student takes, we try to group our hearing impaired students together as much as possible—

at least for the basic required courses. That way one staff person can interpret for several students at a time. All our interpreters have to use sign because that's the only universal way for them to interact with all the students. If Heather can't understand what's being communicated to other deaf students, she's going to miss out entirely on one of the primary resources we provide for our hearing impaired students."

On the ninety-minute drive home from Jacksonville State, Heather and I discussed what Dan had said. "I think he is right, Mother," she told me. "I need to learn sign."

I suspect Heather may have expected an argument from me. And I have to admit, as long and as hard as I'd resisted the "experts" who told me Heather needed to learn sign language, there was a part of me that still wanted to say, "I don't think so!" or at least, "Not yet." However, I think I may have shocked Heather by telling her, "If you want to learn sign, I guess maybe it's time."

Part of my ongoing argument against sign had been that Heather could always learn it later. But only after the oral language skills, which would be much harder for her to master, had been firmly established. The truth was, I'd always known the day could come when she might want to use sign as a second language to bolster her primary language— oral English. If and when that happened I figured she'd then have the best possible chance to access both worlds—the hearing world all of us live in *and* the smaller deaf world with its own rich and unique heritage.

I remained (and still remain) convinced that Heather could never have attained that dual-access goal if we hadn't started with the oral approach and then stuck to our acoupedic guns. But I no longer worried that learning sign would hinder her oral communication. Heather had proved herself on that score. She was certainly old enough now to make up her own mind.

I didn't yet realize how hard it would be at this point in life, even once she learned sign, for Heather to enjoy ready access to and acceptance in the deaf culture. But I have to say, even if I had understood all the stakes from the start, when it came to Heather's education I'd have made the same choices anyway.

When Lisa Armstrong heard that Heather wanted to learn sign, and why, she talked to the high school administration and got permission to organize and teach a course in Signing Exact English (SEE) that next semester for any interested Berry High students. While Heather was the only deaf person in the class, more than a dozen hearing students signed up and took the course with her.

One of those, a bright and popular girl by the name of Misha Jones, became Heather's closest and dearest high school friend. The two of them found their growing proficiency in sign a distinct advantage for their budding relationship. Not only did they have a secret language which enabled them to conduct private conversations that could never be overheard in crowded hallways, they could talk anytime during any class without drawing a teacher's wrath, and after school they could drive down the road, conversing back and forth between cars until the intersection where they finally parted ways.

I think that the two girls became such good friends because Misha's continuing efforts to learn sign proved her commitment to their friendship. And in another way it affirmed and symbolized to Heather Misha's complete acceptance of her—handicap and all.

I know Heather didn't feel that same ready acceptance from everyone. Yet, like most teenagers, she wanted to belong and not stand out from the crowd. Usually she wore her hair in a style that covered her hearing aid. As a result, many of her high school classmates never realized Heather was deaf.

I remember the afternoon she picked me up after school and told me about an acquaintance who'd asked her, "Are you too big a snob to speak when I say 'hi' to you in the hall?"

"I just did not hear her," Heather complained to me. "Now she thinks I am a snob. I feel awful about that. Do you think there are other people who think that?"

"There might be," I told her. "But the only way to avoid that is to be open about your hearing. Tell the people you meet that you are deaf; remind all your friends that if they want you to understand they need to speak directly to you when you are looking."

Heather finally tried the open and straightforward approach. But that had its drawbacks as well. Lunchtime was especially miserable for Heather; she found it nearly impossible to pick voices out of the constant roar of cafeteria commotion in her ear. That meant she had to rely almost totally on lipreading around the lunch table. "I get tired of asking my friends to repeat what I don't hear," she admitted. "And I think sometimes they get tired of me asking. So I just laugh when the people around me laugh. That makes me sad. I want to be part of the conversation. But I'm not."

I nearly cried when she told me that. It hurt so much to see and hear her pain at feeling excluded.

While Heather had a number of friends at school, I realized her social life remained fairly limited. But that didn't worry me much. What with her daily commitment to dance and the long hours of schoolwork every night, Heather didn't have time or energy to devote to a social life anyway. She did have the church youth fellowship, where she usually felt very much accepted and took part in every group activity her schedule would allow.

Heather never really participated in the high school dating scene. And that didn't bother me. But I was glad to see the determination in her eyes when she told me she'd made up her mind she was going to the prom, even if she had to ask a boy herself. She had a candidate in mind, but she didn't know if the boy would go with her.

I realized she dreaded the rejection she might feel if he turned her down. So did I.

I tried to reassure her that any boy in his right mind would be glad to go out with her. But I also knew there are some boys who aren't in their right minds. So I asked around until I learned from a teacher friend at my school that her handsome college-age son, who had recently broken up with his girlfriend, would be thrilled to go to the prom with Heather if she asked him. Once I had that backup plan in place, I encouraged Heather to go ahead and ask her first choice.

However, I warned her that there could be any number of reasons a boy might say no. Some high school boys are simply scared of beautiful girls. Others might not be mature enough or possess the self-confidence needed to feel comfortable on a date with a girl who is deaf. So if the boy did say no, I hoped she wouldn't take it as a personal rejection.

I needn't have worried. David accepted the first invitation and took Heather to her first prom. They evidently had a good time because he asked Heather out again a couple times before the school year ended.

All in all, Heather's prom experience turned out a lot better than the first time Heather ever "went out" with a boy. But then that memorable fiasco hardly qualified as a "date." I believe it took place when Heather came home for spring break during her last year at CID. For some reason I'd been telling the girls about dating an identical twin in high school—wondering the first couple times we went out if he really was the one I thought he was. Once I really got to know him, though, he and his brother didn't look that much alike after all.

I think that's what gave Stacey the idea for a great practical joke. She and Heather, despite the four years of difference in their ages, looked enough alike that a number of Stacey's high school friends did a double take when they saw her little sister. So Stacey wanted to see if they could fool her friend Ben when he came to pick her up for a date that evening.

We all thought it would be a terrific prank. We dressed Heather up in one of Stacey's outfits and fixed her hair just like her oldest sister's. When Ben rang the doorbell, I invited him into a dimly lit living room and told him Stacey would be ready momentarily. Stacey called from the back of the house to apologize for running late and said she'd be out in just a minute. Then, seconds later, Heather hurried into the room and headed straight for the front door. She didn't say a word, so Ben never suspected a thing as the two of them crossed the porch and started down the sidewalk toward his car. Stacey watched them go, wondering how long it would be before Ben caught on.

I don't know exactly what went through Heather's mind— maybe it was the sight of that car and the realization that she was seconds away from driving off with a boy she'd never met before who thought she was Stacey. Maybe it dawned on her that she wouldn't know what to say in what was soon going to be a very awkward social moment. I don't know. But Heather suddenly panicked.

"Oh . . . oh! I cannot do this!" she shrieked as she turned and raced back toward the house, leaving a very startled and bewildered teenage boy on the walk with his mouth hanging open. I was standing out on the porch by this time about to die laughing. When Stacey came out of the house laughing behind me, the look of complete and total confusion on Ben's face cracked us both up.

It took Stacey and me some time before we managed to stop laughing and explain to Ben what had happened. I don't think he ever did see much humor in it; maybe that's why he never asked Stacey out on another date.

I realize now I probably should have apologized to the boy, but I never did. At this point I can only hope he finds some consolation in knowing that he took a future Miss America on the first (and shortest) "date" of her life.

CHAPTER 16

Caught Between Two Worlds

Between her junior and senior years of high school, Heather went to Jackson, Mississippi, for a summer workshop conducted by a touring Christian dance company called the Ballet Magnificat. What she experienced there seemed to reinforce everything Heather had learned during the preceding year in her classes at Briarwood: that dance could be a beautiful and powerful way to witness for and worship God.

During that time in Mississippi, the Ballet Magnificat members and staff talked to the young people attending the workshop about their dance company's history, present ministry, and future goals. Telling how their ballet troupe lived, worked, and traveled together around the country performing for churches and schools, these young professional dancers painted an exciting, enticing picture of their ministry. By the last day of the workshop, when the director of the Ballet Magnificat thanked the participants for coming, praised their progress, and expressed the hope that when they finished school some of them would consider coming back to join the group's dance ministry, Heather was ready to sign up on the spot.

"I think God is calling me to be a dancer," she told me when she got home.

"That may well be, Heather," I told her. Who was I to contradict God? "But I'm sure he also wants you to get an education."

Perhaps Heather wanted to dance because her education had been such a long and grueling ordeal. Maybe she was drawn to the glamour of life as a professional dancer—the fulfillment of her grandest dreams. Or maybe it was a combination of both. Whatever the reason, Heather began to question her need for higher education. If God wanted her to be a dancer, why not get a jump on a professional career? Maybe she'd just become a dancer with the Ballet Magnificat.

I created some real tension between us when I told her, "God may indeed be calling you to become a professional dancer, Heather. I don't know. But so far the Ballet Magnificat hasn't contacted you specifically to offer you a place in their company. And until they do, you need to be planning on getting an education."

My saying that seemed to set me against God in Heather's mind. She obviously took the Ballet Magnificat's blanket offer for workshop students to "come back and join our troupe" as a personal invitation. The fact that I saw it differently made her feel I was questioning her talent as well as resisting God's will for her life. Having worked so hard and so long to be encouraging and affirming of Heather, I hated to be cast in the role of an unsupportive mother trying to throw a wet blanket over her dreams. And that's just what I felt like.

All Heather's life I'd encountered and fought people who thought me unrealistic—for wanting to teach her to communicate orally, for enrolling a deaf girl in dance, for insisting on a mainstream education, and for so much more. Now I was the one wanting to inject a note of realism.

Recognizing the irony of my position didn't make it any more comfortable for me. So I tried to keep our ongoing discussions focused on the central issue: the importance of getting an education.

"Suppose you are offered a place with the Ballet Magnificat when you graduate from high school," I said. "Let's say the doors do open for you to begin a professional dance career, and you even go on to become a prima ballerina. What happens ten, fifteen, or twenty years down the road? Very few professional dancers can perform forever. You need to have something else to fall back on. Which means you need the education."

That argument seemed to carry little weight. But then I suppose the specter of "retirement" hardly seems a relevant or compelling argument for anything when you're seventeen. I quickly took a different tack.

I'd checked out the Ballet Magnificat. I had been impressed enough with what I had learned about the company's professionalism and ministry to think I'd be very happy for Heather to join the group if that's what she wanted to do after college. But I also learned that this Christian dance troupe was not yet self-supporting. The dancers themselves, like "missionaries" in many other outreach ministries, were expected to provide or raise a significant portion of their own personal support.

So I told Heather, "If you're thinking about this in terms of a long-term career, you need to consider the financial implications. Can you be happy always being dependent on family and friends for your financial support? Or do you want the independence that comes from having another career to augment what you can make as a professional dancer?"

I figured "independence" would be a better hot button for any teenager than concern over "retirement plans." And I was right. Heather considered independence a very high priority.

"Then you need to be thinking about possible careers," I told her. "And a good place to start is to consider your strengths. What subjects have you always enjoyed and done best in?" I knew the answer to that one.

"Math," she replied. "But I'm never going to be a math teacher!"

When I sensed the defenses coming up, I quickly backed down. "I'm not saying you ought to be a math teacher just because it's what I do," I assured her. "There are lots of other jobs that utilize math skills. Remember our interview with Dan Miller at JSU?" When we'd asked his recommendation for college majors best suited for deaf students, he'd told us a number of his hearing impaired students did very well in accounting.

"I remember," Heather said.

"With your strength in math, that might be a very good option for you," I told her. "I know a number of CPAs who make a very comfortable living. You could do that full-time or maybe part-time for a while and still keep up with your dancing on the side. And when you get older you might want to start your own school and teach dance at night or on weekends. Trained accountants are always in demand. It seems like a solid, dependable career that would allow you to keep all your other options open."

165

Heather agreed that made a certain amount of sense. And while I'm not sure she ever quit hoping the Ballet Magnificat would call and make her an offer she couldn't refuse, we were at least talking in terms of college plans again. Heather even signed up for an elective, introductory course in accounting her senior year just to get a feel for the field.

Whenever Heather and I talked about college, the subject of money usually came up. Even a state school like JSU would cost more than I thought I could afford. Heather knew enough about our financial situation to understand it wouldn't be easy.

"Lots of college students work to help pay their expenses," she said. "I could get a part-time job."

I appreciated her willingness to help, but Heather's hearing impairment had always made her education a full-time job in itself. I had no reason to think college would be any different. And when I talked to her about it, she conceded that point.

But knowing Heather, I suspect she never quit hoping and trying to think of some way she could help out financially. Fortunately, that fall of her senior year we stumbled on a most unusual financial aid strategy.

As a colleague working in the Hoover City School System, I already knew Kathy Matusak as a casual acquaintance when she approached me one day at work to say she'd been talking about Heather with Lisa Armstrong (Heather's academic advisor) and Frances Moon (a wonderfully dedicated guidance counselor at Berry High). She told me she had heard about Heather's remarkable dancing abilities. She also knew we'd been looking for sources of college scholarships. In fact, that's why she'd come to talk to me. "Do you think Heather might consider entering our upcoming annual Jefferson County Junior Miss Scholarship Pageant?" she asked.

I told her I honestly didn't know. "What would be involved?" I asked. She handed me a program booklet from the previous year to look over. Quickly flipping through, I read the pageant's statement of purpose and goals. The booklet said they were looking for young women with poise, leadership ability, talent, and a number of other valuable character traits. While I could see Heather qualifying on those points, a quick scanning of last year's contestant profiles raised a red flag. There seemed to be a big emphasis on extracurricular activities—things like cheerleading, chorus, band, student council, yearbook staff, honor societies, debate squads, interscholastic sports, and all manner of student clubs.

"Heather hasn't done any of these things," I told Kathy. "Her studies eat up so much of her time and energy she isn't really involved in anything else besides her dance and church youth group."

"Oh, that won't matter," Kathy assured me. "Junior Miss is a lot more concerned with the character issues than they are about all the stuff kids are into. From what Lisa and Frances tell me about Heather, she's just the kind of young woman Junior Miss wants to attract. And with her strong dance background I think there's every reason to hope she could win some scholarship money in the talent portion of the competition."

I told Kathy I'd share the information with Heather and see what she said, but that I had no idea how she would react.

As it turned out, Heather reacted pretty much the way I had at first. "I haven't done any of these things," she said as she looked over the contestant profiles. "I don't think they would want me."

I told her what Kathy had said, including the part about the scholarship money available for talent. That was enough for Heather to agree to attend a preliminary informational meeting for the Jefferson County Junior Miss Pageant at school the following week.

When I went with Heather to that meeting, I was very much surprised by her obvious interest. We were both extremely disappointed at the end of the session, however, to learn that Heather did not qualify to enter the Jefferson County Junior Miss Pageant because we actually lived outside of the district.

I thought that probably meant the end of that. But Heather surprised me by wanting to get in touch with the people in charge of the Junior Miss program in Shelby County, where we lived. After we did, Heather surprised me even more by deciding she did indeed want to enter the Shelby County Junior Miss Pageant—despite the fact that she wouldn't know any of the other girls in it.

I helped her fill out all the application forms. Then the two of us began learning just how much was involved in preparing for a pageant. So many plans, so little time. I took the sleeves out of the green bridesmaid dress Heather had worn three years before in Stacey's wedding, added some rhinestones, and made a few other alterations to transform it into an evening gown. In preparation for Heather's talent we adapted one of the costumes she'd previously worn in a Briarwood Ballet performance, and then spent hours recording and editing down a taped version of Twila Paris's Christian inspirational hit "How Beautiful!" to the required length for the talent segment of the pageant. Then, in addition to practicing her own talent, Heather had long, nightly rehearsals with all the girls in the competition for a full two weeks prior to the November competition.

The preparation nearly exhausted me. But the anticipation, excitement, and demanding schedule actually seemed to energize Heather.

I worried a little the evening she drove off to her first rehearsal, at a strange school, with a group of girls she'd never met before. I think Heather had a few doubts of her own. Neither one of us knew what to expect.

But the pageant director and a number of the Shelby County girls took a special interest in making Heather feel included and welcome. And her background in dance served Heather well when it came to rehearsing the production numbers involving the entire cast. When she got home after 11:00 that first night and then spent almost an hour giving me a blow-by-blow report of her evening, I realized that neither of us had needed to worry. Heather had enjoyed herself so much that she could hardly wait for the next rehearsal.

Evidently not all the girls were having such a wonderful time— at least when it came to the group's big production numbers. While the dance requirements of the rehearsals seemed rather simple and fun to Heather, those girls without a dance background were at a disadvantage.

One contestant in particular, whose talent was singing, and who like Heather had entered the pageant in quest of the talent scholarship, really struggled with even the most basic dance steps. "I just can't do it," she complained after she'd messed up the routine for the umpteenth time. But when the director called the next break, Heather hurried over to the frustrated girl.

"Come on," Heather told her. "I'm going to help you do this. I know you can. Here, watch me. Like this. . . ." And every chance she could after that, Heather encouraged and worked with her new friend until the girl began to catch on.

I didn't find out about any of this until later. I just knew that something very positive seemed to be happening with Heather during those days leading up to the actual pageant. Every night she came home late from practice, not exhausted, but excited and happy, and with an air of contentment I hadn't seen in her before. So even before the big night finally arrived, I'd made up my mind that the whole Junior Miss process had already been a great experience for Heather.

The pageant itself was icing on the cake.

Like a lot of large pageant competitions, Shelby County Junior Miss was a three-night affair. One-half of the contestants performs their talent while the other half models their evening gowns on each of the two preliminary nights. At that point, the judges narrow the field to ten finalists, who are announced soon after all the contestants are introduced on the final evening. Then, in the course of that last night's program, each of the finalists performs her talent, models her evening gown, and answers an impromptu question onstage as a measure of her poise.

During the preliminaries, Heather danced beautifully and looked elegant in her green evening gown. As far as I was concerned, they could have crowned her after those two nights. While I have to admit to being a bit biased, my mother, my sister Stephanie, her six-year-old son, Trey, and even my dad, who'd been roped into his first-ever pageant, all agreed. We felt certain she'd be a finalist with a real shot at the title.

The butterflies I felt going into that final night caught me by surprise. And they really got going once Heather was named one of the ten finalists. I could barely sit still when she walked across the stage in her evening gown. I'm not sure I breathed even once during her dance routine (which the audience obviously loved). But the worst moment of the night for me came when Heather walked out to a microphone onstage and stood waiting for her impromptu "interview" question. *Will she even hear the question? Will she know what is being asked? Will she answer clearly and distinctly enough to be understood? If she doesn't understand, will she be too embarrassed to ask for the question to be repeated? Or will she try to guess what was being asked? If she does misunderstand or misspeak herself, will she be too humiliated to go on?* So many things to worry about!

But when the emcee asked Heather to explain to the audience what orienteering was (we'd listed her Missouri state championship on the application form), I knew from the way Heather immediately launched into her answer that she'd understood the question. Her response was clear and concise. *We're home free now. She might actually win.* But that seemed almost too much to hope for.

The butterflies returned in force when the entire group of twenty-nine girls lined up at the end of the evening for the announcement of all the scholarship winners and the crowning of the Shelby County Junior Miss. As I recall, every participant won something. So the announcements began with the smallest, $100 scholarships. The first time Heather's name was called, it was for being voted the "Spirit Award" by the other girls in Group B. Next she won the overall "Spirit

Award," the only scholarship awarded by the girls themselves—for the contestant they thought exhibited the best attitude or "spirit" of cooperation, encouragement, and friendliness. In addition to that, Heather took first place for the talent competition.

Once all the other scholarships had been announced, it was finally time to announce the winner. *Could it be?*

"Second runner-up, Miss Heather Whitestone!"

So she didn't win. But her entire family, including Bill who had driven up from Dothan for the evening, proudly hugged and congratulated her. And while I'm sure she felt a tinge of disappointment for not having won, Heather was absolutely thrilled to total up her winnings and realize she was taking home $1,400 in scholarships to apply toward next year's college expenses. That was more than she might have made from any part-time job flipping burgers after school.

I went home that night feeling terribly proud of my youngest daughter. For winning the talent competition, sure. And even more for receiving the "Spirit Award." But I think what made me proudest of all was when Jim Davis, one of the pageant officials, walked up to me after the program to introduce himself and say, "You don't know what an inspiration your daughter has been these past weeks—for all of us involved in the pageant." He was the one who told me how Heather had helped the girl who just hadn't been able to master the dance routines. "You have a very special girl there," he told me. I thanked him and agreed.

As I talked there with Jim, his wife walked up, and I realized he was the husband of Vicky Davis, who had been an assistant principal at my school the first year I'd taught in Hoover. Vicky had since become principal of a nearby elementary school, and we'd lost touch. As Vicky and I quickly caught up with each other that evening, I had no idea how fortuitous that renewed acquaintance would eventually become. Only later, looking back, would I begin to see how God was working, how he had turned our initial disappointment over Heather not qualifying for the Jefferson County Junior Miss into a wonderful experience in Shelby County. And then how he'd brought us together with Jim and Vicky Davis, who were to become such invaluable and supportive friends— for both Heather and me—in the years ahead.

But as proud as Jim Davis's report made me and as pleased as I was about the scholarship money Heather had won, what encouraged me most was seeing what that first positive pageant experience did for Heather's self-esteem. Totally on her own and without my running interference, Heather had walked into a brand-new setting and not only found acceptance, but had also earned the admiration and respect of the entire group. Perhaps for the first time in her life Heather had proven herself—to herself. It gave her a self-confidence I had never seen in her before.

Not that everything was perfect Heather's senior year. I knew there were still times at school when her hearing impairment made her feel as if she didn't belong. When friends hurt her feelings, when classmates didn't make a point of including her in a conversation, and when she sat at home weekend after weekend without a date, she was deeply hurt. At times she hurt so much she began questioning my decision to give her a mainstream education. She wondered if maybe she would have been better off had we gotten her into deaf education—where she would have grown up with other kids who shared her handicap and could understand her frustrations.

I knew she was proud, though maybe not as proud as I was, the night she graduated with honors from Berry High School. But I also knew some of her self-doubts remained. And it was out of those doubts, in the midst of what I only later realized was an almost classic adolescent search for identity and a sense of belonging, that Heather shocked me by announcing she wanted to enter the Miss Deaf Alabama Pageant to be held at the Alabama School for the Deaf in Talladega that June.

I don't know where Heather learned about it. I told her I'd never known there was such a pageant. "But if you want to enter it, that's fine with me," I told her. When I learned that the winner would go on to represent our state at a Miss Deaf America Pageant in Denver I thought, *That will be a great excuse for a visit with my sister Deborah out in Colorado.* Because frankly, after her success in the Junior Miss Pageant, knowing her talent, and figuring the field of competitors would be pretty small, I just assumed Heather would win.

I certainly had a lot to learn.

And I learned fast—starting with Heather's real motivation for entering the Miss Deaf Alabama competition, something I only began to understand as we talked on our drive to Talladega.

"This weekend will be good for you, Mother," my daughter told me. "You will see what it's really like in the deaf world. You will be the one who doesn't belong." When I realized that Heather viewed this as a turning-of-the-tables and was relishing that prospect, I just smiled to myself and listened. But I had a hard time not responding when she said

171

something about my "learning that hearing might not be as important or as necessary as I'd always thought."

When she finished talking, I thought for a while before responding. "You may just be right, Heather. This probably *will* be a very educational experience for me. Maybe for both of us. I'm really glad we're doing this. And I'm eager to see what I will learn this weekend."

The first thing I learned was that I was right to think we both might gain something from the experience. When we reached the campus of Alabama School for the Deaf, we had a little difficulty getting directions to our dorm, so we stopped to ask an elderly couple. While I think they understood what Heather asked in SEE (Signing Exact English), they responded in ASL (American Sign Language), which Heather didn't know well enough to follow. Obviously confused, she asked again. And again the man tried to indicate the way—this time using a combination of ASL and directional gestures. Heather still couldn't follow him. Even though I didn't know any sign whatsoever, I was able to read enough into the man's body language and gestures to figure out what he was trying to tell us.

Heather acted a little irritated with me when I nodded, smiled, thanked the couple, and pulled away. "Come on," I said to her. "I think I know where we're supposed to go." I stifled a laugh as I thought, *I guess we'll see who feels out of place these next couple of days.* But I decided Heather seemed frustrated enough without my saying anything more.

Once we'd found the dorm and checked into our room, I took a walk while Heather went to a meeting of pageant contestants. When she finally returned to the room, I could tell something was bothering her.

"What happened?" I wanted to know.

She told me she had met the other girls who would be in the pageant—just six of them. And they'd made fun of her for bringing her mother along. Heather said they seemed even more irritated to learn I was a "hearing" mother. They angrily told Heather it was time she grew up and left her "hearing family." They said she didn't need us. And they insisted that the deaf community was her "only real family."

My first inclination at that point was to march out, find those girls, and give them a piece of my mind. But I bit my tongue. Heather went on to say that the girls had told her that absolutely, under no circumstances should she attempt to use her voice onstage during the pageant the next night. "They told me only sign!" she said.

That ultimatum clearly didn't sit well with Heather. Before she left the room for the pageant the next evening she told me, "I don't care what they say. I am going to speak!"

I must say that Miss Deaf Alabama was indeed a unique pageant experience—for Heather as well as for me.

True to her word, Heather did speak out loud while simultaneously introducing herself to the audience in sign at the beginning of the program. I didn't see how her competitors reacted to that affront; at least no one chased her off the stage.

My first look at Heather's competition did nothing to dispel my initial assumption about her chances. Beauty is always in the eye of the beholder, but I felt confident about Heather's talent program.

It wasn't until the first contestant came out and performed her "talent" for a very enthusiastic and responsive audience that I began to think that maybe I'd misjudged the situation. And when the second girl came out and received another warm response to a very similar skit full of pointed and angry declarations of deaf pride and self-worth, I had a sinking feeling that Heather's classic dance routine wouldn't be what this crowd was expecting.

And I was right about that. When Heather came out onstage, took her position, and began her routine, I realized this mostly deaf audience wasn't hearing the music at all. Instead of enjoying the ballet for its graceful interpretation of Twila Paris's gorgeous rendition of "How Beautiful!" they merely saw a girl flitting and spinning and jumping around the stage in no discernible pattern. They weren't at all impressed. Heather finished her wonderful routine to a smattering of polite applause. And this was not even audible applause like we were used to; this was "deaf applause," which consisted of raising both hands in the air and shaking them back and forth.

I looked first at my parents, Stephanie, and her son, Trey, who'd come to lend Heather support. Then I glanced over to three of my teaching friends—Wayne, Amy, and Mandy—who'd driven all the way to Talladega to support Heather and me that night. When we made eye contact, I knew they knew what I knew. This wasn't going to be Heather's night.

Still it proved an interesting evening. I got a particular kick out of the man who'd been flown in from the East Coast to entertain the audience with "hearing people jokes" while the girls changed backstage between sets and the judges finally tallied their scores.

By the end I wasn't at all surprised Heather didn't win. But I couldn't believe she didn't even get one of the three runner-up spots. _It certainly has been a learning experience_, I consoled myself.

Heather didn't act visibly upset when we talked to her after the program. She thanked family and friends for coming and told me that all the girls who'd been in the pageant were going out for pizza. She'd meet me back at the room.

I didn't know what to say when she finally returned an hour or more later. I did tell her, "I thought you should have won!"

"It's okay," she said with a little smile.

But I could tell she didn't want to talk. So we dressed for bed in silence. And when she slid under the covers I turned out the lights and got into bed myself.

A few minutes later I heard a tapping at our first-floor dorm window. "What's that?" I asked out loud.

"What?" Heather wanted to know. She hadn't heard anything.

"A noise at the window." I got up to investigate. A couple of deaf parents of one of the other pageant contestants were outside. The dorm doors had already been locked for the night, and they needed someone to let them in. I motioned for them to wait, left the room, and walked down the hall to let them in the back door.

When I got back to the room, I explained to Heather what had happened. But I'm afraid I couldn't resist by concluding, "Yep, it just goes to prove you don't need hearing people around here."

Just moments later I heard another _tap, tap, tap_. I let those girls in as well. I was enjoying this. When I returned to the room that time, I asked Heather, "I guess maybe it's a good thing you didn't leave your old hearing mother at home after all, huh?"

When a third group came tapping at the window a few minutes later, I couldn't believe it. _Was everyone on campus this weekend informed where our room was? Would they all have ended up sleeping outdoors if I hadn't been here?_ Walking back into the room that third time, I laughed out loud. But Heather had turned her face to the wall and pulled the covers up over her head so she wouldn't hear anything I might say.

She didn't feel like talking on the long drive home either. In fact, Heather moped around—crying and angry—for two days after we got back. To hear her talk, I'd ruined her life so that she didn't belong in either the hearing _or_ the deaf world.

As bad as I felt for the tough time Heather had had at the Miss Deaf Alabama Pageant, I quickly tired of that attitude. Finally I walked into her room on that second day and said, "You and I need to talk."

I said I was truly sorry her feelings had been hurt, but I also told her, "I'm going to do for you what God has had to do to me a couple of times in my life. This pity party has got to end!

"It seems to me you've come to one of life's crossroads. And you've got an important choice to make. It's time you make your own decision about which world you plan to live in—the hearing world or the deaf world. It has to be up to you. So take a careful look. Stop and think this through very carefully. But you need to realize there is no paradise here on earth. You'll have problems to deal with either way you go.

"If you decide you want to live in the hearing world, you can go to JSU like you planned this fall and start preparing for the rest of your life. If you're convinced your future lies in the deaf world, maybe you want to consider going to Washington, D.C., and checking out Galludet [the country's leading deaf college]. That decision is up to you now. I won't make it for you.

"But I do have to tell you that I did learn something very important this past weekend. I was convinced once and for all that the choices I made for you when you were two years old were the right choices. I have never been more glad than I am right now that we didn't put you in the deaf world. Especially if people in the deaf culture say that your hearing family shouldn't be a part of their world. I did what I did because I loved you too much to do otherwise. I wanted more than anything else for you to be a part of my world and for me to always be a part of yours.

"You're an adult now. I can't tell you what to do anymore. But I'll always be your mother. And until the day I die, you'll hear what I think. Whether you accept my opinion or take my advice will be up to you, but you are going to get it. Ask your sisters. I'm not saying this because this is you or because you're deaf. I'm saying it because I'm your mother and I love you.

"What you choose to do now is totally and completely up to you."

That was when Heather cried and told me how the other girls at the Miss Deaf Alabama Pageant had shunned her and given her a difficult time. That's also when she told me about the post-pageant trip to Pizza Hut, how none of the other girls could make the waiter, who didn't know sign language, understand what they wanted to order. Finally

Heather, who did understand enough sign to know what the others wanted, ordered orally for everyone at the table.

"It would have been so much easier if they had just known how to speak," she concluded. "I see it is an advantage if deaf people can speak. Then you can communicate in both worlds."

"I agree," I told her. "That's what I've always thought."

"I've been thinking," Heather said. "Maybe God wants me to be a bridge between the two worlds. Like I was in that Pizza Hut between the waiter and those other girls."

I thought that was a wonderful dream. "How do you want to do that?" I asked. "Are you ready to start at JSU like you planned? Or do you want to start in the deaf world and maybe go to Galludet?"

Without hesitation Heather replied, "I want to go to JSU."

The decision was made. Whether she would become an accountant, a professional dancer, or maybe something else entirely, remained to be seen. But from that day on we both knew one thing for sure.

Heather wanted to be a bridge between the hearing and deaf worlds.

And we had to believe that dream would come true someday.

CHAPTER 17

Miss JSU

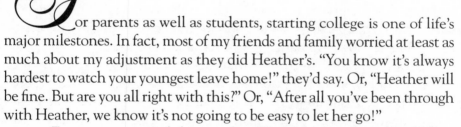

For parents as well as students, starting college is one of life's major milestones. In fact, most of my friends and family worried at least as much about my adjustment as they did Heather's. "You know it's always hardest to watch your youngest leave home!" they'd say. Or, "Heather will be fine. But are you all right with this?" Or, "After all you've been through with Heather, we know it's not going to be easy to let her go!"

Everyone assumed that sending Heather to college would be a traumatic ordeal for me, but it wasn't at all. No one seemed to remember that when Heather was an emotionally immature and vulnerable eleven-year-old with extremely limited communication abilities, I had let her go for three long years to attend school halfway across the country. Now *that* had been traumatic!

Compared to enrolling her at CID, sending a strong, determined, and independent eighteen-year-old like Heather off to a college merely an hour and a half drive away seemed like a piece of cake. I actually enjoyed helping her pack.

In fact, I was pleased when Heather told me that she wanted to arrive on campus several days early to participate in Sorority Rush Week. After our recent discussions about the hearing versus deaf worlds, I saw this as a valuable testing ground for Heather. "That will be great!

Maybe you can be a Zeta Tau Alpha. You know I was a Zeta when I went
to the University of Alabama."

"Mother!" Heather protested, "I'm not going to be a Zeta if I
don't want to be!"

"Of course not," I assured her and let the subject drop.

I naturally wondered how Heather's handicap might affect her
chance for acceptance by her peers in such a socially charged, peer-pres-
sured setting as Rush Week. But there were evidently enough hearing
impaired students on the JSU campus that Heather had little trouble fitting in. By the end of the week, just before school officially started, she'd
decided to pledge to Alpha Omicron Pi.

Although Heather enjoyed her sorority friends and experience, she
very quickly learned the downside of being a pledge. Sorority ties and
responsibilities took time—more time than she felt her studies would allow.

Within a month Heather formally resigned from her sorority. She
told me she wanted to concentrate on her studies and spend what free time
she had with the Baptist Campus Ministry group there at JSU. I knew giving up her sorority affiliation wasn't an easy decision; I could understand
and share her disappointment over that. At the same time it reassured me
to see Heather make such a swift and sure choice regarding her priorities.
I thought she showed remarkable wisdom and maturity.

What I didn't know was that Heather had begun to do a lot of
serious thinking about her priorities, her future, and her goals. On October 2, 1991, in a journal writing assignment for a required freshman class
called "Learning Skills 102," Heather began a short essay entitled "My
Life Goal" with this opening statement: "What I want most to accomplish in my life is to become Miss America."

In her essay Heather went on to describe how she had watched her
first Miss America Pageant on TV when she was seven. She had been
thrilled to see one of the contestants dance a ballet routine, and for years
as she practiced her own dance she would imagine performing in Atlantic
City herself one day. Winning the talent in the Shelby County Junior Miss
Pageant the year before had rekindled her dream of becoming Miss America. As Miss America, she concluded, she could witness for God and be an
encouragement to others, "especially the little deaf children."

I didn't see a copy of that essay until three years later. I had no
idea at the time that Heather had set her sights so high. Neither did I
know that the first pieces of the foundation upon which Heather would
build that dream were already being laid.

One early fall day Heather walked into the JSU Welcome Center to return some class notes to a friend who worked there. The friend introduced Heather to her boss, who happened to be standing there in the admissions area. "Heather, this is Teresa Strickland." Heather must have gotten a puzzled look on her face, because the girl pointed to a row of photos on the office wall of all the former JSU students who had been named Miss Alabama. "That's Teresa up there!" she said.

Looking quickly from Teresa to the photo and back to Teresa, Heather's face lit up. "You were Miss Alabama?" Heather asked. "I was in a beauty pageant last year. But I only came in second runner-up. Would you like to see my pictures sometime?"

"Sure," Teresa told her. "Next time you come by, bring your photos. I'd love to see them."

Within the week Heather returned to the admissions office to show Teresa her photographs from the Shelby County Junior Miss Pageant. When Teresa spotted the picture of Heather *en point* her curiosity was piqued. "You dance ballet, Heather? That's great. But tell me, how do you hear the music?" After Heather explained that we had started her in ballet as listening therapy and how she'd gone on to dance at ASFA and with the Briarwood Ballet, Teresa was obviously impressed. "So many girls in pageants today are singers," she told Heather. "With your ballet, maybe you ought to think about entering the Miss Jacksonville State Pageant this year."

The two of them talked awhile longer. Heather asked a lot of questions and learned that not only had Teresa been Miss Alabama, but she'd gone on to be named first runner-up in the Miss America competition. "Did you win a lot of scholarship money?" Heather wanted to know.

Teresa explained that her scholarship money had paid all her grad school expenses, even though, when she competed back in the seventies, the Miss America system had been more of a "beauty" pageant with a lot less "scholarship" emphasis than there is today. "If you're interested in scholarship money, Heather, that's a good reason to go out for 'Miss JSU.' The winner gets a full year's tuition. And the prize for talent is a free semester."

That really got Heather's interest. She told Teresa she'd certainly think about it.

Believe it or not, Teresa Cheatham Strickland wasn't the only former Miss Alabama Heather encountered at JSU that fall. Soon after she met Jane Rice Holloway, the wife of a minister at the Baptist

179

Campus Ministry fellowship, Heather learned that Jane too had been Miss Alabama—a few years before Teresa. So the two of them also talked about pageants, with Heather again expressing interest in the potential for scholarships.

Later that year, Jane served as a judge for the Miss Wallace State Pageant at a nearby junior college whose competition (like JSU's) was a local, qualifying round in the Miss Alabama Pageant system. She asked if Heather wanted to go along just to check it out. Heather did. And the experience made up her mind.

When Heather told me she wanted to enter the Miss Jacksonville State Pageant, I was pleased. And when she told me that she would also like to enter the Miss St. Clair competition (another local pageant scheduled only two weeks prior to Miss JSU) for the added experience, I agreed that her strategy seemed to make sense. *A little extra practice never hurts*, I thought. I saw Heather's continuing interest in pageants as further reassurance that the doubts and questions of the previous year were a thing of the past. She now seemed intent on firmly establishing her place in the hearing world.

I thought that was good. But neither of us knew yet what would be involved: lots of time, even more money, and loads of paperwork.

Heather could wear the same costume for the talent routine she'd worked up for the Junior Miss Pageant the year before. But she needed a new evening gown and other clothes to wear for the interviews with the judges. The Miss Alabama/Miss America Pageant system requires each contestant to have her own individual platform—some significant social issue of the day that she is willing and able to speak out on, and a practical plan for implementing that program. So Heather had a complete personal platform to pull together on top of all the other applications and forms to fill out regarding her family, school, personal history, and any past or present community service involvement.

Stacey helped with the shopping. (When her husband took an early out from the military, she and Tom and my baby grandson, Shane, had moved in with me temporarily while Tom explored civilian career options.) During the week Stacey would take Shane and scour the malls looking for suitable outfits so that when Heather came home on weekends, we'd already know where to take her to try something on. Stacey had an eye for fashion and a real knack for finding bargains. Still, even at half price, Heather's new blue evening gown cost us $500. And that was just the start.

With all of us working together, we had Heather primed and everything ready to go for the Miss St. Clair Pageant on February 29, 1992. That was a night none of us will ever forget.

The emcee for the pageant that evening just happened to be Teresa Strickland. Heather bumped into her backstage before the program and greeted her warmly, only to have her friend get a funny, uncertain look on her face. When we found out later that Teresa hadn't immediately recognized Heather, I wasn't at all surprised. I've always been amazed at the transformation that takes place when Heather fixes her hair on top of her head and puts on makeup. She changes from this "cute-little-girl-next-door" her friends and classmates see on campus every day into a very sophisticated, stunningly beautiful young lady.

I thought Heather looked great during the swimsuit and evening gown portions of the competition that evening. She danced well, too.

The trouble came with the impromptu questions on stage. As always my stomach churned fastest in the eternity of seconds that Heather stood in front of a microphone awaiting her question.

"Heather," she was finally asked, "as someone who obviously knows and loves ballet, tell us, who is your favorite dancer? And why?"

I winced because I knew the "who" she was going to say. I could only pray she'd be able to pronounce his name so the audience and judges could understand.

Heather turned toward the audience and smiled. "My favorite dancer is Mikhail Baryshnikov." She spoke with such poise and the words came out so clearly, I wanted to cheer. I breathed a big sigh of relief as the question was repeated.

"And why?"

Maybe Heather panicked at that point. Maybe her brain vapor-locked. We'll never know because Heather can't explain it herself. All she managed to say in response to the question about *why* she admired the great Russian dancer Mikhail Baryshnikov so much was: "He jumps high!"

That was all she said; she made no attempt at recovery. I couldn't believe it. *He jumps high?* That sounded like something she might have said back in the third grade.

Heather didn't win anything that night. When our usual large contingent of family and friends hurried up to greet her after the program, she acted subdued and embarrassed.

As the audience quickly filed out of the auditorium and I waited in front of the stage for Heather to get dressed, Teresa Strickland sought me out, pulled me aside, and reintroduced herself. "I don't know if you remember meeting me when you and Heather first came to JSU?"

I told her I did.

She said, "I just wanted to see you and say—please don't let Heather give up on pageants, even though I have a feeling she might want to after tonight." She went on to tell me how moved she'd been by Heather's dance. And how shocked she had been standing out on stage when she had announced Heather's name and realized the beautiful girl she'd bumped into backstage was the same little freshman student who'd stopped by her office early that fall to show off her Junior Miss photos. "I see tremendous potential in Heather," Teresa concluded. "She'll do better in the Miss JSU Pageant."

"I'm not going to be in the Miss JSU Pageant!" Heather declared when I told her what Teresa had said. "I am never going to enter another pageant."

"It's too late to drop out now," I told her. "I already mailed your registration fee. And I didn't pay that $35 for nothing. Besides," I laughed, "we spent $500 for that dress, and I intend to get at least two wearings out of it!"

"I was so embarrassed!" Heather complained. "It was awful! I was terrible!"

I stopped her at that point and finally got her to admit that she'd done fine in the swimsuit, evening gown, and talent portions of the pageant. "The only problem was the interview question," I assured her. "You might want to practice a little more for that. But everything else was fine."

"It's no use. I don't think that the judges like me because I am deaf," she argued. She complained about her afternoon interview with the pageant judges. "No one even looked at me. They acted so awkward. Like they thought I shouldn't be there."

"My guess is that they were just ill at ease with themselves because they didn't know how to interact with you," I told her. "I know it may not seem fair. But maybe *you* are going to have to be the one to set *them* at ease."

Fortunately I wasn't the only one trying to encourage her. Tom talked to Heather about how her pageant experience seemed a lot like his current job search. "When I go in for an interview with a potential employer, I have to try to sell myself the same way you have to sell yourself to the judges in that interview session. I think this is great practical experience for later in life."

Stacey took a different approach. "I don't think you should enter a pageant unless you're going to enjoy it, Heather. But I think you ought to give it one more try. If the Miss JSU Pageant isn't fun, then by all means, don't enter any more pageants!"

When Heather left to go back to school that next Monday, I wasn't sure what she planned to do. But the combined weight of her family's arguments had evidently changed her mind. I didn't know it, but she asked Janet White, one of JSU's deaf support staff, to find a political science instructor to come up with some sample current-events questions for her. And she spent all her spare time the next two weeks preparing for that ever-worrisome bugaboo, the impromptu questioning.

Twenty-three girls entered the one-night pageant for Miss Jacksonville State University. The program was long, because we had to see every single one of them go through every aspect of the competition— swimsuit, evening gown, talent, and questioning. As we had during the Miss St. Clair Pageant, Stacey, Stephanie, and I took copious notes in our programs—because we knew that Heather couldn't hear any of what the other girls said or did on stage. If she was going to learn anything from her competitors' strengths and weaknesses, we had to be Heather's ears before and during the pageant in order to give her a full report sometime after the pageant was over.

Once again Heather made a fine appearance in the swimsuit and evening gown portions of the program. And as the long night wore on, I decided she had a great chance to win talent. I knew that would make her feel a lot better. I only hoped that she would make it through the question portion without being embarrassed again.

When the long-dreaded question time finally came, Heather stepped confidently to the mike. "Heather, do you think it's right for our U.S. congressmen and senators to be able to vote themselves pay raises? Tell us why or why not."

Oh, man! I thought. *What I wouldn't give for that question about Mikhail Baryshnikov!*

But Heather nailed it this time. I was so nervous I don't remember exactly what she said, but she didn't hesitate at all, and whatever she said sounded logical and clear. *All right! She made it through!*

Finally the program wound to a close. All twenty-three girls lined up for the announcement of winners. The first contestant called was fourth runner-up. Then the emcee realized she should have started with the talent winner and backtracked saying, "The winner of the talent portion of tonight's competition and the recipient of one semester's tuition to Jacksonville State University, Miss Heather Whitestone."

I knew from the confused look on Heather's face she didn't know what she'd won. Perhaps she figured they'd called her name for third runner-up. I knew she'd be thrilled with the semester scholarship as soon as we explained it all to her afterwards.

The rest of the announcements followed in order. Third runner-up. Second runner-up. First runner-up. And then "Miss Jacksonville State University for 1992 . . . Miss Heather Whitestone!"

Suddenly our family and friends were all shouting and cheering. When my mother, who was holding Stacey's baby, started screaming, so did Shane. But none of us noticed for a while because we yelled much louder than he could cry.

I was absolutely and totally shocked Heather had won—not because she was deaf, but because she was just a freshman. I'd expected the title to go to a junior or senior. I didn't know if there had ever before been a freshman selected as Miss JSU.

Later Teresa told us Heather had simply blown the judges away in the pre-pageant interview. "She seemed so relaxed and at ease," she commented.

Heather explained that she'd taken all the family's advice. She'd practiced answering questions ahead of time and tried to set the judges at ease. She had tried to approach that initial interview session as if she were applying for a job. But mostly, she'd decided to simply relax and have fun. "And it *was* fun," she laughed.

Good thing. Because like it or not, Heather was now committed to at least one more pageant. As Miss Jacksonville State University, she automatically qualified to represent her school at the Miss Alabama Pageant in Birmingham three months later.

We soon received a competition packet at least an inch thick filled with material and information. The good thing about it was that it went into incredible detail telling us the what, when, where, why, and how of everything that had to be done before the Miss Alabama Pageant. The troubling part, however, was *everything that had to be done before the Miss Alabama Pageant.*

There seemed to be some kind of deadline, with paperwork due, every week or so from the end of March until the middle of May. We needed two edited copies of Heather's "How Beautiful" music on reel-to-reel tapes. She needed a portfolio of professional glamour photos.

They wanted a more complete and refined treatment of her platform. The list of things we had to do, prepare, and plan seemed endless.

The number of clothes alone that Heather needed would challenge the capacity of my credit cards. She would require at least one new outfit for every day of the week before the pageant. And each of the girls was expected to wear a different cocktail-style dress for meeting the public at receptions following the three preliminary nights of competition.

People kept telling me to just borrow the outfits we needed. But I didn't begrudge Heather all the new clothes. For most of her life her wardrobe had consisted primarily of hand-me-downs from her older sisters. I kept reminding myself that much of what we bought in the way of suits and casual wear would serve her well for years. But still I don't know what we would have done without Stacey's time and bargain-hunting skills. Fortunately, selection seldom presented a problem; there weren't enough people Heather's size to ever buy out the stock of cute outfits in sizes 2 to 4.

Still, in all that winter, spring, and summer, I spent roughly $5,000 on clothes and other pageant-related expenses. The new evening gown required for the traditional all-white finale of the Miss Alabama Pageant set me back a cool grand all by itself.

Adding to the financial strain and our incredibly pressured deadline schedule was the fact that our Miss JSU Pageant director, who was supposed to help mentor Heather through the state pageant process, got married, abruptly resigned, and moved away. We would have been lost if Teresa, Jane, Janet, and a few other wonderful folks hadn't jumped in and taken up some of the slack. Because as much as Heather's family wanted to help, none of us had been through the complicated state pageant process before.

I felt a little more prepared after Heather and I attended the annual pre-pageant orientation workshop that the Miss Alabama board conducted the first of May. The most valuable part of that weekend for me was the chance I had to talk with other mothers who'd been through the process before and who freely shared their wisdom with us rookies. But by then we had only six weeks left to follow their voluminous advice and make our final preparations.

For the most part, all the hours of planning and preparing seemed a positive bonding experience between mother and daughter. But on one issue Heather and I had a very real difference of opinion—her hairstyle.

Heather preferred it down because it was simpler; I argued that it made her look far too young, like a naive little schoolgirl. I thought she looked so much older and more sophisticated with it up; she thought it a pain to fix and keep her hair on top of her head. We'd gone round and round on the subject until the afternoon of the last day before I was to deliver her to the pageant officials on the Samford University campus in Birmingham.

Because every contestant in the Miss Alabama Pageant was required to fix her own hair, Heather was sitting in front of the mirror in her bedroom, fretting and fussing. Her dark hair was so fine that no matter how she pinned it, large strands kept slipping out of place.

Frustrated with her hair and irritated with me for preferring it up, Heather finally declared, "I am not wearing it up, Mother! I can't get it to stay!"

"You can't wear it down," I told her.

"It's my hair!"

"Just take that banana clip with you. You need to wear it up!"

"I don't want to wear it up! I like it better down!"

I think we were both ready to scream when Stephanie stopped by. "Could you please go see if you can help Heather figure out what to do with her hair?" I pleaded.

It took awhile. But with me staying out of the way, the two of them finally came up with a style variation Heather thought she could manage by herself. I wanted to shout hallelujahs and hug my little sister for her help. But I didn't dare say a word, for fear it would change Heather's mind again.

Stephanie had actually come by that day not just to say goodbye and wish Heather good luck, but also to help me finish up some little surprises she and I had planned. During the pageant workshop for mothers, one of the women had suggested that we send a special little creative gift or note of encouragement for our daughters to open each day of the week that they spent preparing for the pageant.

The surprise Stephanie and I had cooked up for Heather's first day at the pageant was our biggest. Someone had advised Heather early on that she might practice her interview by placing stuffed animals in chairs around a room and talking to them like pretend judges. She'd been doing that for weeks and had actually packed a couple small animals to take with her for extra practice that final week. But Stephanie and I knew she'd be too embarrassed to show up at Miss Alabama carrying her all-time favorite stuffed animal—her old, love-worn friend, Pooh Bear. So we packed Pooh Bear into a big box with a note saying, "After I've been with you all these years, I knew there was no way you were going to make it through this week without me. So I stowed away, and here I am!"

I could imagine her acting a little embarrassed and exclaiming, "Oh, Mother!" when she opened the package Stephanie and I had wrapped with colorful paper and bows. But I also knew she'd be pleased to have Pooh Bear with her for the duration.

Once I dropped Heather off at Samford Monday morning, I hardly saw her again all week except on stage. The pageant officials kept the girls sequestered on campus for an intensive week of rehearsing, interviewing, and preparation for the four nights of competition. We did get a few moments together at a public reception each night after the preliminaries. But what time we had in the middle of that crowd was spent with Heather giving me a list of things she wanted me to drop off at the dorm for her the next day, things like disinfectant spray, bathtub cleaner—and pantyhose. It seemed every time we talked she asked for more pantyhose. She must have run through twenty-five pairs that week.

After the months of hectic preparation, pageant week itself seemed surprisingly quiet—almost anticlimactic. Almost. Until the preliminary competition began on Wednesday night.

Family and friends were there in force all four nights. Mom, Stephanie, Stacey, and I were nervous wrecks. (Although Stacey and Tom had moved to Colorado by this point, they came for the week of Miss Alabama.) Dad kept up a steady stream of good-natured complaints: "After four straight nights of this, you're gonna really owe me! Big time! This beauty pageant business is costing me a lot of my own beauty rest. All I can say is, this better be worth it."

When Heather walked across the stage on the night of her preliminary swimsuit competition, my father leaned over and whispered, "Seeing her up there like that tells me just how badly she wants this!" I knew exactly what he meant. It didn't seem possible to me either that the beautiful young woman walking confidently across that stage in front of two thousand people wearing nothing but a swimsuit and high heels was the same daughter who modestly insisted on wearing a long T-shirt over her swimsuit whenever I took her to the beach.

This was definitely different from anything any of us had experienced before. And I think the entire family felt the added tension that comes along with the higher stakes at any state-level pageant. Everyone, that is, except Heather. Once again she seemed to be having a ball. When she took first place for talent in her group during the preliminaries on Friday evening, we figured she would have to be one of the finalists. As we began to hope for even more, the tension only got worse.

The last evening began with Heather indeed among the finalists. That meant she went through every part of the program again that night on stage. The crowd warmed to Heather from the start. She got sustained applause when she came out in her blue sequined evening gown and made her twenty-second platform summary statement: "With positive self-esteem, courage, inner strength, and God's help, the impossible is indeed possible."

By the time she finished dancing to "How Beautiful," she had the entire audience entranced. *Maybe, just maybe, she's got a shot at winning!* I thought.

When they announced that Heather was the overall talent winner, I felt even better about her chances. So when she got first runner-up, I couldn't help feeling a little disappointed knowing she'd come so, so close.

Heather herself was absolutely elated. She'd already decided she would go for the title again the following year.

The very next morning Heather awakened complaining of terrible pain in her jaws. Early Monday morning, less than thirty-six hours after the Miss Alabama Pageant ended, I made an emergency dental appointment for Heather to have four impacted wisdom teeth removed. That same afternoon Heather, unable to talk herself, insisted I call the officials of the Miss Point Mallard Pageant up in Decatur, one of the first qualifying competitions in the state for next year's Miss Alabama, to inform them that she planned to compete there on the Fourth of July weekend—now barely a week and a half away.

I made the call. But as I looked at my daughter's swollen face and shook my head, I said, "Too bad there's not a Miss Chipmunk Pageant starting somewhere tomorrow. You couldn't lose."

At least she didn't hurt too much to laugh.

CHAPTER 18

"*Via Dolorosa*"

*E*very year, Point Mallard, a large recreational park located just outside Decatur, Alabama, hosts a two-night pageant over the Independence Day holiday. As soon as Miss Point Mallard is crowned on the park's big outdoor stage, fireworks explode overhead and drift down through the night sky over the Tennessee River.

The setting makes for an exciting and impressive ending to a pageant. The fact that the competition has a reputation for always being well-organized and for offering some of the best prizes of any local pageant in the state makes Miss Point Mallard one of the most coveted titles in the Miss Alabama system. Additionally, as the very first open local competition for the following year's state pageant, the Miss Point Mallard program appeals to any young women in the pageant circuit eager to get that first required step in the Miss Alabama qualifying process out of the way early.

So it was that Heather's competition for Miss Point Mallard included a half dozen or more very familiar faces—girls she'd competed against in the state pageant in Birmingham just two weekends before. These competitors, like Heather, had already decided to pursue their dreams another year.

Because this was Heather's fourth pageant experience in less than five months, our family felt like true pageant veterans. While we warned Heather and each other not to be overconfident, I for one was not surprised when they crowned Heather Miss Point Mallard 1992.

Evidently I wasn't the only one to anticipate that result. The mother of one of the other girls walked up to congratulate me that evening saying, "Good for Heather! Now that she's won this title, the rest of the girls will have their chance." In her mind at least, Heather was an early favorite to become the next Miss Alabama.

I hoped she was right. But doubts were raised when I learned that not everyone felt as charitable toward my daughter.

Later that summer I received an unexpected long-distance call from Beverly, one of my closest friends in Dothan. She had just that minute learned that a mutual acquaintance of ours had overheard one of the officers of the Miss Alabama board of directors tell a Dothan business proprietor, "There will never be a deaf girl chosen as Miss Alabama! Heather Whitestone doesn't stand a chance next year!"

I knew the woman Bev had heard this from. She had no reason to make the story up.

Beverly was furious. "Isn't there anything you can do? Maybe go to court and sue him for unfair bias or something."

"No," I told her. While I wasn't exactly happy with what I'd heard, I just chalked it up to petty ignorance and prejudice. "I think the best course of action is simply to let Heather prove him wrong. Let's just see what happens."

Somehow the word must have gotten back to the man that people had heard what he said. (It's amazing how fast communication flies in the pageant circuit.) He called me one day just a couple weeks later to say, "Daphne, you're not going to believe the latest rumor going around. I have no idea how this got started, because it's certainly not true. But supposedly, according to this rumor, I've been going around the state and publicly saying that Heather will never be Miss Alabama because she's deaf. Ha, ha. Of course, I felt sure that you'd know that's a preposterous story. But I wanted to call and assure you there is nothing to it—before you heard it from anyone else."

I could honestly tell the man I wouldn't want to believe such a story of anyone. And I thanked him for his call. But I have to admit that I hung up thinking, *Yeah, right!* Any doubts I might have had about the story before he called were gone. I've been a teacher long enough to recognize a guilty party who's trying desperately to cover his own derriere.

I never did mention the incident to Heather because I knew it would only upset her. I was thankful that I didn't need to worry about her finding out on her own. One of the few advantages to Heather's handicap is that her deafness effectively filters out most rumors and gossip—automatically shielding her from a lot of the pain such pettiness often causes. I figured what she didn't know, and wouldn't know, couldn't hurt her.

The positive side to Heather's having won the title of Miss Point Mallard was that she had almost a full year to get ready for the next state pageant. Although we wouldn't get the official information and application package until spring, we'd been through the process once and knew the ropes. So there was a lot we could do throughout the year to prepare for next summer's Miss Alabama Pageant.

Heather had wanted the Miss Point Mallard title because it was one local pageant that demanded a lot from its winner in the way of community service and public appearances. Heather thought that experience would stretch her and help her grow. And it did.

She had to drive to Decatur (a six-hour round-trip from Birmingham) one or two weekends every month. Add to that the occasional demands placed on her as Miss JSU (her two reigns would overlap until March of 1993), and I thought it amazing that she found time to attend class, let alone earn the same A and B averages she had her freshman year. While I totally supported what she wanted to do, there were times that I worried she was overdoing it. Some weekends, if her final engagement in Decatur wasn't over until Sunday evening, she'd be exhausted by the time we finally got back to Birmingham. I'd send her to bed and set my alarm for 3:30 or 4 in the morning so I could wake her up in time for her to drive on to JSU for her Monday morning classes.

There was one other very positive benefit to knowing so early that Heather would be competing in Miss Alabama again. This second time around I would have more months to spread out the expenses. I needed all the time I could get because I'd maxed out my credit cards the first year and was now pretty much limited to a strict pay-as-you-go policy.

But even with the extra time, I knew I couldn't bankroll Heather's pageant quest on my teaching salary alone. I had to figure out some way to raise the necessary funds. I already earned some extra income by tutoring a number of students a couple days a week after school. But I needed something more.

I'd always been an artsy-craftsy person, so it seemed only natural to try to turn that interest into a money-making idea. And Stephanie, loyal sister and aunt that she is, volunteered to form a partnership venture to make a variety of decorative wooden country-style buildings that doubled as handy index card organizers when you lifted off their roofs. Our little gingerbread house held a Christmas organizer; our miniature country church made a great wedding planner/organizer. Our country schoolhouses were organized for teachers with room inside for class lists, schedules, and cards for individual students. Our basic country houses (in various pastel colors) served as perfect recipe files.

Stephanie's father-in-law, Tom Ward, not only loaned us his backyard workshop, he also taught us how to use the equipment—band saws, jigsaws, routers, and sanders—needed to transform 4' x 8' sheets of plywood into the mass-produced walls and roofs of our buildings.

My parents' basement also served as paint shop, construction site, inventory warehouse, and mailroom for shipping. Mom and Dad helped a lot with painting and the endless tedium of sanding.

Heather joined our assembly line whenever she could. Many were the times she and Stephanie and I spent the better part of the night (and a portion of the early morning) with glue gun, paintbrush, or fine sandpaper in hand, laughing at the way we looked—our hair dusted with sawdust, drips and dabs of paint on our faces, and carpenter's glue caked under our fingernails. As usual, the pursuit of Heather's dreams required extended family commitment.

Unfortunately, our family's miniconstruction business paid only modest dividends on a maximum investment of time and energy. We sold a ton (literally it seemed) of those little buildings that year at craft shows and gift shops. But it just wasn't enough. Once again I had to scrimp, scrape, and squeeze more out of those thin little pieces of plastic than I did from that huge stack of half-inch plywood.

I don't know how Heather managed, but on top of everything else that year, she somehow found time for a social life. At first I was happy for her. She obviously enjoyed the attentions of her first-ever steady boyfriend. And like Heather, I saw the boy's efforts to master sign (so as to communicate with her more easily) as an impressive measure of his commitment to her. But I didn't appreciate the fact that he seemed to think his willingness to learn sign proved he loved Heather more than her nonsigning family did. So I can't say I was sorry to see him go when they finally broke up.

While I didn't for a moment think Heather doubted her family's love, her boyfriend's attitude toward our family did prompt some questions from her. She started by asking my father, "Granddad, why didn't you ever learn to sign?"

"I'm sure we would have if it hadn't been for the acoupedic philosophy," he told her. "But your mother convinced us that you would never learn to speak unless we all forced you to use your hearing and your voice."

She then pressed me for an explanation of why I had never learned sign even after her speech had been established. "I thought about learning sign when you took that sign class in high school," I told her. "I believe it's been good for you. It's certainly a beautiful language.

"I guess after all those years I spent resisting the pressure to teach you sign, I can't help feeling a little like I'd be selling out. But the main reason I haven't learned sign and haven't wanted the rest of the family to use sign is because I know oral speech is more difficult for you. Like any champion figure skater or gymnast who has to train every day to keep sharp, you will always need daily voice stimulation to stay in training as an effective oral communicator.

"All your life we, your family, have been your coaches and training partners. If those of us who are closest to you learn sign, we might be able to communicate a little easier at times, but there would not be any place left in your life where you are regularly forced to practice oral communication. I don't ever want that to happen."

One other crucial development took place in that long eleven-month stretch between the time Heather won Miss Point Mallard and her second Miss Alabama Pageant. We decided we had time to make some major changes in the talent portion of Heather's game plan.

Step one would be regular private dance lessons for Heather. At Jacksonville State during the week, Heather was just too far from Birmingham to continue participating regularly in her Briarwood Ballet classes. And her unpredictable schedule, even on weekends, made any consistent class time in Birmingham impractical. Private, individual lessons seemed the only logical alternative.

That's when we found Monica Barnett Smith. Not only had Monica competed in some Miss Alabama pageants herself, she had also been the official choreographer for several Miss Alabama pageants. Monica knew the pageant system well. That, and her willingness to work with Heather late Friday nights or whenever on Saturday best fit Heather's schedule, made her a perfect fit for our needs.

Step two was a significant change in Heather's talent program itself.

People thought we were crazy to consider any alteration whatsoever. After all, with the exception of Miss St. Clair, Heather had won the talent portion of every pageant she'd ever entered. As they say, *If it ain't broke, don't fix it.*

But Heather and I both agreed that if she hoped to become Miss America, her dance routine could stand to have a little more excitement and emotion in it. "How Beautiful," a smooth and elegantly flowing musical backdrop to her routine, didn't have the variety of tempo or the abrupt changes of pace that might inspire dramatic interpretive movement or call for sudden jumps and turns.

For weeks I went from one store to another in quest of another contemporary Christian song that would fulfill all our requirements. Not only did we need a beautiful song with appropriate lyrics and dramatic changes of pace and mood, but it had to be sung by a singer whose voice Heather could hear. And we had to be able to cut it down to the exact length allowed for each talent portion of the competition—two minutes and forty-five seconds.

Twila Paris's voice had always been in the perfect frequency range for Heather's hearing. So I looked a long time for another suitable Twila Paris number—with no luck. I spent a fortune on tapes because I could only do so much screening in the store before I brought the best options home, for Heather's reaction (How did she like the song? Could she even hear it?) and to see how easily we could edit them down.

By late summer, we'd made no progress. Then Heather and I attended a Miss Alabama Musical Revue where Kim Wimmer, the girl who had beaten Heather out for Miss Alabama 1992, sang her own version of the Sandi Patty hit "Via Dolorosa." As Kim stood on stage in a filtered spotlight of soft yellow tinged with red and belted out that gorgeous number, I suddenly knew. God had given me the answer. In my mind I could already envision Heather, dressed in a yellow costume tinged with red to symbolize Christ's blood, dancing ever so dramatically to Sandi Patty singing "Via Dolorosa."

After the program ended I told Heather, "I have it—the perfect song. You can dance to 'Via Dolorosa.'"

"No way!" Heather replied.

"Why not? It's perfect!"

194

"It's Kim's song!" Heather said.

"Kim didn't sing it in the Miss Alabama Pageant."

That didn't matter to Heather. "She sings it now. It's one of her regular numbers."

"But you're not going to sing it, you're going to dance to it."

"It's still Kim's song. I can't use it."

I went out and bought a tape of Sandi Patty singing the song. Using my own tape player, I edited it down to the required length. I thought it sounded great. With a professional editing job done in a studio, the breaks would be nearly seamless.

I kept playing and replaying the song for Heather. She loved the music and the lyrics. But she still insisted, "I can't dance to Kim's song."

I kept looking, but I couldn't find anything else that I thought worked nearly as well. So I enlisted Monica's input. She agreed "Via Dolorosa" had everything Heather needed for her talent routine.

Heather told Monica what she'd told me. "It's Kim's song."

Monica responded, "It's actually Sandi Patty's song, Heather. And lots of other people use it."

"Like Kim!" Heather said.

"But you're not going to sing it like Kim does. And it's not like Kim even sang the song at Miss Alabama. You're talking about a totally different talent. You would be dancing—with Sandi Patty herself singing the song. You wouldn't be duplicating anything. I don't see the problem."

Heather finally came around and decided to dance to "Via Dolorosa" after all. She and Monica began choreographing the movements early that fall. Once in a while they'd let me see their progress and ask what I thought. The only advice I had for them was that Heather might want to sign, "Let me see Christ," as she crossed the stage at the very beginning of the routine. I thought everything else looked great.

Heather and Monica perfected the routine for months. Fall, winter, and spring Heather worked on it almost every day.

It wasn't until March or April that we suddenly realized we might have a serious problem. When we'd filled out the official Miss Alabama Pageant application forms the year before, we'd simply listed "How Beautiful!" as the music we'd selected for Heather's talent routine. No problem. It now dawned on us that if one of the other contestants filed first and wanted to sing "Via Dolorosa" (we knew one local pageant winner had used it for her vocal talent), Heather would be forced to choose another number. We'd already choreographed and costumed the song. If we couldn't use it, months of hard work and hundreds of hours of practice would go down the drain. And I hated to think how Heather would react if her talent plans had to be changed at the last minute.

We decided we had only one hope. Heather would have to file her application first. And since application packets for all contestants went out at the same time—after the last local pageant every spring— we figured out what we had to do to manage it. The minute Heather's package was delivered to the Point Mallard Pageant director in Decatur, we arranged for Beverly Walker to call my parents with the message (I was at school). Beverly filled out all the forms required from her before she and her husband, Julian, drove to meet Dad and me late that night at a rest stop halfway between Decatur and Birmingham. There the two of us spread the papers on the counter, and Beverly went over everything Heather and I needed to do to complete all the remaining forms. I stayed up most of the night typing in everything I could do by myself, and the next day after school I drove to Jacksonville with the packet to get Heather's input and signature. At home again that night I typed up everything Heather had given me. And the next day I took personal leave from school so I could get everything notarized and delivered in person to the Miss Alabama office in downtown Birmingham soon after it opened.

"Hi, Daphne." Sandra Gardner, the secretary and only paid employee for Miss Alabama, knew me well. She'd been such a wonderful help the year before when we'd negotiated the complicated application process for the first time without the help of any local pageant director. "You've got Heather's application forms? Great. You're just the second one to file."

"Second?" I felt a sudden panic.

"The first one came in just a few minutes ago."

"Who was it?"

When they told me, I felt my heart sink clear to my shoes. It was the one girl we'd been most worried about—the very one who'd sung "Via Dolorosa" to win her local qualifying pageant.

What are we going to do? How am I going to tell Heather?

CHAPTER 19

First Runner-up

 ell, Daphne," Sandra Gardner said as she paged through the application forms, "let's make sure everything is in order here before you go."

"Oh." She paused. "Heather's decided to change the music for her talent routine! She wants to use 'Via Dolorosa'?"

Oh, boy! I thought. *Here it comes now!*

"That should be fine."

What? "What?"

"That will be a beautiful number for Heather's dance. Tell her good luck, everything looks in order here."

Thank you, Lord! It seems the other girl had changed her mind and was singing a different number for her talent in the state pageant.

I called Heather and Monica the minute I got home. "You're not going to believe this. . . ." I told them what had happened.

With the exception of that one scare, Heather and I both felt much better prepared for Miss Alabama that second time around. I was now one of the seasoned veterans with advice for the new girls' mothers at the annual pageant workshop.

But it's a good thing we felt we had everything under control on the pageant front, because we had a couple other major family events to plan for that spring. Heather and I went with my parents to Colorado for six days at the end of May through the beginning of June to stay with Stacey and Tom for Melissa's graduation from the Air Force Academy and her marriage two days later to Tony Gomillion, one of her graduating classmates.

Stacey had made arrangements for Heather to use the studio of a local dance instructor for her daily workouts while we were out in Colorado. Unfortunately, the altitude change really got to Heather. She was so weak by the time we returned home that I worried she wouldn't recover in time to be at her best for the pageant. But she did.

Pageant week seemed both better and worse the second time around. It helped to know what to expect. It didn't help that so many people now considered Heather one of the favorites. Higher expectations make for added pressure and a lot more gossip.

Early in the week I heard from a couple of pageant mothers who wanted to console me about the tough time Heather had during her preliminary interview with the pageant judges. "I haven't heard anything about that," I told them.

"We're sorry. We assumed you knew."

"No. I haven't talked to Heather at all." Evidently some of the other girls were not as conscientious as Heather in abiding by Miss Alabama's strict "no telephone calls to parents" policy.

"Well, we felt bad when we heard how upset Heather was about some of the judges and their questions."

I politely thanked my informants for their *concern*, admitting again that I hadn't heard a thing from Heather. "There's nothing to be done now anyway. We'll just have to trust the Lord on this."

Inside I wasn't quite so calm about their news. I realized how difficult the pre-pageant interviews were for Heather. We'd paid an extra $175 to get an individual video of everything Heather had done during the Miss Alabama Pageant the year before. We'd sat and critiqued every aspect of her first year's performance several times.

I had seen in that first year's tape what the preliminary interview was like. Heather had walked into the middle of the room, taken her seat in front of five judges, and then spent the next ten minutes answering whatever questions any of them wanted to ask. One of the first-year judges had asked her about the role her hearing impairment had played in her life and how she felt about her handicap. She had smiled at the judge and said, "I don't suppose I feel much different about my handicap than you do about yours. Mine you can see; maybe yours is not so obvious. But we all have handicaps of some kind. The more important question is how we deal with them."

I'd winced when I'd first heard that on tape. While it encouraged me to see that she'd internalized the lessons I'd tried to instill in her over the years (I'm afraid I could hear the echo of my own words in her answer), I wasn't sure how that particular judge would react to her candor. As it turned out, that man became one of Heather's staunchest supporters. But I didn't know that yet, and I wondered and worried what curve the judges might have thrown Heather that second year.

It turns out, I learned later, that Heather had indeed felt her precompetition interview didn't go very well. One of the judges looked down at her notes while she asked her question and another had a mustache; Heather had difficulty understanding both of them. But what had upset Heather most was her own answer to a question she thought she clearly did understand.

One of the judges asked, "How many people are there in your family, Heather?"

"Oh. . . ." she hesitated. "I don't know exactly. Thirty. Maybe forty."

"I was so embarrassed!" Heather told me later. "I did not realize at first that he was asking about brothers or sisters. I was including my grandparents, aunts, uncles, and all my cousins."

"I don't think you have any reason to feel embarrassed," I told her. "In fact, I think you answered that question the way God intended it to be answered, because he's given you a very big family of people who care about you."

But that chance for reassurance didn't come until later. During pageant week itself I could only wonder what had happened in the interview and worry about what little I'd heard. And of course I prayed for Heather and hoped the little one-a-day gifts Stephanie and I had sent along would help bolster her spirits.

I liked the figure of Sebastian Crab (from Disney's *The Little Mermaid*) that we sent on the day of her swimsuit competition and the note that reminded Heather (who was never a morning person): "Don't be crabby today." But my favorite gift, because I knew it would make Heather laugh, was one of those ugly little plastic troll figures with the wild fluorescent hair. I'd carefully rolled the doll's bright red tresses into a tiny bun on top of its head and attached a little sign that said: "Troll Hair Patrol: Wear it up!"

We had a bigger entourage of friends and family than ever before that year. They all came all four nights. And we weren't the only ones who thought Heather would win.

The grapevine was buzzing all week. Saturday morning at home I received a phone call from a good friend who had volunteered to work during the pageant. She'd overheard backstage talk that some insiders were saying Heather Whitestone could not win because she was deaf. "I'm not calling to upset you," she said, "but I wanted you to be prepared because I know a lot of people consider Heather the favorite."

"It's okay. It's in the Lord's hands now," I said with a lot more confidence and faith than I really felt.

To tell the truth, I was seething inside. That night, when Heather was named first runner-up again, I felt intensely frustrated and angry with the whole pageant system. Ironically, she had lost to Kalyn Chapman, the same girl who'd been her first runner-up at Miss Point Mallard the summer before.

I knew Heather well enough to tell how terribly disappointed she was. But she maintained her composure through all the usual post-pageant congratulations and picture taking. It wasn't until she came out into the auditorium itself to talk to her personal throng of well-wishers that she finally broke down and burst into tears. I'd never seen her so devastated.

"I thought you should have won," I told her. "But since you didn't, we will just have to believe it wasn't God's timing. If you want to try again next year, I'm with you. If you don't, fine. Either way," I assured her, "it will be your decision."

After everyone else had gone, while Stephanie and I waited for Heather to gather the last of her things from backstage, our friends Jim and Vicky Davis, who'd been so supportive and encouraging all year, walked up. "Do you think she'll go again?" Vicky asked. "She shouldn't give up!"

"To tell you the truth, Vicky, I don't know," I replied. "I'll certainly back her if she decides to try next year. But I've never seen her this discouraged. So I don't have any idea what she will decide to do."

Stephanie made the depressing ride home with Heather and me that night back to my parents' house, where all our out-of-town family and friends were gathered. After that rather lifeless party finally broke up and the two of us were headed home, Heather noticed the boxes of fresh-baked donuts (her favorites) I'd bought earlier in anticipation of a celebratory breakfast. "Those look wonderful," Heather told me. So when the two of us finally got home we tried to raise our spirits to an all-time sugar high as we pigged out on Krispy-Kremes and Coca-Colas while watching a video of the Carolyn Sapp story. (Carolyn, the 1992 Miss America, didn't win her Miss Hawaii state competition until her fourth try. In previous years, she came in fourth and twice was first runner-up.)

When the movie ended sometime before dawn, Heather jokingly said, "If I go out again, I'll have to write Carolyn a letter to let her know she won't be the longest running first runner-up in history much longer. I may be."

We were so tired we had to laugh.

A few weeks later the Davises approached me again. "Has she decided yet?"

When I told them she hadn't, they said, "We have an idea we'd like to propose. We think that for Heather to have a chance at becoming Miss Alabama, the board is going to have to get to know her—to see her outside the competitive setting and realize she can handle the job.

"We've talked about it, and we'd like to pay her way to the Miss America Pageant in Atlantic City in September as part of the official Miss Alabama delegation. Not only will that give the right people a chance to get to know Heather better, it'll give her a chance to see what goes on at the national level. Maybe that will help her make up her mind about next year."

I thanked Jim and Vicky. And when I told Heather about their generous offer, she agreed to go.

Stephanie and I had a grand total of $400 left in our craft-house account. She thought I should take the money and accompany Heather to New Jersey. I told her, "We've been in this together so far. Let's both go with Heather." So Stephanie paid her plane fare. I paid mine. And we liquidated the remains from our joint business venture to spend on meals, pageant tickets, and our share of Heather's hotel room.

A lot of encouraging things happened on that trip—starting Thursday afternoon when we sat near several members of the Alabama delegation in that cavernous convention center. As we all watched the pageant rehearsal action unfolding on stage, a man with a distinctive Texas accent walked up to ask Heather if she happened to remember him. She said she did; he'd been the judge for her first Miss Alabama pageant the year before. There in front of several members of the Miss Alabama board, this former pageant judge—the same one who'd asked her about her handicap—told Heather he hoped that she would try out for Miss Alabama again because he thought she had the potential to become Miss America one day.

There was also a reporter there looking for behind-the-scenes stories from the pageant. He thought it interesting that Heather was there to support the girl who had beaten her out in the state pageant and was even more intrigued to learn that Heather was deaf. He interviewed her on the spot and wrote a nice human interest feature that appeared in the New Jersey papers the next day.

That made Heather feel good. So did the fact that people stopped us everywhere we went in Atlantic City those next few days to ask if Heather was one of the contestants. "No," she'd tell them. "I'm just here to watch the pageant as part of the delegation supporting Miss Alabama, Kalyn Chapman."

Then there was the Atlantic City oddsmaker, a personal acquaintance of one of the Miss Alabama board members, who leaned over at one point to whisper to his friend. "I tell you what," he said, nodding toward Heather. "You bring that one back next year, and you'll have yourself a Miss America."

I don't know how much any of this influenced anyone. I'm sure the Miss Alabama officials got to see Heather in a different light on that trip. But whether that had the positive impact Vicky and Jim hoped for is impossible to say. I do know that Heather, Stephanie, and I had an absolute blast.

By Saturday morning, after three nights of preliminaries and the big traditional, Friday night parade, the consensus in the Alabama delegation was that Kalyn had made a very good showing. We all assumed she'd earned a spot among the ten semi-finalists and maybe even had a shot at the crown.

But the possibility that Kalyn would become Miss America really made Heather feel torn. Part of her was rooting for her friend. But I knew that wasn't the way she wanted to become Miss Alabama! As first runner-up to Miss Alabama, Heather would be required to take over Kalyn's duties for the coming year if Kalyn were crowned Miss America. And that would make Heather, as reigning Miss Alabama, ineligible for the next year's state and national pageants.

"We've said all along that we had to trust the Lord and his timing," I told her.

"I know," Heather said, "but it really bothers me to feel this way. Do you think you and Stephanie could pray with me about it just before we go to the pageant tonight? That whatever happens, the Lord will give us peace about it?"

Stephanie and I agreed that would be a great idea.

But in the hurry and hubbub of dressing in time to get to our seats early that night, we forgot all about our planned prayer time until we were actually hurrying through one of the lobbies of Caesar's Palace.

"Uh-oh!" Heather stopped suddenly in her tracks. "We forgot to pray!"

None of us wanted to walk all the way back to our room. I looked around that crowded hotel and thought, *This is not what you'd call an inconspicuous place for a prayer meeting—even a short one.*

"We'll have to find some place we can stop on our way to the convention center," Stephanie said. And we set out walking again.

Constant streams of people flowed up and down the corridor outside the main casino hall. *No quiet spot here either.*

Just then we passed a small gardenlike alcove, set off from the hotel lobby and shops by a cluster of potted greenery. I grabbed Heather's arm. "Over here," I nodded, and the three of us slipped out of the crowded walkway into the quiet sanctuary of this little corner garden. *Perfect.* We could stand facing the garden as if we were admiring the plants and flowers, and maybe no one would even notice us.

"Why don't you pray for Heather, Steph?" I suggested. When she nodded agreement, we held hands, I closed my eyes, and Stephanie began to pray. I don't remember everything she said, but the prayer wasn't particularly long. She thanked the Lord for the chance we had to make this trip together, the good time we'd had, and for all the blessings he had bestowed on our family. She thanked the Lord for Heather, the way he had worked in her life over the years. She also asked that whatever happened at the pageant tonight, that the Lord would help Heather accept and deal with it. When she finished and we opened our eyes, Stephanie almost screamed.

There, standing less than six inches away and staring intently into Stephanie's face, was a dark-haired man wearing an exquisitely tailored suit, with several gold chains draped around his neck. I glanced quickly at Heather, who was obviously trying not to laugh at our surprise. Since she'd had her eyes open during the prayer in order to read

Stephanie's lips, she'd seen the man walk up and had been waiting with bated breath to see how her aunt and mother were going to react.

I thought my sister showed amazing restraint not to have screamed. But she did gasp. The man politely apologized and then startled us further by saying to Stephanie, "That was beautiful. Would you please pray for me, too?"

Stephanie looked at me in a panic. I shrugged. *What else can we do?* Fifteen feet away, over by the bushes, stood two burly fellows who looked like bodyguards. When my eyes caught Heather's, I could tell she was on the verge of cracking up.

"What exactly did you want me to pray about?" Stephanie was asking the man. "If you want me to pray that you'll win big at the tables tonight, I can't do that."

"That's okay," the man replied. "That doesn't matter. Just pray. No one has ever prayed for me before."

"Okay," Stephanie agreed. "We'll pray for you." So we all bowed our heads and Stephanie prayed again, as short a prayer as she dared for this man we knew nothing about—not even his name. (I wondered from the look of him whether he was some mafia don or a South American drug lord, come to Atlantic City to gamble away his ill-gotten gains; we would never know.)

By the time Stephanie finished praying and we opened our eyes a second time, I realized we'd drawn quite a bit of attention to our "quiet little corner" of Caesar's Palace. *So much for trying to be inconspicuous!*

"You could have warned us!" Stephanie and I scolded Heather as we hurried on toward the convention center. "That guy nearly scared us to death!"

"I couldn't say anything, Aunt Stephanie," Heather protested. "You were praying."

"You could have coughed or something," Stephanie told her.

Heather was still laughing when we got to our seats.

Kalyn Chapman did make the semi-finals that night. But she wasn't named as one of the five finalists. Kimberly Aiken of Columbia, South Carolina, was crowned Miss America 1994.

Membership in the official Miss Alabama delegation gave us backstage privileges. So when most of the crowd filed out the back of the auditorium, we headed upstairs to a ballroom jammed with friends and fans anxiously awaiting their first post-pageant look at the new Miss

America. I think it was well after midnight before Kim finally arrived for a brief appearance and a very short victory speech.

When we'd finally wormed our way through the mob scene and out of the ballroom, Heather asked if we could go back down to the convention hall for "one more look." Stephanie and I nodded and tagged along.

The cameras and the crowd were all gone. The massive hall was empty by this time, except for a small crew of workmen dismantling the sets and readying the stage for the next big event.

"Do you think they'd let me walk out on the runway?" Heather wondered.

"You'll never know unless you ask," I told her.

So she walked up the stage steps and over to one of the crew. "Is it okay if I walk out on the runway?" she asked.

The guy looked up and nodded. "Sure, why not?"

"Is it okay if my mother goes with me?"

I saw the workman give a shrug. "What do I care?"

Heather motioned for me to join her. "Come on, Steph. Go with me," I said to my sister.

"You go on. I think I'll just watch from here."

As I made my way up onto the stage and looked down that famous runway my first thought was, *It's slick as glass. I hope I don't fall!*

But then Heather took my arm and we walked together down that long shiny runway in that empty convention center. First we waved down at Stephanie (who was giving us a singular standing ovation). Then we began waving out at thousands of empty seats as if they were full of screaming, adoring fans.

I'm sure those workmen on stage, if they noticed us at all, must have been thinking, *Those people really need to get a life.*

But afterwards Heather told me it was at that moment, walking down the runway in that darkened Atlantic City Convention Center, that she finally made up her mind. *I'll give it one more chance. I'm going to commit this year to do whatever it takes to come back here as a contestant in the Miss America Pageant next year.*

CHAPTER 20
The Unspoken Question

When we came home from Atlantic City and Heather told me she'd made up her mind to enter Miss Alabama again, we immediately checked out the list of upcoming local pageants. Among the upcoming "open" competitions (meaning it didn't have any residency or enrollment requirements) was the Miss Cullman Area Pageant. The timing would be right, and Cullman was only an hour north of Birmingham, so we quickly filled out and sent in Heather's official entry forms.

Dancing again to "Via Dolorosa," Heather took the top talent award for her fifth straight pageant. And when the winner was announced, Heather was crowned by Leigh Sherer, the outgoing Miss Cullman Area whom Heather had crowned as the new Miss Point Mallard over the Fourth of July, when Heather's previous reign had come to an end.

With the Miss Cullman Area title already in hand that fall of 1993, we once again had the better part of a year to get ready for our third Miss Alabama Pageant the following summer. And since Heather had decided to make this an all-or-nothing year, one of the first things we did was sit down with the support team to do a detailed evaluation and analysis of

Heather's complete pageant history. Could we see any weaknesses we needed to correct? Any refinements we might want to make?

We'd changed Heather's music once; we saw no need to do that again. But we planned to alter the dance costume this year. And Monica wanted to work with Heather on more technically and physically demanding steps to add excitement to the dance routine.

The Miss Alabama Pageant decided to change swimsuits that year. Contestants could choose from four different styles in five or six different colors. That was not a major change.

We felt better than ever about the evening gown portion of the competition since we'd learned we could rent (for $250 to $300 a wearing) Heather's evening dresses instead of paying a thousand or two thousand apiece to purchase them outright. The previous winter, a few months prior to her second Miss Alabama Pageant, Heather and a few other state pageant contestants worked a charity fashion show for Ann Northington, a remarkably gifted Alabama designer who specializes in one-of-a-kind creations. Ann and Heather really hit it off; Heather called her "my fairy godmother" because, as she put it, "Wearing Ann's gowns always makes me feel so wonderful—like Cinderella going to the ball."

Ann had already begun work on designing the gowns that Heather would wear for the Miss Alabama Pageant the following summer, so we felt that we had the evening gown segment of the competition well covered.

The only real weakness that we saw when we considered Heather's total pageant package was the community service requirement. We felt that we'd never been able to create a clear connection between Heather's volunteer work and her stated platform. We thought that if we could make those two things tie together somehow, we might strengthen Heather's showing in both areas.

The first year we'd been so rushed between the Miss JSU Pageant and the Miss Alabama Pageant that we had no choice but to count something Heather had already done as her community service. So we had listed the freshman spring break trip she took to St. Louis with her Baptist Campus Ministry fellowship group to work with a homeless shelter and refurbish an inner-city church.

For her community service requirement the second year, we'd used her yearlong work with "Silent Expressions," an organization that Heather had revived, managed, and directed as a student outreach of Jacksonville State University. This music group, made up of hearing and deaf collegians, performed motivational and inspirational programs promoting better communication and self-esteem among elementary, middle, and high school age students (both hearing and deaf, in public and private schools) throughout the eastern part of the state. Heather saw it as a way to help bridge the gap between the hearing and deaf worlds. But even though the basic thrust of Silent Expressions paralleled Heather's platform on the importance of self-esteem, there was no clear integration of themes.

After her year leading Silent Expressions, Heather said she thought she'd rather concentrate her community service efforts on younger children. She felt that too many of the teenagers she'd encountered had already solidly established their basic self-image—whether good or bad. There seemed a lot better chance to impact the lives of younger kids.

I thought Heather's observations were accurate. "But you know," I told her, "in education we're always taught that the younger the group you're working with, the more you need something concrete to get across your lesson. So if you want to design a program for younger kids, you're going to have to come up with some tangible idea that will help them relate to and remember your message."

For a time Heather tried to think of some way she could incorporate rainbows to illustrate her themes. Nothing seemed to click. Finally I said, "Why don't we approach this from the opposite direction? Try listing the basic points you want to make for kids about achieving success and building self-esteem. Then we'll work backwards from there to see if we come up with something."

So that's what she did. When Stephanie, Stacey (on the phone long distance), and I helped Heather boil her message down to five main points, we thought, *A star has five points!* And that's how we ended up with Heather's STARS program: **S**uccess **T**hrough **A**ction and **R**ealization of your dream**S**. In her program for kids she emphasized one main point for each of the five points in a star:

1. Have a positive attitude.
2. Believe in your dreams.
3. Be willing to work very hard.
4. Be honest with yourself; face your weaknesses and obstacles.
5. Build a support team you can depend on.

These lessons all grew out of, and were illustrated by, Heather's own life experience. She could deliver this advice with conviction and power because she'd seen it work. The entire program was a summary of the strategy our whole family had used to help her overcome her obstacles to achieve success in life against incredible odds.

When we ran the new outline of Heather's platform past our friend Vicky Davis, she offered Green Valley Elementary (where Vicky is principal) as a pilot school where Heather could refine the program. "It sounds perfect as a values unit for any grade level," she told Heather. "Let's give it a try."

We came up with a STARS booklet (my brother Mike and his wife, Lois, helped us design and lay it out on his computer one weekend), which Heather could hand out to older elementary students as a follow-up reinforcement of her message. Then Vicky remembered that her school had a huge box of plastic sheriff's stars left over from some long-forgotten occasion. "If we spray paint those badges, Heather could use them as STARS pins—something concrete and memorable to hand out to kindergartners or first graders who are too young to appreciate her booklet," Vicky suggested.

We all thought that was a great idea, so Heather went over to Vicky and Jim's one evening to paint those stars. The night grew so late they were all getting tired and acting a little silly. Vicky was the one who held up a freshly painted gold star in front of each eye like a zany mask and started saying, "Glow, Heather, glow." They all laughed. But then they decided that might work somehow. After all, STARS shine, STARS glow.

That's how "Glow, Heather, glow!" became something of a slogan, a rallying cry. The students of Green Valley Elementary used the slogan on posters and banners throughout their school to welcome Heather, show their support for her Miss Alabama goal, and remind themselves of the STARS program's message. The Green Valley kids not only adopted Heather as part of a mutual support team that year (part of her point #5), they responded so enthusiastically to Heather's message that she soon had offers to expand the program to other schools in our area and up around Cullman. So the decision to "go younger" with Heather's youth motivation program of community service paid off in many ways. Heather learned that she loved working with kids, and the kids certainly loved her.

One other aspect of Heather's pageant strategy concerned us that year: the interview. We weren't concerned as much with the onstage questioning, because there was only so much you could do to prepare for such an unpredictable, impromptu thing. We were more concerned with how Heather might improve her in-depth, offstage interview conducted by the judges early during pageant week. Not only did those pre-pageant interviews pose a real challenge to Heather's communication skills (with five different judges talking, she often found it tough to understand their questions), but the judges themselves seemed awkward and uncertain about what to do when Heather didn't understand a question. Watching the videotapes from her first two Miss Alabama competitions, we noticed several times when Heather had misunderstood a question, or part of a question, but the judges had simply allowed her to answer what she thought they had asked. They never tried to clarify for her what they'd really wanted to know. The judges were obviously trying to be considerate and cut Heather a little slack in allowing for the fact that she hadn't heard everything they said. But we thought that the fact that they felt the need to "help" her in that way probably hurt Heather's scores in the long run. We just didn't know how to solve the problem.

Some people we'd encountered during the course of Heather's pageant experience had adamantly advised us never to mention the fact that she was deaf. "But she is!" we said. "We can't pretend she's not. This isn't a handicap that goes away when you ignore it." We'd been open about Heather's hearing impairment (Point #4: We'd faced that obstacle) all her life. We weren't about to change our philosophy now.

So the second year she'd competed in Miss Alabama we'd attempted to confront the issue head-on. She carried a small pad of paper and a pencil into her interview with her so that when she had trouble understanding a question, she could relieve any awkwardness simply by handing the pad to that judge and saying something like: "I'm sorry, but my hearing loss makes it difficult sometimes to catch everything that is said in a room like this. But I want to answer as many questions as possible. If you'd write that one down for me, it might save us all a little time." Still, we felt some things slipped by Heather that the judges just let go.

It was Jim and Vicky Davis's son-in-law, Brandon Blankenship, who finally helped us pinpoint the problem we needed to attack. The Davis's original connection with pageants had been through their daughter, Donna Lee, who had competed in Miss Alabama herself a few years before Heather. Donna Lee was now a frequent volunteer with Miss Alabama; so their whole family was active in, and very familiar with, the process and the people involved in the pageant scene.

Brandon approached us soon after Heather made her decision to pursue the Miss Alabama title a third year. "I don't know how you're going to take this," he said. "You know we're all fans and supporters of Heather. But I think there's one problem that has to be solved before she will ever be Miss Alabama. And that's the interview with the pageant judges."

We told Brandon we'd been wrestling with the problem for two years already. We just didn't know how to solve the problem.

He told us he felt the underlying problem wasn't the questions the judges asked. "The real hurdle for Heather is the one question they don't ask! And never will ask. In fact, I can't imagine even the meanest, ugliest pageant judge in the world ever asking it. But I know the question is always there in every pageant Heather enters. It's on the mind of every judge. And until Heather can answer that question to their satisfaction, I don't think she will ever win at the state or national level. And that question is this: Can a deaf girl handle the responsibilities of a Miss Alabama? Or a Miss America?

"I certainly believe Heather can. But she has to convince the judges first. To do that, she's first going to have to find a way to address that question no one wants to ask."

We all knew in our hearts that Brandon had indeed pinpointed the problem. Yet we still didn't know the best way to approach it. We thought and talked about it off and on all year.

Not that we didn't have other things going on in our lives besides pageant plans. I still had a teaching job that kept me busy. And Heather had her toughest year of college yet—by far.

Back before Heather had made up her mind to take another run at Miss Alabama, she'd decided to transfer to the University of Montevallo for that junior year. While she'd been very happy at JSU, one of Heather's scholarship prizes as talent winner in the Miss Alabama Pageant had been a full, four-year tuition package to Montevallo. Part of our thinking, in addition to the very appealing monetary factor, was that the school's proximity to Birmingham (only a thirty-minute drive south of the city) would enable Heather to better keep up her private dance lessons with Monica during the week as well as on Saturdays.

My brother Mike, who'd graduated from Montevallo, and my dad visited the school with Heather when we first talked about the possibility of her transferring there. The admissions people told them about their deaf-support program, and they had all been impressed by the sign-language interpreter supplied for their tour of the campus.

So Heather and I were both surprised when the transfer didn't turn out as well as we'd anticipated. While Montevallo did have a support program for its hearing impaired students, the help offered there just didn't seem to meet Heather's needs the way JSU's resources had. The only way we could figure out for her to fulfill the requirements of one of her lit courses was for me to go with Heather to the play performances she was assigned to attend and critique; that way I could take notes and explain what was happening on stage in order for her to have enough information to write up her reports. She struggled so much to keep up with a number of classes that, for the first time since her junior year of high school, Stephanie and I found ourselves transcribing or at least taking notes for Heather from tapes of many of her class lectures. Heather and I had to work a lot harder to survive that year academically without letting her grades slip too badly.

But it wasn't so much the academic workload that concerned me (we'd faced that before) as it was the unprecedented pressure I was feeling about my personal finances. I thanked the Lord for Heather's free tuition and for the ongoing funds we received from the State Department of Rehabilitation Services to help with the cost of room and board, because I had reached the very end of my own financial rope with last year's pageant expenses. The credit cards were all at their limits. I still had a long list of expected expenses for the upcoming Miss Alabama Pageant. And if Heather won that, who knew how much it would cost to get her ready for Miss America?

It seemed to me the best option, my only option really, was to sell my house. I could use what equity I had to pay off some of my debts and maybe have enough room left under my credit card limit to cover some upcoming pageant expenses. I told myself, *You don't really need a house. It's just you and Heather now. And she's away at school most of the time. An apartment would suit you better. Less upkeep. No maintenance. Why, this isn't so much of a sacrifice as it is a smart move!* That's what I told everyone, including Heather, when I put my house up for sale that spring.

Fortunately, our bigger pageant-related problem proved far simpler to solve than we could ever have hoped. When we received the usual thick information/application packet from the state pageant office in April, we learned there had been a procedural change in the judges' interview. On previous interviews, Heather had been expected to walk into the room, state her name, and immediately begin fielding whatever questions the judges had for her. This year, for the first time, each contestant was given two minutes to make an opening statement during which time she could say whatever she wanted to say before the formal questioning began.

We knew immediately that those two minutes would provide the chance we needed for Heather to address that crucial question none of the judges wanted to ask. But what exactly should Heather say? We prayed and talked and thought about that question constantly until pageant week.

But we didn't have many spare moments between packing to move (the house had sold), finishing out another school year, attending another pageant workshop weekend, and making all the other final, frantic preparations for the big, annual state-level competition. The last hurdle came the Sunday afternoon before pageant week: The zipper broke on the white evening dress Heather was to wear for the pageant competition. Finally, after some frantic phone calls, we found a friend of Mom's who was able to make the last-minute repairs.

Despite all that, when Monday morning came and we left our new apartment to drop Heather off at the contestants' dorm, I think we both felt as confident and ready as we could possibly be. *This is it!*

We never said it out loud. But we were both realistic enough to know this was probably Heather's last chance at winning Miss Alabama. And her last shot at her Miss America dream.

Early that week Heather had her interview with the judges. When she walked into the room, this is what she said:

"I am Heather Whitestone, Miss Cullman Area. When I was eighteen months old, I became very ill. The medicine given to me to save my life left me profoundly deaf. My mother was told that a normal life for me would be impossible. For example, that I'd never drive a car or go to a public school. But thank goodness the word *impossible* is not in my family's vocabulary. On Wednesday night you will see the results of believing in your dream. Now it's my turn to take all my resources and energies to bring about my dreams.

"I want to be Miss America, and I want to graduate from college. But I know each of you has a question in mind, and I want to answer it for you right now: Can a profoundly deaf woman fulfill the duties of Miss Alabama and Miss America? To this I say, yes. I can do it! Because I realize that everything is possible with God's help. I don't see my deafness as an obstacle, but as an opportunity for creative thinking. My STARS program has made it possible for me to go into elementary schools to express this message.

"I do want you to know that lipreading at its very best will only give me about fifty percent of what you say. So I may repeat the question just to make sure I understand. Or I may ask you to write it down to save time.

"I'm excited about our interview. So let's begin."

Of course we had no idea what would happen after Heather's opening statement. But we felt that the introduction would let the judges know where Heather was coming from and answer any unasked questions and doubts they might hold against her.

This year I didn't hear the kind of backstage gossip I'd heard before. I could only watch what happened on stage during preliminaries and hope Heather's spirits stayed up. Stephanie and I had sent our traditional one-a-day surprises for Heather to open.

I knew she'd have the biggest surprise and laugh on Thursday when she opened her gift to find that little troll with the red hair bun again. I'd noticed Heather had thrown the doll in the trash after our pre-move garage sale. But I'd saved it from its terrible landfill fate with the thought of recycling it one more time for this year's state pageant. I sent it along with a little sign that said, "Just when you thought it was safe to let your hair down, the hair patrol is back. Keep it up!"

For Saturday, knowing Heather was planning to wear her favorite Ann Northington gown in the final that evening, I'd wrapped a special little gift. I'd found a beautiful glass miniature of a coach and horses. With it I sent a note: "Like Cinderella, may all your dreams come true tonight, Heather. Love, Mom."

I didn't know about Heather, but I was a nervous wreck that night for the Miss Alabama Pageant finals. Knowing this was possibly Heather's last chance multiplied the pressure for me. None of the previous pageants could even begin to compare.

I don't think I had ever been more excited in my life than when I found out that Heather had won Miss Alabama 1994. I know I'd never been more relieved.

However, because of an Alabama state pageant tradition, I didn't actually hear the announcement. I wasn't even there to see my daughter crowned Miss Alabama.

Unlike the Miss America Pageant where there are only five finalists, the Miss Alabama Pageant has ten. Those ten girls are lined up onstage at the end, along with all the other contestants. And the emcee begins: "Fourth runner-up, Miss. . . ." When the applause dies down, "Third runner-up. . . ." And so on.

The moment the first runner-up is announced, a pageant officer who has slipped into the audience literally grabs the parents of the about-to-be-announced winner and whisks them out of the auditorium. So the last part of the pageant I experienced that night was the voice of the emcee announcing, "First runner-up, Miss Amie Beth Dickinson."

At that moment the exit door nearest my seat opened, and a pageant official pulled me out of my seat. Of course all the family and friends around me, seeing what was happening, turned into a crying, cheering mob. They were screaming, "It's Heather! It's Heather!" even before the final word came from the stage.

But I was long gone when the big moment came. I wasn't there to witness the audience's reaction or my daughter's emotional reaction. I never got to see Heather's victory walk across that stage with the Miss Alabama crown on her head. I could only imagine it all while being escorted quickly down a deserted stairwell and then around backstage. There behind the scenes, impatiently waiting for my chance to hug and congratulate my daughter (an opportunity which wouldn't come until later at the official reception), it hit me. *She did it! Heather really did it!*

With tears of joy streaming down my face, I thought to myself, *It's all been worth it.*

I had no idea that in the weeks ahead I would begin to wonder if it had been.

CHAPTER 21

A Dream Come True

The family saw Heather for only a few minutes at the big post-pageant reception. I got a little extra time with her when we went upstairs in the Wright Center for a quick tour of the Samford University guest apartment where she would be staying that next week. She and the team of Miss Alabama officials would use that time to take care of all the application business for the Miss America Pageant in Atlantic City in September.

The week after that, Heather began a whirlwind schedule of Miss Alabama appearances throughout the state. I could only imagine how thrilling all this must be for Heather; it was exciting for me just to see her picture in the papers or to hear about her on the radio. She kept so busy to start with I hardly even got to talk with her on the phone.

I was so excited for Heather that first couple of weeks that our lack of contact didn't bother me too much. But as the weeks dragged on, I began to feel that maybe my being ushered out so quickly at the end of the Miss Alabama Pageant had been a precursor of things to come. By this time it seemed clear to me that I was being very effectively shut out of my daughter's life.

Evidently Miss Alabama officials were feeding Heather the "baby bird in the nest" analogy: "There comes a time when a mama bird shoves the baby bird out of the nest. You're ready to fly on your own now, Heather. You need to leave that nest and break free of your family." They even told her, "Miss America is looking for independent young women," implying that Heather could never win that crown if she came across as too dependent on her family.

The trouble was, the people telling Heather all this didn't know my daughter. A veteran pageant volunteer told me about a conversation she had with a Miss Alabama official who complained in an exasperated tone, "I'm getting sick and tired of telling Heather Whitestone something over and over again and not having her do it!"

"You know," my volunteer friend replied, "if you wrote down what you wanted Heather to do, you wouldn't have that problem. Heather *is* deaf. And she doesn't hear nearly as much as you might think she does because she covers for it so well."

According to my friend, the official had just rolled her eyes at that suggestion. Whether the woman thought the advice ridiculous or was simply expressing her frustration with having to cope with Heather's deafness, I'll never know. Either way, that incident worried me.

On very rare occasions, the family was given a chance for brief visits with Heather. I remember one visit distinctly.

Mom, Dad, Stephanie, Trey, and I had been invited to share a Sunday dinner with Heather and one of her chaperones. Our time began pleasantly enough as we chatted before the meal. But when we began to ask Heather such natural questions as "How are your dance workouts going?" "What shopping have you done for clothes?" or "Have you started preparing for the interview yet?" it became very clear that someone had told Heather that any discussion of her Miss America plans was taboo. The more times Heather responded, "I don't want to talk about it," "I can't discuss this," or "I was told not to say anything about that," the more irritated I became.

But the topper came at the end of the dinner. When Heather mispronounced a word, Stephanie, instinctively and very casually, stopped and corrected Heather, just as our family had corrected her speech all of her life.

The chaperone suddenly became indignant. "Enough with the English lessons!" she admonished Stephanie. "Let's have dessert!"

218

I very slowly and deliberately pushed my plate back away from the edge of the table. Stephanie said later, "It was like you were clearing the field for battle."

There was no battle, however. Although I would have liked to have said a few choice words at that point, I didn't. A few minutes later, after we'd finished what turned out to be a very strained dessert time, we said our polite good-byes.

That encounter confirmed for me what my mother's instinct had been telling me for weeks: *Something is very wrong here!*

Now I was more worried about Heather than ever. I knew the people who were "handling" her preparation for the Miss America Pageant didn't understand Heather or her needs. And they certainly didn't understand or appreciate the role her family had always played in her life. They seemed to view me and the rest of Heather's admittedly conspicuous and loyal entourage (comprised of grandparents, sisters, brothers-in-law, aunts, uncles, cousins, and friends—several of whom were often furiously taking notes on anything and everything) more as a negative, interfering presence rather than a positive source of support for Heather.

We were never provided with an advance copy of her scheduled public appearances so we could inform family or friends when they could see her. Some events we did learn about we were strongly discouraged from attending.

People would naturally call to inquire about Heather. "She must be so excited! How is she feeling about the upcoming Miss America Pageant? What's she doing to prepare for that? Where is she this week?"

It got downright embarrassing always having to say, "I guess she is getting excited; I haven't talked to her about it this week. I expect she's doing a lot of dance rehearsal. I know she's out of town today and tomorrow, but I don't have any idea where."

During the last five weeks before Heather took off for Atlantic City (by way of Disney World and a big week there with all the other Miss America contestants) I was not allowed to see Heather even once. I was not told what outfits the Miss Alabama board had chosen for her to wear at the national pageant. I wasn't even allowed to help Heather pack for pageant week or see her off at the airport.

Looking back now, what hurts most is that we have no memories to share of that time. My family and I have many wonderful memories we've shared with Heather over the years, including many fond recollections from Heather's pageant experiences. But from the three months between the state pageant in June and the national pageant in September, her entire reign as Miss Alabama, there are no such recollections. After sharing Heather's dream for so long, after a lifetime of pursuing goals together, as mother and daughter and as a family, we were robbed of the chance to share any of the planning, the excitement, or the anticipation of those last three months—the last leg of Heather's remarkable journey toward her ultimate dream. What should have been the most wonderful, rewarding, and happy time in our lives was instead an emotion-wrought period of pain, separation, and worry.

I worried about Heather's health. I knew the summerlong demands of her Miss Alabama schedule had exhausted her. She'd been promised days off she never got. She sometimes made so many appearances in a day that she couldn't finish practicing her dance routine until 10 or 11 at night.

I also worried as much, if not more, about her emotional well-being. How were her spirits? She could always put on a good front for strangers, and the people around her now were almost all strangers. They couldn't know how she really felt. How would she react when she had to go into her first pageant without her usual support group? Who would encourage her? Who would even know when she needed encouraging?

I worried so much about so many things that I lost thirty pounds over those three months—even more than I'd lost in the emotionally devastating aftermath of my divorce. I could only hope things would get better when we reached Atlantic City.

They did . . . and they didn't.

I had very serious questions about just how emotionally prepared Heather was for the Miss America competition. What I didn't realize at the time was that Heather's deafness had in effect shielded her from much of the anti-family messages and other negative attitudes being conveyed by the people around her. She knew there were tensions, of course. But she hadn't picked up on all the nuances and innuendos. Her hearing impairment actually proved an advantage, a natural cocoon, sheltering Heather from the air of tension and conflict that seemed so obvious to me all summer.

Only now, looking back, can I see how wonderfully God used not only Heather's personal strength of character, but also her "weakness" to keep her focused. Even in spite of the potentially devastating effect of having her established support system (#5 in her STARS program) suddenly and totally removed, Heather arrived in Atlantic City fully prepared to pursue her dream.

As things turned out, our time in Atlantic City was everything we'd hoped for. And more.

I had a terrific time creating many great memories with all the family and friends who helped make our time at the Miss America Pageant one of the most exciting and wonderful weeks of my life. What a crew we had: my parents; Stacey and her baby daughter, Tessa; Melissa and Tony; Stephanie and Trey; my sister Deborah and Heather's closest cousin, Holly; my brother Jim and his wife, Debbie; Jim's mother-in-law and his oldest son, Ben; Jim and Vicky Davis; Brandon and Donna Lee Blankenship; Heather's friend and former Miss Alabama, Teresa Strickland; along with a bunch of my teaching friends who took a week off from school to share this experience with me—Wayne, Martha, Charlotte, Tricia, Camille, and Annette. We created quite a stir wherever we went together—whether it was walking into a restaurant, climbing on a bus for one of the many Miss America-sponsored day trips, or just strolling down the beach in front of our hotel, the Trump Regency. And our "little group" was just a portion of the huge Alabama delegation (over 250 strong) who'd come to support Heather in her pursuit of the Miss America crown.

The Miss America preliminaries always begin on Tuesday evening of pageant week and run three straight nights. The contestants are subdivided into three groups (the Mu, Alpha, or Sigma groups named after the Miss America sorority), with each girl participating each night in one of the three main segments of the competition.

On Tuesday evening Heather and the rest of her Mu group appeared in the evening gown segment of the program, while the other two groups competed in their swimsuit and talent divisions. Since the results of the preliminary night's evening gown competition are never publicly announced (they are held as a secret wild card in the judges' balloting), we had no official measure as to how she did that Tuesday night. Of course, our unbiased group thought she was tops.

The first positive public indicator of Heather's chances came as a nice surprise Wednesday morning. I was climbing onto a bus with all the family and friends for a day trip to a nearby historical town when a Miss America volunteer caught up with me. She asked if I wanted to attend a special press conference and award ceremony announcing the "Fruit of the Loom Quality of Life Award," which is given to the top contestants in the area of community service. Heather had been named first runner-up in that competition and was to receive an award and $2,000. I skipped my family excursion to sit in the back of that press conference and watch proudly as Heather received her first individual recognition of the week.

Then Wednesday evening our entire group went crazy when Heather won the swimsuit preliminary. None of us had expected that.

By Thursday morning the buzz up and down the boardwalk was about Heather: how being first runner-up for the Quality of Life Award and then placing first in the swimsuit preliminary suddenly made her the girl to beat. The local newspapers were carrying human interest stories about the deaf contestant from Alabama. The odds makers made her a favorite.

The *Atlantic Press* featured the pageant with cover-to-cover reports all week. And since Heather seemed to get more than her share of coverage, my dad took it as his job each day to buy enough copies of the daily newspaper for everyone in our group. He even had a favorite little out-of-the-way newsstand that always seemed to have a big hot-off-the-press supply. By the end of the week, when the proprietor would see Dad walking up, he'd wave and automatically pull out a stack of twenty papers bundled and ready to go.

As much as we enjoyed the good press Heather received that week, we knew that what happened onstage was a lot more important. So of course we were all thrilled when Heather won her talent preliminary on Thursday night.

However, while having the unusual distinction of being a double preliminary winner (swimsuit and talent) definitely put Heather in the running for the crown, some veteran pageant observers warned us this could be a jinx. Half the time it had happened, they said, the double-preliminary winner had been named first runner-up on Saturday night.

I knew I'd be proud of Heather no matter what happened in the finals. So I told myself, *It doesn't matter.*

But it did. Heather's dream had always been to become Miss America, not first runner-up. I couldn't imagine the disappointment she'd have to deal with, the "if only" and "what if" questions she'd have to face if she came so close to the goal and fell one step short.

By Friday even Heather's family and friends were minor celebrities. Wherever we went in Atlantic City, people wanted to talk to us about Heather. Reporters left piles of phone messages requesting interviews. Television cameras cornered us in our hotel lobby. If it hadn't been for the fact that the last name of "Gray" on my pageant ID badge made it easier to slip unrecognized through the media lines, I'd have spent my entire week speaking into microphones.

The Miss America Organization (MAO) puts on a terrific and well-orchestrated show all week long. I think everyone in our group had an absolute ball.

The only damper on our wonderful week was my continuing frustration about Heather's isolation from her family. The mother of a former Miss Alabama had warned me ahead of time that the girls would have such an unbelievably grueling schedule all week that there would be precious little time for family to see them except in public onstage and in the crazy crush of the big ballroom reception after each night of preliminaries. So we didn't expect much contact with Heather.

But because this same mother had told me there would be one block of free time for girls to be with their families on Monday evening, most of our group flew in early Monday, a full day ahead of the competition, in anticipation of eating dinner and spending part of the evening with Heather. I'd called Heather's room as soon as we arrived in Atlantic City Monday afternoon to let Heather's chaperone know we were in and would meet them for dinner wherever they wanted to go. She told us she would tell Heather when she got back, but she never did. When our hungry gang finally got tired of waiting in our rooms and went in search of food, we saw many Miss America contestants wandering up and down the boardwalk with their families. But by the time Heather herself called to check on us after 9:00 that night, it was too late to make the cross-town connections for any family get-together.

When the family still hadn't had any face-to-face time with Heather by Friday afternoon, Stephanie cornered one of Miss Alabama's executive officers to complain. In tears she explained that Melissa (who was on leave that week from the Air Force and hadn't seen her sister in over a year) desperately wanted a little time to talk with Heather. The man simply shrugged, said he couldn't help, and told her to talk to the chaperone.

Stacey, Melissa, and I were finally given permission to come to Heather's hotel that evening after the Miss America parade. My brother Jim and his wife, Debbie, volunteered to drive us across town. But when we rang Heather's room that night, at first no one answered. But after I told the front desk who I was and that I knew Heather had to be somewhere in the hotel, one of the clerks finally got an answer. Minutes later the chaperone came down to the lobby to say Heather couldn't meet with us after all because Heather had insisted on practicing her dance routine with her instructor. She didn't know that earlier in the evening, I'd talked to Monica, who had told me that Heather didn't want to rehearse that evening.

When she realized I wasn't going to take no for an answer, the chaperone finally backed down and allowed us to go up to Heather's rehearsal room "for a few minutes." But if I hadn't been willing to bulldoze my way in, Melissa, Stacey, and I wouldn't have had any time with Heather all week.

As frustrated as I was by the Miss Alabama officials' treatment of our family, I kept my mouth shut all week. I didn't even protest the fact that Bill and his new wife had been allowed to purchase the "parent box" tickets allotted by the pageant to the parents of each state winner. I didn't want to create any controversy that might get back to Heather and upset her chances.

As things turned out, I can now look back and honestly say that the Lord worked everything out for the best. If I had been able to buy those special "parent" tickets, I would have watched the entire pageant seated with the families of the other contestants—all of whom were strangers to me. Instead, I got to spend four of the most exciting nights of my life surrounded and supported by people I love more than anyone else in the world. And I wouldn't give a million bucks for the memories we share from that 1995 Miss America Pageant.

By Saturday night there was such an incredible air of anticipation running through town, through the Alabama delegation, and especially through our family entourage, that the level of excitement was truly indescribable.

Minutes away from airtime, thousands of people were still milling around near their seats, looking for friends, making final predictions about who might win. From the stage, the audience was being briefed about what would happen during television commercial breaks and where to watch monitors for cues on when to applaud.

About that time I leaned over toward my dad and whispered, "I can't believe I'm not nervous. You know what an emotional wreck I always am the final night of a pageant. It makes me wonder if something is wrong."

My dad grinned back at me. "It's only because things haven't started yet. Don't worry. You'll be a basket case soon enough! The show's about to begin."

I grinned back at Dad and sat back upright in my seat thinking, *He's probably right.* I was sure I was about to be hit with the worst case of nerves in pageant history.

But that next moment the strangest sensation came over me. A river of warmth started at the top of my head and flowed all the way down through my body and out the tips of my toes. And in my mind, as clear as day, I heard a voice saying, *Relax and enjoy. Tonight is hers.*

I didn't breathe a word to anyone about what I'd just felt and heard. I didn't dare. Besides, there wasn't time.

That's when the orchestra began and the live pageant broadcast went on the air around the country. And around the world.

For most of those next three hours I was able to *relax and enjoy* that Miss America Pageant like no other pageant Heather had been in before. I grew a little anxious when it was time for that onstage interview with Regis Philbin, in front of those 13,000 people packed into the convention center and millions more clustered in front of television sets around the world. And then there was that nerve-wracking wait through the final commercial break and the slow announcement of fourth . . . third . . . and second runners-up.

To tell you the truth, I didn't exactly *relax* when Regis said, "And the new Miss America 1995, Miss Alabama, Heather Whitestone!"

But I certainly did *enjoy* those next few minutes as I watched my grown-up daughter take her long walk out on that same slick runway again, by herself this time, wearing a crown and waving to the world.

It wasn't until I'd been ushered behind stage and was sitting— with Stacey, Melissa, and my parents—in the back of Heather's first official press conference as Miss America that I remembered the message I'd received and thought, *Heather's dream* has *come true. Tonight* is *hers!*

The rest of that night was a wild and wonderful blur. Not until sometime between one and two in the morning, after a press conference and two or three public receptions, did Heather make it back to her new suite of rooms in Harrahs Hotel for an informal celebration just for family and MAO officials.

When our party wound down an hour or so later and everyone else had straggled out, Heather and I stepped into her bedroom to talk. When the door closed behind us and we were alone together for the first time in months, we looked at each other and exclaimed, almost in unison: "Do you believe this!"

As we sat together on the edge of her bed, Heather began to tell me about all the telegrams she'd gotten that week wishing her well, "Sandi Patty sent one! And I got another one from. . . ." and she excitedly ran off a long list.

When she wound down a little I decided I had to tell someone, so I said to her, "The strangest thing happened to me tonight, Heather. You know how I'm always such a nervous wreck before pageants?"

She nodded. She knew me well.

"Well, tonight I wasn't the least bit nervous. And just before we went on the air, this strange warmth just washed over me, and it was like I heard a voice saying, 'Relax and enjoy. Tonight is hers!'"

Heather got the strangest look on her face. "You're not going to believe this, Mother. But just before the pageant started tonight, I was standing backstage when this strange warmth passed through my body and I heard a voice say, 'Relax and dance for me tonight.' And I wasn't a bit nervous all night!"

I don't know how Heather felt at that moment. But as we looked at each other in silent awe, I felt chills running up and down my spine.

And it wasn't because my daughter had just been crowned Miss America.

CHAPTER 22

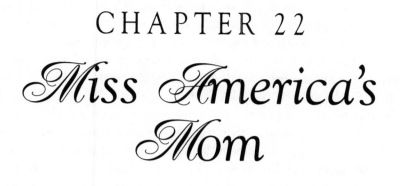

Miss America's Mom

❦

O f course, September 17, 1994, was merely the beginning of the fulfillment of Heather's Miss America dream.

By the end of the first month of her reign, Heather had already
been granted a personal audience with the President of the United
States, met twice with the First Lady, and launched her official platform
Anything Is Possible! in a Capitol Hill press conference, accompanied by
Alabama Senator Richard Shelby and the rest of the Alabama congres-
sional delegation. She interviewed with a host of national advocacy
groups—all appealing for her time, her voice, and her working knowledge on overcoming physical challenges. President Clinton appointed
Heather to his Executive Committee for Employment of People with
Disabilities, and she also met with the Secretary of Education to discuss
ways she could work with his department over the coming year.

Newsweek, U.S. News and World Report, the *New York Times*, and
a host of other national publications ran features on the new Miss America. And Heather crisscrossed the country several times making numerous
public appearances and speaking to a wide variety of audiences.

Things began to get really busy the second month.

The public response to Heather and her message of inspiration and hope has been absolutely mind-boggling. Within four months, the Miss America Organization (MAO) announced that Heather has been one of the most requested Miss Americas in pageant history.

By the time her year of service comes to an end, Heather will have traveled a staggering total of over 250,000 miles as Miss America. Thankfully, the staff at the MAO offices in New Jersey has been very good about sending me copies of her imposing itinerary. Heather travels to a different city every other day, and in each place, she meets with the press. At times, she has been known to have breakfast in one city, lunch in another, and dinner in still another. And she has only one day off a month. After reading through one of Heather's schedules, I often get an overpowering urge to lie down and take a long nap.

It's been very interesting for me to see how many of my family, friends, and acquaintances have expressed their concerns about the way I'm coping with all that has been required of Heather as Miss America. "How are you holding up, Daphne? It must be hard to let her go! Don't you miss her?"

I have found myself responding to these questions the same way I did when Heather went off to college. "Compared to the heart-wrenching experience of sending a vulnerable eleven-year-old daughter away to school for three whole years, Heather's year as Miss America, however hectic, seems like nothing."

Heather's a grown woman now. She's dreamed her whole life of becoming Miss America. I know she's ready. Sure I miss her, but it is only a year. And I know she'll be coming home when it's over—a better person for the experience. For I'm convinced Heather's Miss America adventure has been every bit as enriching and broadening, every bit as invaluable for her development, as those three turning-point years at CID.

In all those years that our family focused so much of our time and emotional energy on Heather's dream, I don't think I once stopped to imagine what life would be like as Miss America's mom. To be so suddenly thrust into the public eye has certainly been an eye-opening, and not altogether positive, growth experience for me as well.

Among the first lessons I learned was that it only takes one little misquote to create a major big-time controversy. During interviews at the Miss America Pageant, when asked about the cause of Heather's deafness, she and I had explained: At the age of eighteen months, shortly after her DPT shots, Heather became very sick with a fever. (We never did know whether or not there was any connection there.) While she was hospitalized, Heather became deathly ill, and the medication given to save her life left her profoundly deaf.

Evidently at least one reporter's story omitted any mention of medication, and that report led to follow-up stories all over the country which "informed" readers that the new Miss America and her mother said she became deaf "as the result of a DPT shot."

Heather and I both tried to refute that story immediately. We repeatedly explained that we had never said that a DPT shot caused Heather's deafness; we never believed it did. But the damage had already been done.

Routine vaccinations declined so drastically in the following week that public health officials across the country sounded an alarm. The American Academy of Pediatrics even issued a statement from the pediatricians who originally treated Heather, saying the DPT shot had nothing to do with her hearing impairment. I was recruited to make public service announcements clarifying the issue and endorsing childhood vaccinations. Then we began hearing from the anti-vaccination lobby, which accused me of selling out to the medical establishment by changing our story.

For months, I received angry mail from people on both sides of the childhood vaccination debate. I couldn't believe it.

My brief "Hollywood experience" also proved to be enlightening. As you might expect, a number of producers saw "made for TV movie" written all over Heather's story. A couple actually sent contracts. But the studio representatives who talked to me all wanted to hear more about Bill's and my marital troubles than anything else. One person actually said, "Give me all the dirt on your divorce!" They seemed to lose a lot of their initial interest when I told them: (1) I didn't think her parents' divorce was really the focal point of Heather's story; and (2) I wasn't interested in reopening old wounds and publicly sensationalizing my family's heartache for any amount of money.

I don't know what kind of rube they took me for, but one of the provisions of a proposed contract was that the studio would have complete creative freedom to fictionalize the story any way they saw fit "for dramatic purposes." As if that weren't bad enough, that same contract also included a clause stating that I would be held personally liable for any legal damages should anyone decide to file suit over the contents of the movie. Needless to say, I wouldn't sign any such contract.

I guess there aren't many people interested in making upbeat, positive, and inspirational movies anymore. I can't say I'm surprised.

Neither was I surprised about the controversy that erupted when many people in the deaf community criticized Heather for using oral communication rather than sign during most of her public appearances as Miss America. They accused her of selling out to the hearing world, and some spokespeople actually went on record in the national press complaining that "speech is just a tool, a verbal trick. . . . Hearing people give her so much credibility." She "doesn't belong to the hearing or the deaf community. . . . But her signing skills show she was brought up in a hearing world." And the problem with that, according to these same critics, is that "among the deaf, status comes from using ASL, attending [deaf] schools, and coming from a deaf family. That's our culture. . . . That's why there's this disappointment in Heather."

I think Heather was taken aback and a little hurt by the intensity of this reaction. One hearing impaired magazine writer even went so far as to accuse me of "child abuse" for the "cruelty" of attempting to teach a deaf child to listen and understand instructions given from behind her back.

But because I'd been exposed to the whole oral versus sign controversy long ago, and was well aware of the volatile feelings on the subject, my only real surprise was that the arguments and questions raised in the wake of Heather's selection as Miss America 1995 merely rehashed the very arguments I'd encountered when I first researched educational options for her. That saddened me—to see that the same antagonism and intolerance persist today, and to realize so little progress has been made in the twenty years since I chose the oral approach.

While I'm sorry to see Heather caught in the middle of such a controversy, I am very proud of the way she's been willing to take the criticism and still try to share her message in the deaf community. I know that the choices I made for my daughter when she was young have shaped the person she is today. I know that because she is deaf she will always face special challenges living in the oral-hearing world. And because of her oral training, she faces special challenges relating in the deaf world.

My prayer is that people—both hearing and deaf—will see Heather for who she is. I hope they will understand and appreciate the fact that Heather's becoming Miss America has enabled her to pursue an even more worthy dream—to be a bridge between our two worlds, so that hearing and deaf people throughout our country and around the earth will have a better understanding and appreciation for each other, and for what we can learn from one another.

By referring to these various controversies I certainly don't intend to leave the impression that Heather's reign as Miss America has made for a bad, or even a particularly difficult, year. There have been some tough things about it. But it's been extremely exciting and always interesting. Much of it's been wonderful. And most of it, by far, has been good.

What has been the most rewarding for me as "Miss America's Mom" has been the joy of seeing my daughter have such a positive impact on so many lives. I've heard from countless people who want to tell me how inspired they have been by Heather's story and by her message of acceptance, encouragement, and hope. Particularly touching are the letters from kids who say that Heather's "Anything Is Possible!" campaign has shown them that they don't have to be limited by their handicaps. Or as one physically handicapped girl wrote to Heather, "Since you spoke here, for the first time ever, I feel accepted at my school."

Heather's being named Miss America has also had a very positive impact on our extended family. It's drawn us even closer together as we all share in the joy and excitement of her experience.

This Miss America dream has opened up doors for me to speak and share the memories we have with so many other people. Even writing this book has afforded me a privilege I might never have had—to be able to go back, remember, and relive so many joys I'd long forgotten.

I tell my daughters that they need to keep written accounts or diaries of the days when their children are little, because it's so easy to forget. I wish I'd done that for all three of my girls when they were young. But I didn't.

Only the fact of Heather's deafness forced me to keep such detailed records for her. Through those records and the recollections of so many people graciously willing to share their memories, I've been able to reconstruct this story as a gift to Heather. And a tribute to God, who has taught us both that with his help, anything is possible indeed.

I've always tried to believe that.

I know there were lots of times when people thought I wasn't being realistic. A few years ago when I was shopping for a CD player for Heather, I received a typical reaction from a sales clerk. Friends had told me that the sound quality of CDs was much better than you could get from tapes, and I hoped Heather would be able to hear and enjoy music better with CDs. As I examined several different models out on display, the sales clerk seemed attentive and eager to answer all my questions—until I mentioned I was Christmas shopping for my daughter who was deaf.

"You're buying a CD player for your deaf daughter?"

When I saw the incredulous look on her face, I tried to explain, "She loves music. And I thought she might enjoy CDs better than tapes."

"Oh . . . kay," the woman replied. But I knew she thought I was crazy and was probably wondering whether to call store security.

She hasn't been the only one to question my grip on reality over the years. Many experts, doctors, school officials, and even some family and friends have thought my goals for Heather, and those she set for herself, simply weren't reasonable.

What none of those people knew, and what kept me going in the face of the doubts and hurdles they sometimes created, was that I had seen Heather's future. Not that I have any special gift of sight. What I had, what I clung to all those years, was the gift of God's guidance.

In those dark days after we learned of Heather's deafness, when I didn't know where to turn, he assured me he would go with me. And he did. He led me to Doreen Pollack's clinic in Denver, where I saw, for the first time, deaf children who could actually communicate effectively in an oral-hearing world. From that day on I could always envision the future I wanted for Heather.

God was there each step of the way. When we encountered the biggest obstacles and experienced the greatest discouragement, I felt his presence most, reminding me of that vision he'd provided me of Heather's future. That gave me the determination to go on.

So many times this year I've thought of my dreams for Heather. Even though I always told her, "Yes, you can, Heather. Anything is possible!" the reality of all that has happened is almost too much to believe. Some days I've wanted to pinch myself to make sure it was all truly happening.

Then I see my daughter's face on the cover of a national magazine, I hear her familiar voice on the radio, or I watch her being interviewed on network television, and I realize both our dreams have come true.

There she is, Miss America.

Resources

Parents and families with hearing impaired children can obtain information from the following sources I have mentioned in this book:

Alexander Graham Bell Association for the Deaf
   (publishers of *Volta Voices* and *Volta Review*)
3417 Volta Place NW
Washington, D.C. 20007
(202) 337-5220 (V/TTX)
(202) 337-8314 (FAX)

John Tracy Clinic
806 West Adams Blvd.
Los Angeles, CA 90007
(213) 748-5481
(213) 747-2924 (TTY)

Porter Memorial Hospital
Speech and Hearing Department
   (where acoupedics began)
2525 South Downing Street
Denver, CO 80210
(303) 778-1955

Central Institute for the Deaf
818 South Euclid
St. Louis, MO 63110
(314) 652-3200

Photo Credits

Page 1
J. M. Frank/CP News

Pages 2–3
Gray family collection

Pages 4–5
Gray family collection

Pages 6–7
Gray family collection

Page 8
Top and inset top: Gray family collection
Bottom: Dothan School of Dance

Page 9
Background: Briarwood Ballet
Inset: Dothan School of Dance

Page 10
Inset: Ray Hathorn Photography
Background: Mark Davis Photography

Page 11
Top: Gray family collection
Middle: Esco Olinger Photography
Bottom: Mark Davis Photography

Page 12
Top: Gray family collection
Middle: Gray family collection
Bottom: Charles Sides Photography
Inset: Charles Sides Photography

Page 13
Background: Charles Sides Photography
Inset: Charles Sides Photography

Pages 14-15
1. N. Rokas/CP News
2. S. Jaslecki/CP News
3. S. Jaslecki/CP News
4. S. Jaslecki/CP News
5. K. A. Frank/CP News
6. S. Jaslecki/CP News
Right: Harrahs Hotel Photography
Middle: J. M. Frank/CP News
Bottom: N. Rokos/CP News

Page 16
Charles Sides Photography